A FASCINATING JOURNEY TO SUCCESS

A PROFESSOR AND CEO TRUE STO

STRUC
AND SUCCESS

FIRST EDITION

RICHARD T. CHENG

ISBN 978-1-952835-25-4 (softcover)
ISBN 978-1-952835-26-1 (ebook)

Printed in the United States of America.

Book Vine Press
2516 Highland Dr.
Palatine, IL 60067

Contents

FOREWORD

The *Struggle and Success* described how he had overcome the shortage of fund. With $30 in his pocket, he had to face the day-to-day expenses. He had found a part-time job during his first week in the United States. He worked and studied and sent $10–$20 back to his wife every month. After two years in the United States, he fell in love with this country, so he asked his wife to come and live here temporarily. After they had been here for a few years, they wanted to become citizens of this country. In 1971, they were sworn in as U.S. citizens. After he received his PhD in 1971, he started to build new computer science departments for various universities. From 1971 to 1975, he was promoted to full professor rank, and in 1979, he was appointed eminent professor. He was appointed as the UNDP as a lecture and went to China to give talks to groups of scientists, He also was appointed the senior consultant to the ministry of interior of Saudi Arabia to consult on the National Network and establish a computer science college in King Saud University. In 1985, he started a small company, and in 1988, the company had multimillion revenue.

CHAPTER 1

My First Impressions of the USA

As I entered the country, I felt like a water lily uprooted and floating on a vast new pond. I had to reach the place to anchor myself.

It was Menomonie, Wisconsin, the place I had known only from letters I received from the college. I had come through high waters, and now I was on my way to my destination in the United States. It was hope, excitement, and worrisome all presented in my mind. I was not intimidated but had to resolve any matter confronting me one at a time, in this totally new land.

The Greyhound bus ticket agent was an African American. That was the first time I ever talked to a black person face-to-face. He was very nice and helpful to me. In general, my fear of the people in the new country was diminishing rapidly as the day grew. My immediate goal was to go to Menomonie, Wisconsin, to report to the school. At this moment, I was not certain what lay ahead of me. Until I was registered with the school, I would not feel secure in this country.

I was impressed by how clean and how well equipped the Greyhound bus was. The seats and the curtains were first-class as I saw them. I found an open seat near the front row next to a window. I just took the seat since the seating was not numbered. The bus was about half full that day. Most of the passengers were older folks. Of course, at the age of twenty-seven, I considered people over forty as elderly. I did not try to talk to anyone on the bus throughout the trip. I did not know how people conducted casual conversations in this country. The Greyhound bus was very roomy, quiet, and comfortable. To my surprise, the bus was heated too! Comparing with what I had experienced in China, during and after the war, the Greyhound bus was the most luxurious and enjoyable bus to ride. Of course, I could not forget the charcoal-burning stove on the truck that provided the fuel to run the truck. Or in wartime China that winding, wet, muddy road where the real danger of rolling off to the bottom of the valley was always present. Here in the United States, the contrast of what I saw in front of my eyes and what I recalled was like heaven and earth—an understatement.

It was amazing to me that this huge bus had only one person who handled everything—the ticket person, the baggage man, and the driver. The uniformed bus driver was very polite, authoritative looking, responsible, and confident. I felt quite safe to ride in the bus. I was comfortable to give him my luggage, and I was sure he would not run away with my belongings!

Looking through the side window constantly as the bus headed eastward, I was trying to learn as much as I could in this new country. The bus entered the expressway after about ten minutes of winding through the city streets. That was the first time I had ever seen such wide four-lane highways with all cars going the same direction. Across the nicely trimmed medium was the same wide highway with all cars and trucks going the opposite direction. At that moment in time, traffic on the expressway was very light. Everything I saw along the road was so magnificent, clean, and orderly. I was in awe for what I had seen in the short few hours that morning in this completely new land for me.

Back home, people used to say that the United States was paved with gold on its roads. But as I saw it, the road in this country was paved with blood and sweat by visionary and dedicated people. It was not by luck or accident that this country could become so wealthy and the strongest in the world. I began to secretly admire the people that I was going to mingle with.

Maple leaves had just turned bright red or golden yellow in Washington State. The United States' northwest was truly a vast scenic wonder under the bright, sunny, autumn sky. Among the patches of colorful trees were houses painted white or in red bricks. A few farmhouses had cows, horses, and lambs fenced in nearby fields. It was peaceful and beautiful. I enjoyed every bit of the picturesque scenes along the expressway. When the bus reached Montana at the end of the day, a fresh snowfall had just blanketed the great mountains and valleys that presented such a sense of purity and striking beauty of the landscape. For someone who just came from a subtropical island, this was something beyond my imagination. The bus was going east without overnight stops and only made short meal stops and fueling every few hours. Sometime in the evening they switched the driver. A white man in his forties was taking over the driving first. There were serval changing of drivers along the highway, but I couldn't tell the difference - the Americans all looked the same.

At one of the meals stops, I tried the famous hamburger for the first time. I found it was very tender, unlike the beef I had in Taiwan and China where beef was really buffalo meat, a very tough variety. The hamburger tasted good, but I did not like to see the red, bloody juice seeping into the buns. All the beef I had in the past were well cooked. It cost me over two dollars for that meal and was too pricey for me. For the rest of the trip, I had just cookies and cold drinks, but I really had a very good time. I was so excited about seeing everything along the way, for most of the time, I kept myself awake and only dozed off for a few minutes at a time. I tried to capture everything that came into my view, day or night. I found these Americans on the bus to be friendly and polite to one another; not one fight or argument had taken place. It sure was quite contrary to my perceptions of American people before I met them.

The bus traveled three days and two nights and arrived in Eau Clair, Wisconsin. The bus driver took my suitcase and the book box from the undercarriage of the bus and placed on the floor for me.

"You need to take the bus at gate 7 to Menomonie," he told me.

"Thank you so much," I said.

"You bet!" he said. I didn't understand the meaning of his reply, but I thought it must be a version of saying "Never mind" or "Don't mention it."

I had no trouble to board the connecting bus at gate 7, after about one hour of waiting. The bus headed for Menomonie on a small highway. The road was a two-way country road, but the condition was excellent and very clean. Finally, I arrived at my destination: the bus stop in downtown Menomonie, Wisconsin. At the bus stop, I saw this lanky elderly gentleman. When he saw me step off the bus, he came straight to me and extended his hand.

Dr. and Mrs. Ray Wigen

"I am Ray Wigen. Are you Mr. Cheng?" he said to me.

I immediately guessed who he was and thought, *Wow! He is the dean of the graduate school and is here to greet me in person!* I was awed by the fact he would meet me himself at the bus stop.

"Yes. I am Richard Cheng, Dr. Wigen," I answered. I put the luggage on the ground and shook hands with him.

"I am glad you informed us of your bus schedule," he said.

"Thank you for coming to the bus station. I really did not expect seeing you until tomorrow in your office." I told him the truth.

"I am very happy to be able to catch you here. Many people from overseas have trouble getting around in the first few days," he said with a smile.

He picked up my luggage from the ground and carried it for me as we walked on the sidewalk of the street.

"We are putting you in the local hotel, right down the block," he said, pointing to the hotel about forty feet away.

A tall, gray-haired man in his mid-sixties, Dr. Wigen was so gentle and kind. I had never expected the dean of graduate studies would greet me in person and carry my luggage for me. I was quite moved. We walked into the hotel. He spoke to the person at the counter briefly. A young man came to me and helped me to take my baggage inside the hotel.

"The young fellow will show you to your room. Go and take a hot shower and have a good night's rest. Come to my office tomorrow morning. We will get you registered," he told me.

"Thank you, Dr. Wigen. I will see you tomorrow," I said.

I saw him walk out of the hotel lobby.

"This way, sir," the young man told me.

I followed him climbing the stairs to the second-floor room. He opened the door for me and put my luggage on the stand. I wanted to tip him, but he refused.

I was truly very touched by Dr. Wigen's presence this evening, his thoughtfulness, and his kindness. I would not even know where to go from the bus station, if he did not come and help me. At this moment, all my fear of being in a strange and rough country had totally evaporated.

The hotel I stayed in that first night was an old but elegant and well-kept place. Again, this was a brand-new experience for me. The room was large with a double-size bed. Everything in the room was very fresh and clean. That night, I slept on a bed with mattress and box springs for the first time in my life. In the past, the best bed I had slept on was the two-inch-thick straw mat, the mat made from braided bamboo strips, or the hard wood floor. Those were all single narrow beds. The hotel room included a full bathroom that was also new to me. I had never stayed in a hotel that was not using a shared facility. The room was furnished with a fancy dresser with a big mirror, a desk, a chair, a sofa, and a nightstand. It was too luxurious for me! Why did people need all this just to stay in the room overnight?

I was wondering how I would be able to pay for it all. Well, I decided not to worry about it until the next day; while I had to pay for it, I might as well just enjoy it. I took a hot-water bath in the big tub and soaked for a solid fifteen minutes. Another surprise to me was I did not even need to use the towel I had brought all the way from home; it was furnished. There were several large and small towels. I used just a medium-sized towel. I had not seen a large bath towel like the one in the room before. That reminded me of the scenes I had seen in American movies—those luxuries! Now I was right in it. The bed was so soft and comfortable it did not take more than a few seconds before I fell into deep sleep.

The next morning, I woke up at seven o'clock. I washed up and dressed in the best clothing I had brought with me and was ready to do business.

When I went downstairs, the young man who had helped me the previous night was there to greet me. He took me to the coffee shop and ordered a big breakfast for me. That was the first real meal I had had in America since I left the ship. I finished every bit of it and found everything was just delicious. The young fellow helped me at the counter to check out, and the clerk told me that the school had taken care of all my bills. A surprise and a relief, for I knew how little money I had to sustain my life before I could start earning some money. I asked the clerk to keep my luggage in the storage while I went to school. I found out later that Dr. Wigen had paid all my bills from his own pocket. He really did not have to do that. I was just moved emotionally by what he had done for me and felt speechless. If I had to pay for that room and the breakfast, I would be close to—if not totally—penniless at that moment.

Under the bright morning sun, the town looked quite different from what I had seen last evening. It again was a very clean and orderly town. It was a college town with commercial district built around the campus. The campus was larger than the commercial establishment in the town. The campus was just a block from the hotel I stayed in.

I walked to the administration building that was just another two blocks away from the hotel. It was very easy to find Dr. Wigen's office. The administrative building was an old building of more than fifty years. The all-brick, four-story building was well built and well maintained. I was very impressed by its stately looks and how clean it was.

Dr. Wigen's office was just down the hall from the main entrance. Catherine Olson was his secretary. She was a very nice and patient person who spoke very slowly in order to be understood by newly arrived foreign students. I entered the reception room and introduced myself. "Good morning. I am Richard Cheng from the Republic of China," I said.

"Good morning, Mr. Cheng. Dr. Wigen is expecting you," she told me while she got up from her chair. She opened the door leading to his office and announced my arrival.

"Come on in. Have a seat and make yourself at home," Dr. Wigen said with a broad smile.

I sat in a side chair in front of his huge desk.

"Dr. Wigen, thank you so much for taking care of my hotel bills and the big breakfast. I must repay you for that soon," I said.

"Don't worry about that. You need the money to get settled in. You can buy me a lunch when you make some money later," he said with a heart-warming smile.

"I will buy you more than just one lunch when I make some money," I promised.

"Good! We have a deal," he said.

After a short conversation, he took me to the office of Dr. Price, the dean of men. He told me that I was granted a scholarship that covered tuition, fees, and a year of dormitory room rent, but I had to pay my own meals and expenses. That of course was good news to me. It was better than the letter offer I received when I was in Taiwan. Dr. Wigen then took me to see the registrar and formally registered me as a graduate student at Stout.

"Thank you, Dr. Wigen, for helping me in person this morning," I said.

"Anytime. If you need anything, just come and see me," he said.

"I am going to move into the dorm now. Thank you again. See you later."

I went back to the hotel, picked up my luggage, and walked the four blocks to Lynwood Hall.

My next stop that morning was to the bank. Before I left Taiwan, I had borrowed money to show the United States Consulate and the immigration service upon arrival. I promised my mother-in-law and my aunt to send the money back as soon as I arrived at the school. They were paying interest on the money they helped me to raise. That was why I had to send the money back right away. I went to a local bank on the main street to wire the sum of seven hundred dollars—five hundred to my mother-in-law and two hundred for the aunt.

At that point, I had only the twenty dollars that Mrs. Koo gave me at the Taipei train station plus some change that totaled another ten dollars. The thirty dollars cash was all I had in my possession the first day after I sent back the money. I knew that I would have all sorts of expenses to pay in the following days, but I had no other options. I had no specific ideas of how to make my ends meet after the thirty dollars were spent. Somehow, I was not at all worried. My skills in radio and electronics should be useful in this technologically advanced nation. I was optimistic that I could easily find some work earning money to support myself. For now, I just had to watch how to budget the thirty dollars for the days ahead.

I was assigned to live in a room in this old dormitory called Lynwood Hall. The building was to be demolished to make room for a high-rise dorm planned for next fall. The room assigned to me was very large—from my own standard. It was completely furnished, including weekly maid services. It was a luxury for me to stay in such a nice, large room alone. However, my friend back in Taiwan, who had been here before, told me about its location that was back against a funeral home. My room was at the end of the hall and the window was directly facing the back door of the funeral home where the coffins entered. And that was the exact room my friend told me to stay away from. I was not a believer of ghosts, but it was not a pleasant scene to watch when there was a service.

Next door to me was a student from Jordan, Ahmed Al-Sani, and the next room down was one from Indonesia. His name was Kumer Borache. Across the hall were two graduate students from Ethiopia: John Fusuii and John Salashi. They were all graduate students. The building had three floors of dormitory rooms. The rest of the rooms on the first floor were occupied by freshmen. The freshmen were white American boys without exception. All the dormitory occupants had lived there for at least three months.

I was the only new student to move in currently. I became the center of curiosity to all the freshmen, since I was the only Chinese on the whole campus. They all came to my room to introduce themselves. I was overwhelmed by how polite and nice those young fellows were. My impression of them was that they were all quite tall, healthy, handsome, extremely polite, friendly, and understanding. There were Dick Maiman, a six-foot, seven-inch fellow with short crew cut; Bob Stoeffle, a big and strong wrestler; Mike Smith, a slender, tall, and quiet guy; Jack Buckman, a nice, gentle soul; and Mike Tibbets, a kind and caring person. We became friends quickly and spent a lot of time talking after school. Dick Maiman was an electronics buff. His interests coincided with mine; therefore, we had a lot to talk about and sometimes argued about things that were really a misunderstanding of words on my part. Once, we talked about the Morse code. I declared that I could send over 150 "words" a minute. Dick was extremely upset about it.

"The best operator I know of can't even send forty words per minute. I can do maybe twenty a minute," he said with a smile, but he was not happy.

"It is true I can do 150 words per minutes. I have the certificate to prove it," I said.

"You must have a finger that vibrates at 750 times per minute or fifteen times per second. How can that be physically possible?" he said.

I began to see what the problem was: five English letters make a word.

"You see, in Chinese, we do not have any distinction between a letter and a word. When I said 150 words, I meant 150 alphabets. I was wondering why you thought it was too fast. Sorry that my poor English has upset you," I said.

"I am glad you are just a normal guy like me," Dick said with a big laugh. We all laughed.

The first night in the dorm, Jack Buckman came to my room and invited me out to eat with Bob and Mike. We went to a nearby café and they chipped in to treat me with a dinner. The dinner was pizza and Coke. I had never had pizza before, but I had heard Dean Martin's song "Amore" in Taiwan. The song contained the lyrics "When a moon hits your eye like a big pizza pie, that's amore." I had a really hard time to figure out what a pizza pie was at that time, but it sure sounded very romantic. The food was quite different from what I was used to having, but I thought it tasted pretty good, except after dinner I still felt hungry.

The next morning, I was walking on the campus and bumped into Dr. Wigen on my way to a class.

"Mr. Cheng, where did you eat last night?" he asked me slowly.

"I ate in the cave," I quickly replied.

He thought for a short moment, laughed, and said, "Oh! You mean café. That's what we call cafeterias in a simplified French word," he said as he laughed. "It is difficult for new people to know that."

I could imagine what might have appeared in Dr. Wigen's mind for a short moment: I was eating with a bunch of savages in a mountain cave.

I also tried to learn from Bob Stoeffle, with a few other foreign students, about how to greet professors when we met them on the campus.

"Just say, 'How is your hammer?'" he told me.

I immediately detected that he was pulling our legs. I thought the others must have detected his joke, so I did not say anything. The few graduate students bunched together to learn American customs from our dorm mates. We learned several American slang terms, such as *hit the sack* and *shoot the breeze.* The next morning, Ahmed and I walked on the campus and met Dr. Rudiger. Ahmed wanted to apply his new knowledge just learned from those freshmen.

"Good morning, Professor, and how is your hammer?" Dr. Rudiger was shocked for a second or so and quickly realized that we were only the victims of some kids' pranks.

"We do not ask people that kind of questions in America, and I do not think you do that in Jordan either," Dr. Rudiger told Ahmad. We were taking a course from Dr. Rudiger at that time.

Later I explained to Ahmed what the word *hammers* implied. Ahmed then realized he had made a stupid mistake and was mad at those kids that taught him the ways to greet a professor.

Another day, Ahmed and I went to a nearby café for a cup of coffee. After the coffee was served, he said to the waiter, "Thank you."

"You bet!" the waiter replied.

Ahmed became very angry.

"Those crazy American people! I thanked the waiter, but he said I was bad!" He fumed.

I laughed and told him that the waiter said *bet* and not *bad.* Ahmed was not totally convinced and was still fuming when we walked out of the café.

"If I were not a Muslim, I would have punched that guy o n the nose," he declared.

There were at least one hundred foreign students at Stout in 1961. Dr. Sandra Langford was the foreign student affairs program coordinator of the college. She organized group activities from time to time for all foreign students and for students from certain countries. In the second week after I entered the school, a welcome party was set for the seven newcomers. This was an all-foreign student affair, and everyone should attend, and the turnout was very good. Each of the new students was asked to get up and introduce their country and themselves.

"I am Richard Cheng. I just came from Free China," I got up and said.

Immediately several students from Ethiopia and Sudan stood up and shouted in protest.

"What do you mean by 'Free China'? Do you mean there is a *non-free* China?" That fellow I never met before was hot.

"The island we live on is called Taiwan," I said.

"Taiwan? We never heard of the place," another African student said.

"Well, it is also called Formosa by the Dutch people," I tried to explain.

I did not really know what was so upsetting to them.

"You call your island 'Free China'?" the first guy asked again, still unhappy.

"The Republic of China is on this island just temporarily. We refer to the People's Republic as Red China." I tried to be very patient.

That answer was apparently not satisfactory to them at all. Afterward, I learned that those African students were all sympathetic to Communist ideology. Their homeland either had close ties with the People's Republic of China or was run by their own Communist regime. I learned to keep my mouth shut about politics and tried to be careful of what I said from that day on, especially to those people whose convictions and political backgrounds I did not know.

When I was in Taiwan, we learned everything from the government-controlled press and radio stations. What we learned about the world was totally based on what the government news that was released to us. When I said, "Free China," it was so natural that I did not even give a thought about the terminology. Back home in Taiwan, the head of the state was viewed as a god. We thought nothing about questioning the deeds of the government. My first exposure to the US democracy was when some nightly comics like Johnny Carson joked about the US president—Kennedy. I was quite upset in my mind about Johnny's belittlement of the country's leader. The negative report of the US media about Taiwan sometimes was upsetting me. Those were the kinds of talks I had never heard before about the government. Such was my mental state when I first arrived in the United States. My respect to the old country's leaders collapsed only after I read the book *The Soong Dynasty*, among others, which described the corruption and dirty laundry of high government officials in Nationalist China.

At that time, mainland China was almost at war with the United States when the US Seventh Fleet was enforcing the embargo in Taiwan Straits, and the Vietnamese War was going on hot. Because Taiwan was an ally of the United States, I was totally committed to defending Taiwan when the few African students were fiercely attacking the existence of Taiwan.

CHAPTER 2

Gizzards for the Puppy

Since I had only thirty dollars in my pocket the day after I had arrived Menomonie, I had no deposit in the bank and there was no prospect of any source of income for me. I knew that I must watch my expenditures very, very closely. I bought cookies, bread loafs, canned food, and fruits for the next few days.

One day, just a few days after I had arrived the school, I took a leisurely walk on the main street of Menomonie. I saw a butcher shop with a display counter that was right next to the sidewalk. I went closer to inspect what was displayed on the counter. I saw some pork, beef, and chicken. Piled up in a corner was a mixture of gizzards, livers, and wings.

"How much are the chicken gizzards?" I asked the clerk.

"Nothing. If you take the whole pile, I will just give them to you," he said.

"Sure, I will take them all," I said.

He wrapped up the pile of chicken parts with a brown paper and gave it to me.

"Here you are. What's your name?"

"Thank you. I am Richard Cheng. Very nice meeting you. Oh! What is your name?" I was very, very happy about the findings.

"Just call me Bill," he said with a smile.

"See you. Thank you again, Bill." I rushed out of the shop.

It must have weighed more than two pounds. I hurried back to the dormitory. First, I cleaned my big mug. Then I cleaned about a quarter of the chicken gizzards, livers, and wings and put them in the mug. An electric hot-water coil was put into the mug and the water was filled to the rim. The coil was plugged into the outlet. I waited anxiously, hoping it would work for me. The water started boiling after a long wait and soon the chicken parts changed color and the good smell filled the room. I made sure the meats were well done and tried a small piece with a bit of ketchup. Wow! It was the most delicious food I had had for a long time. I finished the whole mug of food in no time.

I went to the small store down the street and bought a bottle of hot sauce. When I got back to the dormitory, several students were talking about the source of the mouth-watering smell.

"What is that smell?" John Salashi saw me holding the hot sauce bottle.

"Chicken parts," I said.

"Wow! They smell so good." Several others came along.

"Come on in, fellows. See what I am doing here," I declared.

I invited them into my room and cooked another mug of the food. With the help of ketchup and the hot sauce, they finished all of it in just a few minutes. Since there was no refrigerator in the dormitory, I had to finish the entire supply of the meat in the same day. I cooked the rest of the chicken gizzards and shared it with all the tenants on the first floor. Some of the American kids were a bit hesitant in the beginning, but after the first bite, they all liked it.

After that day, I timed myself to go back to the butcher shop every third day or so to collect the chicken gizzards and other unwanted parts by the butcher.

"Richard, since you come here so often, I think I need to charge you some money," Bill told me one day.

"How much do you want for the pile?" I asked.

"I need to charge you a dime for the pile," he said.

"Sure, Bill, it is fair," I said, and I gave him a dime.

Since then, I gave him a dime each time I went to the store to pick up the gizzards.

"Richard, what do you do with that stuff?" Bill the butcher asked me sometime later.

"Oh! I have a puppy," I said. It was not really a lie, since I was born in the year of the dog.

CHAPTER 3

My First Part-Time Job

A week later, my money supply went low—less than five dollars. I was surprised how fast the money was spent. In order to find a job, I thought I'd best go to a place that I could do something not everybody could do. So, I decided to find a radio repair job in town.

I walked into the closest radio and television dealer right across the street from the campus. It was called Red's TV. A middle-aged man with red hair greeted me at the counter.

"What can we do for you today?" the redhead asked me.

"I am looking for a part-time job," I replied.

"What can you do, young man?" he asked with his eyes scanning me from head to toe.

"I can repair radios," I said confidently.

He then called his chief technician, Ray Hansen. "Ray, do you have anything for a part-time student?"

"We don't have much work he can do here. But if he can fix those damned car radios, we have plenty of them," Ray said.

He pointed to the pile of about fifty or so car radios on the top of the shelf.

"Do you know any car radios?" Red asked.

"I have not seen one before, but I will try to fix them," I told Red.

"Good luck!" Ray said.

He pulled two of the car radios from the shelf and gave them to me. The two left for lunch. It was almost twelve o'clock noon.

I took the radios to the bench, found the problems quickly, and repaired both within ten minutes. I then took another five radios from the shelf and repaired them in the next thirty minutes. When Red and Ray came back at one o'clock, I showed the seven repaired radios to them. Red was very happy, but Ray was not impressed at all.

"I will pay you one dollar per hour to fix the radios," Red offered me. *Wow! His is paying me one dollar per hour? It was my daily salary in Taiwan,* I thought.

"I am very happy to accept your offer." I was very excited about the job.

He gave me two dollars for the work I had done. I thought he was very generous because I only worked for less than one hour, but I did not argue with him. I needed the money.

"I think we can use you here. Come back tomorrow after your classes," he told me.

"Thank you. I will be here tomorrow," I told him.

I was very happy to have found the job. I went back in the next three days and repaired all the car radios on the shelf. I was paid thirteen dollars for the fifty-seven radios I fixed.

"Good work, Richard! I will call you when I have more radios to repair," Red told me.

I was very happy to get paid. That thirteen dollars would last me another week, I thought. When I told this repair job to Dick Maiman, he was extremely upset about the way I was treated.

"Richard, you have done a real dumb thing. The guy has cheated you. Do you know how much Red charges people for each car radio fixed? I bet you he charges at least fifteen dollars apiece. You need to charge him by each radio you fixed," he said.

I took Dick's advice. When Red called me a week later, I went right to his shop.

"Richard, we have a couple car radios here for you to fix," Red said.

"I would like you to pay me five dollars for each radio I repair," I told him.

"You are driving a hard bargain. How about three dollars per radio?" he offered me.

"No. Red, I need five dollars per radio or I will be working for Ted's Radio Shop," I said.

Ted's TV was Red's competitor just a couple of blocks away. He immediately agreed.

"Okay, you win! You are driving a real hard bargain. I will pay you five bucks per car radio," he finally agreed. "You sure have learned the American way very quickly!"

But there were very few car radios to fix. The first week, only two needed to be repaired. I had to find something else to do while there was no work for me at Red's TV. Dr. Ruehl introduced me to the head electrician, Simon Olson, from Stout's maintenance department. Simon hired me immediately to work as an assistant electrician at seventy-five cents per hour. The pay was low, but the work was steady, and time was flexible. The work included changing light bulbs and rewiring power lines in a room. The work was not challenging, but there were plenty of hours of work available. The electrician work continued for about two months until the TV repair work took all my working hours. Simon and his aide, Raymond, became very close friends of mine.

I worked for Red's off and on depending on car radios brought in by customers. One day, about three months since I began working for him, Red wanted to give me more work to do.

"Do you know how to fix a TV?" he asked me.

"Not really, but I will try," I said.

As a matter of fact, I had never even touched a TV before. There was no television station in Taiwan at that time. I asked Red to show me how to operate a good TV. "Red, would you please turn on a TV set and tell me what a good picture looks like?"

Red turned on a demo unit and tuned in a local channel. I played with it for a moment to get a feel of a good TV set.

"What do you have that needs to be fixed?" I asked.

He took me to a back-storage room. It was a huge warehouse. In it were over 150 nonfunctional TV sets.

"Those damned TVs are junked by Ray. If you can fix them, I can sell them and recover some of my cost," Red told me.

"Okay, Red, let me try to fix one. I have to play with it for a while," I said.

"Take all of the time you need, but I am not going to pay you for the learning time," Red said.

"Sure. That's fair," I agreed.

I was excited to explore into this new territory. I took a smaller set and put it on the bench. I figured out how to remove the back and the bottom cover of the chassis. That was the first time I had ever seen the guts of a TV. The fundamentals of circuitry were quite universal. I quickly found a burned-out resistor and a shorted capacitor in the power supply section. That was an easy and quick break for me. The TV was fixed in less than twenty minutes. I showed Red the working TV set.

"Red! Come over here!" I yelled.

Red walked over to the bench. Quite surprised by the working TV, I supposed he was almost in a big shock.

"Damn it! I was told the TV was a piece of junk, but it didn't take you much time to get it fixed!" Red was overjoyed and emotional.

He pointed out the picture on the screen was slanted a few degrees to its right.

"I don't know how to adjust it," I told him.

Red came over and, using his hand, simply turned the yoke to straighten out the screen. The TV was working perfectly. Red was very happy and offered me $3.50 per hour to work on radios and TVs. There were so many "junked" TVs to repair. It could take months just to repair them. In addition, there were many TVs brought in the store every day. Ray was making the service calls and I did the bench repair. Red was very happy with my work.

One day for no good reason, he walked to me and talked. "Richard, do you know why I am the boss and you are working for me?" he said.

"I don't really know," I said, and I was puzzled.

"I am the boss because I don't know a damn thing about them circuits. Ha! Ha! Ha!" He was in a good mood that day.

"Red, I know why people call you Red, but what is your real name?"

"My name is Lloyd Katusky. My ancestors were from Poland," he told me.

With such steady and "good" income, my financial need was more than satisfied. Each day I spent about two dollars for food and saved the rest of my income in a savings account. I could send some money back to my wife and children starting at the end of the first month after I had arrived in the United States of America. I sent ten or twenty dollars a month in the first three months after I started working. It was quite a lot of spending money for my family in Taiwan at that time. My monthly salary in Taiwan was only twenty dollars per month. Later when my income increased from TV repair work, I was able to send fifty to a hundred dollars back home and put the rest of my income into a savings account.

Cars and mechanical devices had been my favorite subjects. I always dreamed to have a car, but it was financially out of reach for me while I was in Taiwan. In Taiwan all the cars on the street were imported from the United States or Europe. Only the very rich and high officials could have a car to use in Taiwan. I had been longing for a car since I decided to study in the United States. Driving a car had entered my dream many times before I left home. When I first arrived in the United States, I was attracted by the glaring decorations of used car lots at night and the number of new and used car dealers in such a small town. The flag-draped car lots with bright lights at night were too much of an attraction to me. I visited many used cars lots in town and learned a great deal about different carmakers, models, and their prices.

Judging by the amount of money I could muster, I decided to buy an older car with a good engine and heavy body. There were so many cars to choose from, even at the low-cost category. I was dazed by the large quantity and the variety of models of automobiles priced as low as fifty dollars.

When I was a junior in high school, I was swimming on the beach in Si-Tze Bay one day. A group of Americans came into the water. A dozen or so kids and I were thirty feet away from them. When we left for home, we saw a few cars parked on the street near the beach. One of them had a flag with three stars on the fender. That was a big black car. The driver told us it was a Buick. That name had stuck in my mind. I thought if a three-star general or admiral used the Buick, it must be a good car.

I quickly saved up enough money and bought a 1952 Buick for one hundred dollars. The salesman had pointed me to a group of about ten cars when I told him I wanted to buy a car for about one hundred dollars. I selected this Buick with very soft springs; when one pushed the car downward, it would bounce up and down for a few seconds. I thought a good car was supposed to have such soft springs. The salesman did not tell me that it was unsafe to drive a car without shock absorbers. In fact, I thought the car was very neat, since it rode like sailing on the water with two-foot waves.

I did not have a license and had not even driven a car before. But I drove it away from the lot and parked it near the dormitory that was about ten blocks away from the car dealer. I struggled to make such a dash without bumping into any patrolman. When I told this event to Mike Tibbetts, he was very concerned about what I had done.

"Let me see your keys," he demanded.

I thought he was going to tell me something about the car or about car keys. Instead, he put my car keys in his pocket.

"Richard, you don't want to drive this car until you have passed your road test and have the car insured right away," he told me.

I was a bit upset because I wanted to drive the car for fun, but I knew that he was a true friend who was concerned about my safety.

"You are right, Mike. I will buy the insurance today. Would you show me how to drive when I get my learning permit?"

"I will show you how to drive when you get a learning permit," he told me.

"Could you just sit next to me while I drive now? I mean just in the back roads."

"Absolutely not. You will get on the wrong side of the law," he said with a straight face.

"Okay! Mike, I will do as you say," I said.

The next day, I told Dr. Wigen about my car. He personally walked with me to his insurance agent and had my car insured right away. I took the written examination the following day. It was very easy after reading the pamphlet handed out by the Wisconsin motor vehicle department. I passed the written test easily and received my learning permit.

Mike and Jack took turns to ride in my car while I drove with a learning permit. I supposed that I was natural with driving cars because I had been driving a car in my head for years. A week later, I took the road test. I passed every road operation but failed the parallel parking. I practiced for another week, went back for the road test again, and passed it. I was finally free to drive my car.

The good feeling and the thrill of sitting behind the steering wheel of a fast-moving car could not be described in simple words. I drove the car whenever I could find the time from study and work. I drove to work for Red when his operation was moved to North Menomonie about five miles from the campus. That gave me a good reason for driving the car every day.

Since I was not a seasick type, the car's wavelike motion did not bother me at all. However, no one else in the dormitory would want to ride in my Buick. Another reason I selected the Buick was the safety factor. Based on calculations when two cars collided, the driver and passengers in the heavier car would suffer less injury than the lighter car. This Buick was loaded with heavy steel bumpers plus a lot of chromed ornaments. It weighed over 4,000 pounds. I thought it was the safest vehicle next to a Sherman tank when colliding with another car. Before I left Taiwan, I had heard about so many people being killed on the United States highways each year. A close friend was wounded badly and crippled for life after his car collided head on with a light truck in Indiana just a year earlier. I wanted very much to drive a car, but I must make sure I did everything I could to make safety the foremost consideration.

The old Buick was running fine except the softness of the springs that I had chosen. To repair the malfunctioned shock absorbers would cost me over fifty dollars as estimated by a car repair shop. It was beyond my ability to pay the repair shop to do the repair job. I decided not to spend that kind of money until I figured out what to do. Several friends in the dorm advised me that the shock absorbers were critical to the safety of my car and I should have my Buick repaired without delay.

"Richard, it is stupid to drive a car like that. If you make an emergency stop, the chassis could be separated from the wheels and fly away. I would not want to see you get killed that way. Why don't you get it fixed?" Mike Tibbets told me.

"Mike, I promise to get it done right away." I knew he was genuinely concerned about my safety.

"I will help you to get it done real soon," Mike said.

"Mike, how about come with me to a junkyard and buy some shock absorbers?"

"Sure. Do you have the tools to take the shock absorbers out? They would not do it for you or they will charge you a lot more money," Mike said.

"I just bought a wrench set for car repair. Is it good enough?"

"I will bring my tool box with me. But I want to go with my car," he said.

"Okay! Mike, you drive," I said.

The same afternoon, we went to a junkyard and bought four shock absorbers that we took off two old Buick sedans for twelve dollars. Mike helped me replace the old shock absorbers on my car using just regular wheel jacks and wrenches easily. It took us just one hour and a half to get everything done. The car now rode normally. It became a handy vehicle for people in Lynwood Hall. I was glad to take them out to drive around for fun or go somewhere for their pleasure or for business.

One Saturday afternoon in February, I took Dick Maiman and two other freshmen, Jack and Bob, for a ride in the countryside. It was raining earlier but the temperature suddenly dropped below freezing. I drove the Buick off the main street toward south and down a steep hill on a paved road.

"Watch out!" Dick, sitting next to me, yelled in panic.

I discovered the road was coated with a layer of ice. Ignorant of the rules of driving on an icy road, I slammed hard on the brakes. The car immediately turned into a rapid spin. I tried everything to regain control of the car but to no avail. I tried to turn the steering wheels; it was without any effect. I stepped on the brakes again; it would not respond at all. The car just kept spinning down the hill rapidly. I was frightened but tried not to panic.

"Oh no! Richard, you have lost the control!" Jack screamed.

"My god! We are going to crash!" Bob yelled in the back seat.

That spinning seemed to be forever. Everyone in the car was yelling something. I could hear but would not respond to them. I was totally absorbed by the current crisis. We knew at the end of the road was the big frozen river that was at least a fifty-foot drop from the end of this road. The end of the road was an intersection to another road like a T-junction and the other road was in parallel with the river. There was not a barrier between the river and the end of the downhill road. I heard someone praying in the back seat. Dick sat on the passenger side, his hands covering his face.

Just as sudden as it started to spin, the car suddenly stopped.

"Are we still alive?" Dick said half jokingly, his face pale like a white sheet.

We got out of the car and found the car was less than five feet from the cliff. A snowbank about two feet high had stopped the car. Without the snowbank, the car would have plunged fifty feet into the frozen river.

"I need a beer to calm me down," said Jack Buckman.

"Me too," said Bob Stoeffle.

We all headed to a local tavern to gulp down a few beers. A big lesson was learned in a very hard way for me. My heart kept pounding for quite a while that day. Our faces did not return to the normal flesh tone until after a few drinks of Miller High Light. From then on, I paid great respect to the condition of the roads in the winter seasons.

CHAPTER 4

Schoolwork in the United States

The first few days in school were very difficult for me indeed. All the professors' lectures were way too fast for me to catch the sentences. They all talked so fast for my head to absorb the meanings. I had to listen intensely and translate the words into Chinese at the same time. I often lost the last part of a sentence. I quickly overcame the language barrier by practicing talking and listening in English, both in and out of the classrooms with my classmates. I had no difficulties with reading material in course subjects. From the middle of the first quarter, I was working as a television repairman more than six hours a day, driving a pickup truck to make service calls throughout the city and in the countryside. That had provided me with a very good learning opportunity to practice English. I was forced to speak and to understand what people were saying to me.

I tried to time the service calls in between classes. However, I was often late and most of the time tired from lack of sleep. Often in the afternoon classes, I had so much difficulty to keep my eyelids open. My facial skin became numb and my eyelids were so heavy. I tried to rub my face with my hands but without any good results. The voice of the professor just faded in and out. I knew I must have dozed off during the lectures. One day, in Dr. Rudiger's class research methods, I fell asleep in the back of the class. Suddenly, someone tapped on my shoulder and woke me up. It was Dr. Rudiger.

"Mr. Cheng, I don't mind that you fall asleep in my class. But please do not snore," he said, and he looked at me with a funny smile.

The whole class laughed.

"I am sorry, Dr. Rudiger. I was just too tired. I will try not to fall asleep again," I apologized.

But I was told by my classmates that I did it again at least two or three times after that. I did receive an A grade from Dr. Rudiger at the end of that quarter. I supposed that he was an understanding professor. He might have had some experience trying to keep awake in classes when he was a student!

It was not a surprise to me that I received all A grades from technical courses. But I had to struggle for B grades in most of the nontechnical subjects such as educational philosophy. In addition to language problems and lack of interest in those courses, I was short of several prerequisite courses.

I became acquainted with an African American student, Marshal Fields, in the class who was very well versed with education-related subjects. He helped me out by giving me his notes from classes, since I could not take notes fast enough. He also helped me in writing term papers. Often, I thought he knew the subjects better than some of the professors. Marshal graduated from his master's degree program after the second quarter I was there. I missed him as a friend and his guidance, but at that point, I was able to take notes and write term papers on my own.

My ability in solving electronics theoretical and applied problems was quickly recognized by Dr. Philip Ruehl, the head of the electronic technology department. He assigned me to work as his assistant in his classes and the electronics laboratories—an unpaid and unofficial work. However, it was truly a great learning experience for me. Dr. Ruehl and I became very good friends, since my first month at Stout and for many years until he passed away twenty-five years later. My master's thesis was the design of an infrared detection system for body temperature measurement and for other diagnostic purposes. Dr. Ruehl supervised my thesis. My master's degree program was completed in one year and a quarter.

Dr. Ruehl was a devoted amateur radio operator—ham radio as people referred to this hobby. It was natural for me to become closely involved with radio transmitters and receivers. We spent many hours building and repairing the ham gears. We also went on trips to Minnesota to hunt for surplus electronics equipment from companies like Control Data Corp, 3M, and Honeywell. On the road, we both enjoyed coffee breaks. An order of apple pie with two scoops of ice cream was the favorite for both of us. Our friendship lasted until he died of a heart attack in 1985 when people found him near his favorite fishing hole, where a big fish was still on the hook. He was sixty-eight years old.

Moving from a hot and high humidity environment to the very dry and extremely cold place was quite a change to me. The air in Menomonie was so dry, when I combed my hair it would spark loudly. When I touched my sheet cover at night, I could see the bright sparks flying between the sheet and my body. I was afraid to turn on or off the light switches, for the big spark would zap my fingers. It was a brand-new experience to me.

In the past twenty-seven years in China and Taiwan, not a single place I lived in had the air dry enough to see the static electric sparks. Fortunately, the sparks I encountered here were harmless to the health. The only questions I had was the relation between losing my hair and the sparks. Since I arrived in the United States, my hair could be found on the pillows and in the bathtub. I suspected that the extremely cold weather where my scalp was exposed to had something to do with it. In any event, it marked the beginning of my long-term hair loss and baldness years later. At that time, even with the hair loss, I still had a full head of thick hair. No concern was given about losing too much hair. I thought it would eventually grow back as fast it fell off. Of course, it never grew back.

I was amazed at how wasteful the Americans were. The graveyards of automobiles were filled with cars stuffed with perfectly usable items. Some of them were taken out for replacement purposes, but most of the parts were left to rot. Among the parts were engines, transmissions, wheels, tires, and radios. Most interesting to me, among all parts in those cars, was the radios. I went to a junkyard where hundreds of cars were stacked. "How much do you want for an AM radio, if I take it off the car myself?" I asked the owner.

"A buck," he said.

I took two radios out off the cars and paid him two dollars. He was happy, because there were no callers for such old car radios. I brought them back to the dormitory and made a six-volt DC power supply from used parts taken from junked TVs. My room was filled with good-sounding music. The car radios were better made and had a large speaker built-in. When other students from the dormitory heard and saw my setup, they all wanted to make one for themselves. I took them to the junkyards. Suddenly, the demand for those old radios skyrocketed. I showed Mike Tibbets and Bill Howe how to convert them into home radios. They, in turn, showed most of the other freshmen how to convert the car radios.

The dormitory instantly became an electronics fan club. The price for AM radios taken from junk cars had jumped from one dollar to three dollars in just a few weeks. It was still a great price for a radio with such superb receptions, good bass, and treble responses. In the early 1960s, car radios had only AM band. The FM radio was not installed in a mass-produced car until the mid-1970s.

I was always interested in firearms since I was little. After leaving the infantry school, I never had an opportunity to shoot a gun. In Taiwan, guns were under very strict control; no private citizen could own a gun, whether it was a pistol or a rifle. Also, there was no shooting range for people to rent a gun for target shooting in Taiwan.

As soon as I arrived in this country, I learned that anybody could own guns. But I was not sure if I could buy a gun as an alien. I went to Dick's Hardware Store near the campus and looked at the display of different guns.

"Hi! May I help you?" a nice young man asked.

"I am looking for a rifle, but I don't know if I am allowed to buy it," I said.

"Anyone can own a gun in this country. There is no law to prevent you buying one."

"I am a student and I am not a citizen," I confessed to him.

"You are all right to buy guns. I have sold guns to foreign students before."

"Okay! Please show me the most accurate and inexpensive rifle."

"What caliber would you like?"

"I would try a .22-caliber," I said.

"I recommend the Ithaca .22 rifle just being introduced." He handed me the rifle.

"How much is the rifle?"

"I will sell the rifle to you for thirty-two dollars plus tax. I will give a box of twenty-two rounds to go for free," he told me.

"Okay! I'll take it." I paid him with a check.

It was a simple and inexpensive gun, but it was a very accurate one. I really liked it and kept it to this day. I took a few friends from the dorm to the countryside and practiced shooting with burned-out vacuum tubes and bottles. When the bullets hit the glass tubes, an explosion made the boom, a puff of smoke, and flying glass. It was just a spectacular display. It was fun for all of us. My friends at the range were quite surprised to see that I could hit a small vacuum tube at thirty yards with almost 100 percent accuracy.

Several people from the dorm followed suit and bought .22 rifles from Dick. His .22 rifles were all sold out in a matter of a few weeks. In a short time, the burned-out vacuum tubes and junk television sets from local TV shops were also sold out. The TV shops used to pay people to dispose of the spent vacuum tubes and junked TVs. Now they were selling at a nickel per vacuum tube and two dollars per TV. The spot we picked to practice the guns was littered with a lot of broken vacuum tubes and other debris. Of course, we were not smart enough then to think about the environment problems.

Stout was a small college, but it was truly an international community. There were students from over fifty countries. Several reasons contributed to such an unusually high percentage of foreign student enrollment. First, Stout was a unique school. It enjoyed the worldwide reputation as the top school in industrial education. Second, the school had a very efficient way to deal with foreign applicants. Third, many returning former Stout graduates recommended the school for people seeking schools in the United States. Those were the exact reasons why I had chosen Stout.

I had never become close enough to know any foreigners before I left Taiwan. It was a mystery to me about people from different ethnic groups and religions. The looks of their faces and skin colors certainly were different, but how did they think and react to words and actions? Now I lived among people from all around the world. I observed each of them with great interest and found that they were just the same as people I knew back home. They all had similar desires and dislikes, had the same emotional reactions, and shared the same philosophy in family values and social justice. Although we were different in almost every aspect in life, we had the same human strength and weakness. However, there were noticeable differences in cultural background and personal traits. I easily made friends with students from the States, Europe, Southeast Asia, the Gulf States, and Africa. My deepest memories went to three fellow students: John Long of South Vietnam, Sam Porchinayan of Thailand, and Bill Lindbo from Eau Clair, Wisconsin.

John Long was a very gentle and quiet person. He was by far the most disciplined person I had ever met. From his studying routines to the way he ate in a party, he followed very strict rules. For example, in a dinner party, he would take the same amount of food, usually half of a plate, no matter how good or poor the food was. He said this was his habit for a healthy body. He had such an even temperament that I had not seen him getting mad or complaining about anything in the entire year when we were classmates.

We became very close friends when he was at Stout. He often confided to me about his personal feelings about the United States and his country. He thought that people in this country were spoiled, innocent, and often ignorant about the world outside of the United States. He was unhappy with the South Vietnam government. He left Stout six months after we met. No one at Stout ever heard from him again. I assumed he had gone back and joined the revolution against the South Vietnam government.

Sam, in his mid-thirties so an older guy, was married to an American citizen, a white girl. They had a little boy of two years old when I first met him in early 1962. The couple was very generous to foreign students at Stout. They had parties almost every weekend for foreign students. Sam was a born leader and a natural politician. He was very smooth and talkative. He asked me to look after his apartment when he took his family to Yellowstone for a two-week vacation. I lived like a king alone in his big apartment. Everything was just great for me in the apartment, except I could not find a single sheet of toilet paper, and then I realized that Sam was a Muslim. I left Menomonie in 1963; we had exchanged letters and Christmas cards for a few years. About ten years after I left Stout, I learned that Sam had died of a car crash in Thailand.

Bill Lindbo was a veteran of Korean War and now a graduate student at Stout. Bill was married to Mitze, a Japanese girl he met when he was stationed in Tokyo. Both Bill and Mitze were very nice and generous toward foreign students in the college. They had a six-year-old daughter, Lisa, and a four-year-old son, Glen. Both were lovely children. Bill was an excellent student in school. He tutored several new foreign students to speak English after school. He was the unofficial counselor for me at Stout. He corrected my English, advised me on driving a car, and took me to his relatives' home to get to know the local culture. Bill was quite upset with his mother for pressuring him to go to church constantly. Bill was a god-fearing person but just did not want to go to church regularly. I was wondering why he was like that until one day I met his mother at her home.

"Richard, please don't pay too much attention to my mother. She is weird," Bill warned me.

"I understand. Don't worry. I know how to handle myself," I said.

After the introduction, she did not want to lose any time on me. "Richard, do you go to church on Sundays?" she asked me.

"No, Mrs. Lindbo, I don't go to church on Sundays." I knew it was coming.

"Oh! Richard, you must go to church every Sunday faithfully," she said, sipping her coffee. "You know the earth is going to be ruined soon. If you are a faithful Christian, the Lord will save you. Otherwise, you will be burned in hell."

"Mother, that's enough. Richard has a class and I have to go to meet someone else on campus," Bill cut in. He knew more was coming.

He just dragged me out of the house.

"I am sorry to put you through this. Now you see how I was treated at home." Bill felt bad about his mother's behavior.

"She was trying to put some good sense to my head. Nothing was wrong with that," I said.

"Well, how about someone lectures you all the time, like every day?" Bill said.

"I understand what you mean. Is that why you moved out from your hometown?" I asked.

"To be honest with you, I really want to stay as far away as I could from her. I just could not stand her anymore," Bill said. I felt very bad for both two good persons—Bill and his mother.

Almost every Friday night, the same group of students from Asia would congregate at Bill's house to have dinner. Mitze's fried rice was famous for the group. We also brought different dishes to make the party even more interesting. We had Chinese food, Vietnamese food, Japanese food, Thai food, and Indonesian food. It was a real treat for all of us.

Most unfortunately, after Bill had finished his degree program, he simply vanished into thin air. No one knew where he went and why it had happened. Mitze was devastated and took her two children out of Menomonie. Fifteen years later, I heard that Bill had gone to the wilderness of Washington State and lived a hermit's life. Did it have anything with his mother? No one knew anything about that.

People away from their homes were feeling much more lonesome during holidays—a Chinese proverb. My first holiday in America was the Thanksgiving of 1961. I was alone in the dormitory while everybody else had somewhere to go. The American freshmen all went home. Local families invited all foreign students, except me, for Thanksgiving dinner, because I was new and did not have any local friends. I believed people in town did not even know that I existed. I had this holiday alone in this empty old building. When nightfall came, the dorm was awfully quiet. The dark shadows of the funeral home made this place at night especially creepy. I was not a true believer of ghosts and was not afraid of being alone in the big dorm, but I sure felt very lonesome and homesick in this totally new environment.

All stores, including restaurants, were closed on Thanksgiving. I could not even go anywhere to buy food. That night, I had some cookies and hot tea as my Thanksgiving dinner. A sense of sadness set in. I was homesick and worried about how my wife and my little boy were doing. My wife was pregnant with our second child at that time. My parents had their only son thousands of miles away, and they must be worrying about me all the time. My mind was filled with thoughts about my family far away, and I could not find anything to do to shake loose my persisting concerns.

Right after Thanksgiving, the city quickly filled with Christmas music and decorations. The music and the decorations were new to me and gave me an unexplainable sense of peace and joyous. This was the time for families getting together, exchanging gifts, and catching up for lost time in the year. How I wished my wife and my son could be here and see all this special season. At that time, there were few telephone services in private homes in Taiwan. The only means of communication was through postal mail services. The time for a letter to reach my wife was about ten days by airmail. I wrote at least one letter per week and sometimes more. My wife wrote me at about the same frequency. I had so much to tell her, but how could I describe my feeling on just one sheet of paper?

Dr. Wigen and his wife, Eve, invited me for the Christmas Eve dinner at their home. Dr. Phil Ruehl and wife, Chris, invited me for the Christmas Day lunch. The Christmas season was so important for American families. It was equal to the harvest moon holiday in China when all family members gathered on this day. Both the Wigens and the Ruehls had all their family members back from all over the country.

The Christmas dinner and lunch were my first time to have a chance to taste the turkey meat and the American ham. I had seen the turkey dinner from a World War II movie when John Wayne shared his Christmas dinner with other soldiers in a foxhole. I had that image of a soldier eating a turkey drumstick since my preteen age. I appreciated the kindness of both families and their hospitality. I also learned so much more about American family life.

I liked very much of what I had seen, but I really had problems when I heard a son call his father by the first name. Another phenomenon was the football watching. All men seemed to be totally devoted to watching football during the Christmas and New Year holidays. They seemed to talk, think, and dream of nothing but football games. I was a soccer player and had no notion what rules of the football game were. I tried to watch a little and just could not get myself interested in it. I was glad that I refused many invitations to watch football games, because I knew how I would become obsessed with it as I did with basketball games back in Taiwan!

In this new country, I needed all the time I had to devote to my survival and to enhance my abilities to make a better future. I thought that I could start to watch ball games after I had established myself in this society. But I knew that I was far from it. Many friends thought I was a weirdo who did not know how to enjoy the best thing in life—watching the Super Bowl!

After I stayed in the dormitory for about three months, the city engineers declared that the old dormitory was not safe for occupancy and we must clear out of there within thirty days. Mrs. Mary Green, a secretary at Stout, told me that she had a room for me to rent temporarily. She had two daughters attending colleges in St. Paul, Minnesota. When they came home in May, I must move out. I agreed and moved into her house. She rented me a small bedroom upstairs while she lived in the master suite downstairs. The arrangement was very nice, except I could not stay there very long. I kept looking for a more permanent solution.

Through some friends' referrals, I called and visited a few potential landlords. Many of them were skeptical about taking in foreign students as tenants. Some of the boarding rooms were too expensive for me. I had a hard time to find a suitable longer-term rental place to stay. I met Mrs. Catherine Ott at Vern's general store, where she worked as a saleslady. I had bought some paper and school supplies from her before. One day I went to the store to buy school supplies. Mrs. Ott was on duty.

"Good afternoon, Mrs. Ott," I greeted her.

"Good afternoon, Richard. What can I help you with today?" she said as usual.

"I need some paper, but I really need to find a place to stay." I was kidding.

"Well, I have a room for rent, but I had some problems in the past with renters, so I just let the room stay empty," she said. "But I will take an exception with you."

"Really? That would be nice! Can I see the place?"

"Come to my house after work. I will show it to you," she told me.

"I will come to see the room at six o'clock. Is it all right?"

"That is just swell," she said.

Mrs. Catherine Ott was a very nice grandmother-type person in her late fifties who raised two sons and three daughters by working as a maid, scrubbing floors, and sewing for people after her husband died at the age of forty-three. She managed to send all her five children through college from her meager earnings. She lived with her youngest daughter, Carol, a freshman at Stout, in a two-bedroom house left by her late husband. The attic was fixed for rental purposes. It had been unrented for some time.

When I appeared at six o'clock sharp at the door, Carol opened the door.

"I am Richard Cheng. I am here to see the room," I told her.

"I am Carol, her daughter. My mom is expecting you," she said.

I walked into this small but ultraneat bungalow house.

Mrs. Ott took me upstairs to the converted attic. It was a large and fully furnished apartment with bedding, desk, and chair ideal for a student.

"How much rent do you charge for this room?" I asked, worrying the rent might be higher than I could afford.

"I will take five dollars a month for the room," she said. It was less than I paid Mrs. Green each week for her smaller room.

"Do you mean five dollars per week?" I questioned.

"No. Five dollars per month," she insisted, "but I have strict rules. No parties and no guests without my approval. Do you accept the conditions?"

"Yes. I accept your conditions, and I will take this room. When can I move in?"

"Any time. It's ready."

"How about tomorrow after work?" I asked.

"Sure," said she.

"I want to thank you for taking me in. I will not give you any problems."

"I know. See you tomorrow," she said.

The Otts' house was about two miles east of the campus in a very nice, quiet neighborhood. I moved into the house the next day. I lived there in the attic and seldom went downstairs except to go to the only bathroom in the whole house. I did not use any of the facilities in the kitchen, not even the electric hot-water coil I had. I just wanted to be very careful about what I did. One day about two weeks after I moved in, Mrs. Ott caught me eating cold hot dogs for lunch in the attic and felt very bad about it.

"Richard, it's no good to eat cold food like that. Why don't you eat meals with us? I will take five dollars a week for the meals," she told me.

"That's not enough to cover your cost. I will pay ten dollars a week for meals," I said.

"Five dollars is enough. I know you are saving money to send home each month. Just let me worry about it."

I accepted her offer but would stuff the refrigerator with meat and other food weekly to make up for the low payment of my meals. Starting the next day, I joined Mrs. Ott and Carol for all three meals each day. Mrs. Ott did all the cooking. I sometimes helped washing the dishes. Carol helped cleaning the table.

We got along very well. Occasionally, Carol would tease me on the dinner table. "Do you know why the Chinese fry their vegetables?" she would ask.

"You tell me," I snapped back.

"Because they are full of worms in Chinese vegetables."

"Yeah! Do you know why the Europeans and the Americans eat raw vegetables?"

"You tell me," she said.

"Because the Europeans and the Americans did not discover fire to cook vegetables until many thousands of years later. They just got used to eating them raw."

"You two, just cut it out and eat your food," Mrs. Ott would intervene.

One day in the summer of 1962, Sam, the fellow from Thailand, and I caught two dozen bluegills from Lake Menomin. We took the fish to the house and used Mrs. Ott's kitchen to prepare the fish. I cooked a pot of steamed rice. I had never cooked any fish before, but I remembered the "sweet-and-sour fish" dish my mom cooked was delicious. Based on my memory and a lot of imagination, I cooked the dish.

"Sam, please try some of the fish," I asked.

"You are feared of your own cooking. Right?" He read my mind.

"Sam, I am not scared of my own cooking. I just don't know how it has turned out," I said.

"Well, okay. I guess it wouldn't kill me if I eat some. It may just be tasted awful." He made a funny face, reluctantly took a piece of the fish, and tried it out. Then he took a bigger fish. I waited for him to say something. Instead, Sam took a plate of rice and two larger fish and started eating. I knew the fish must have tasted all right.

Sam and I ate half of the fish and the rice. I put the remaining fish and the rice in a baking pan and kept it warm in the oven. I left a note on the dinner table. "Mrs. Ott: Please try the sweet-and-sour fish and the rice in the oven. I cooked them."

When she came home that evening, Mrs. Ott told me later, she was afraid to taste the food at first. She had to invite her friend Ella from next door to try the food with her.

"The food tasted so good, we finished them all," she told me.

From that point on, I was noted as a good cook. Subsequently, I made peppered beef, hot-and-sour squirrels, and diced chicken dishes for Mrs. Ott and her guests. Bob Ott, the youngest son, and I hunted the squirrels using the .22 rifles. Both of us were sharpshooters. We aimed at the treed squirrels while standing in a formation at a ninety-degree angle. When the squirrel saw a person and hid behind the tree, the other person hit the squirrel with a single shot. The squirrels did not have a chance. It was unfair for them, although the hunting was not a waste; the squirrels were used for the sweet-and-sour dish. I decided that was the last time I would shoot at any living creatures.

Mrs. Ott's children came home visiting her often. I became familiar with all of them. Mary Lee, the oldest, married Ross and had three children. Catherine, the second daughter, had two children. Bill, the older son, had two children: Bob, a senior football player at Stout, and Carol, the youngest. Everybody called her "Mom." I later called her "Mom Ott," because she treated me just like one of her own sons.

Each week I wrote to my wife at least once. I wrote a few lines at a time. I also wrote to Mom and Dad about every two weeks. Dad would write to me once a month. I gave my wife an American name: Nancy. Nancy would tell me what the day-to-day happenings at home were, especially telling small details of our son, including what he did and what he said. I took intense interest in reading every word she wrote about the little boy. She would send me photos taken from a studio of our son once every two months. I could see the difference in him. He sure was growing fast. My wife was quite upset and wrote me that Dad would open the letters I sent to her. I was not upset because Dad would let anybody read his correspondence in the past. Since then, I would write to my wife devoid of any intimate talks. I told her about my American mom, Mrs. Ott. She was happy that I was in a safe and friendly environment.

One night in early December 1961, I was awakened by a nightmare that our new baby was born prematurely. I could not fall back to sleep again. So, I got up at four o'clock and wrote a letter to my wife. In the letter, I reported the news on the campus and my feelings toward this new land. I specifically advised her not to lift heavy things, not to raise her arms high in the air, and to get lots of rest because I would like to see the baby carried to its full term. That letter reached her two weeks after our second baby was born. The baby was born about the same time as the letter was written and was born six weeks premature.

My wife wrote me about the birth and described the new baby in a letter that arrived two weeks later. When she read my letter, she thought it was such a strange coincidence. Although the baby had to be incubated in the oxygen tent for a few days, he was otherwise very healthy. In the beginning, I was concerned that premature babies might have problems with their health when they grew up. But friends told me that many geniuses in the past were premature babies. I just hoped the baby would be healthy. If he should be a genius, I would be even happier.

I had been working for Red for a few months. I was making home service calls in addition to bench repair work. I drove the service truck throughout the northwest Wisconsin small cities and nearby townships. I charged honestly and reasonably on parts and labor to all customers. Sometimes I would charge less money to poor or older folks in the farm country. Red was not happy with what I did, but he was a kind man and did not really care about the few dollars, I thought. Red would only lecture me a bit when he saw the invoices.

"Richard, you need to think for Red. I must pay bills. You know," he would say.

"Yes. Red, I will charge according to your price table. I am sorry!" I said.

However, the word of the "softhearted repairman" was out among the country folks. One day, I made a service call to a rich farmer's ranch. The old farmer was retired and lived on watching television programs most of the day. In his living room was that giant TV set.

"I had many guys come in here trying to fix that damned TV. It never worked right. If you can get it to work like it was supposed to be, I'll sell you my Caddy real cheap," he told me.

"Tell me what's wrong. I will try to do my best," I asked him.

"Everything. The picture jumps all of the time, some channels are snowy, and the sound is lousy," he complained.

I took the big, heavy set apart and found the previous repairman did not put components in correctly. Some wires were not even hooked back to the chassis. I fixed the TV problems and climbed up the roof to straighten out and adjust the antenna system. The picture came up nice and clear. The old man was very happy.

"How did you do it? It has not been so nice for a long time. You know I depend on the TV to get through the days," he told me. "Come with me to my garage. I want to show you my beautiful Caddy."

He took me to his garage. There was that beautiful 1954 light-green Cadillac with only a few miles on it.

"Wow! It's a beauty! Can I afford it?" I asked.

"You can. I will make a deal you will not refuse," he said.

"I really hope so." That's all I could say. My heart and soul were absorbed by the Caddy.

"I start the car every month and spin it around the farm a little. I have had no problem with the car since I bought it seven years ago. It is virtually a new car," he told me.

I was already willing to pay any amount for this all-automatic, beautiful machine.

"I don't know if I can afford it," I said. "How much do you want?"

"I will take $400 just selling it to you. Normally I would ask more than $1,000 for this car. It cost me $7,000 when I bought it new in 1954," he told me.

This old man owned a large amount of land and real estate properties. I believed that he was honest and sincere about it.

"I don't have any money for a down payment today. I will get the money in a week or so. Is it okay?" I asked him.

"I will not sell the car to anyone else," he promised.

I left the farm elated. I wished I could just drive that Caddy away with me.

"Richard, this is a good deal. Don't miss it. I know this old man well and I knew how much he had paid for the car seven years ago." Red offered me his advice.

I always believed in the theory that heavy cars were safer to drive. I was also a worshiper of fine machines. I went to the bank to borrow some money plus my savings in the bank, so I had the $400 for the car. A week later, Mike drove me to the farm. I paid the old man $400 cash and drove the car home with me. It sure drove nicely. Very quiet, comfortable, and had all the advanced electronic gadgets at that time, such as the auto dimmer, electric windows, electric antenna, and all-leather interior. A new Cadillac like that would cost $15,000 in 1962, I was told. I thought I was the luckiest car owner on earth.

Mr. Tsun-Kai Deng, the deputy minister of education from Taiwan, and Mr. Su-Hun Lai, the secretary of education of Taiwan Provincial Government, made a surprise visit to the campus just before the summer vacation. After the reception by the university president and the deans, I was asked to host them and to show them around the little city. Their purpose of the visit was to see how Chinese students from Taiwan were doing in the United States. The trip's result would be reported publicly in Taiwan and would be studied for future policies of sending students to study overseas as well. There were over 10,000 students from Taiwan in the United States at that time. Why they picked me for the visit was a great mystery.

I had argued and complained to Mr. Deng about the incompetence of the staff in the Ministry of Education before I left Taiwan, because the ministry had delayed so much time for my applications to go overseas. I wondered if he still remembered the incident. Anyway, I was flattered by the two big shots' visit and gladly showed them around in my shining 1954 Cadillac. They were both most impressed by the automatic features of the car: electric windows, electric antenna, electric seats, and automatic headlight dimmer. I was not holding back any of the wonderful features of the most luxurious car in the United States. At that time, Taiwan's economy was still very low. Government officials did not have anything even close to a Cadillac to ride, not even for a vice minister!

I took them to the store where I worked. I also cooked a big meal at Mrs. Ott's house. I invited the Wigens and the Ruehls to join the two visitors for dinner. The visitors really had a good time that day, I was told. Some months later, after they went back, they gave a glorified report on this student who was doing so well in the States and was driving a "brand-new" luxurious car. It was also reported in some newspaper articles for a few days with my name in them.

Although their intention was to encourage students to go overseas to pursue their dreams without the fear of facing financial difficulties, I was in trouble from the result of the wrong publicity. I had since received several requests for loans by some students from Taiwan and in the United States. People I had borrowed money from when I was leaving Taiwan also went to see my wife for quick payback of their loans. They did not know that other than the like-new Cadillac, I really did not have anything else to show and I was just making $3.50 an hour on part-time wages.

CHAPTER 5

A Near-Death Trip to a Frozen World

The first snowfall came a week after I arrived at Menomonie. I had never seen such heavy snowfall in China where I lived. In Taiwan there had been no snow at all. It was a fresh experience to me. After putting on my coat, I walked through the knee-deep soft snow on campus, just having fun. It was so beautiful and tranquil after a fresh snowfall. I felt so much at peace looking at the white world. Well, the snow was pretty, but it also could be deadly!

The second Christmas holiday came quickly. Mike Tibbets and I had become very close friends. He invited me to his parents' home near Wausau, Wisconsin, about 170 miles northeast from the campus. For this homecoming trip, Mike spent several days polishing up his old Chevy and did a thorough engine cleaning job as well. We set out on Friday, December 22 in the evening after classes.

That was a very windy and cold day. The forecast was for a snowstorm and strong wind in the making. Mike filled up the gas tank and checked the coolant. We ate a quick dinner in a fast food restaurant and left the campus at seven o'clock sharp. Mike drove the car, heading to a small highway that was supposed to save some time on the road.

"I hope we can beat the storm before we get to my folks' home," Mike said.

"How long does it take to get there?" I asked.

"In a good day, four hours at most. But with the snow on the road, I'd say five hours."

"It looks fine at this time. I wonder which direction the storm is coming," I said.

"I hope it is not from the north. That's where we are heading," he said.

"Let's keep our fingers crossed," I said.

"My folks are excited to meet you. They had never met a Chinese in their life," he said.

"I will be a novelty to your folks. Right? But I don't mind that at all. I appreciate you taking me to meet them. They must be very nice people."

"I think so." Mike was very close to his parents.

We were quite excited about this trip. Mike's folks at home had never seen a Chinese in person ever, and I had not stayed over in any American friend's home before. Mike was such a nice, gentle, and thoughtful person; I wanted to meet his wonderful parents who had brought him up so well. After about one hour on the road, I thought the headlights were unusually dark.

"Hey! Mike, aren't the headlights a bit too dim?" I asked.

"Maybe the snow accumulation on the lamps is making them look dark," Mike said.

"I thought the heat from the lamp would melt the snow away," I said.

"Not when it is this cold," he said.

"How cold is it, do you think?"

"Maybe ten below zero. With wind chill factor, it is much colder, so the snow would not be melted away from the headlights," he said confidently.

"That sounds reasonable. I hope the snowstorm will not hit us before we reach your home," I said.

"I hope so too. But the weatherman said it will reach this area by late tonight," Mike said.

Suddenly, the engine stopped. Mike coasted the car to the side of the road and tried to restart the car. The engine would not turn over and the headlights were awfully dim. It was nine thirty at night.

"I think we are in big trouble," Mike said grimly.

"Is the battery dead?" I asked.

"This a new battery—less than two months old. I hope I did not bust the alternator when I cleaned the engine yesterday," he said.

"The only thing to do now is to get some help from passing cars," I said.

But there were very few cars on the road that night. We first stood on the roadside, waving a blue towel at cars coming our way, but no one even slowed down to look at us. It might be the storm and low visibility so that no one could see the dimmed flashing lights, and no one bothered to stop on the road to assist us. The wind speed picked up since we had stepped out of the car. We felt very cold now. My nose felt funny, and my feet were in pain. We decided to climb back in the car.

"How cold do you think it is now?" I asked.

"I don't know for sure, but I'll say it is twenty below zero now. Luckily, the snow is not coming down too hard and wind is still fairly mild at this time." Mike knew the weather here well. He was from around here.

"I heard the weatherman said earlier that the temperature would drop to thirty degrees below zero. That would make it sixty-six degrees below freezing," I said. "The snow is going to become very heavy, and the wind speed could be over thirty miles an hour."

We knew we were in the middle of nowhere. The last gas station we passed was ten miles away and we had not seen many houses along the road. There was no house light visible in any direction from where we parked. The closest house or shop must have been far away. It would be dangerous to try to find a shelter at that time. By then, we had given up the hope for anyone give us a ride to a warmer place.

"It looks like we are stuck here." Mike was depressed.

"Well, if there is no help on its way, we'd better keep ourselves warm and just stay in the car waiting for the storm to blow over," I said.

"That's what I think we'll have to do," Mike agreed.

"Mike, why don't you get everything you can manage in the car and put them on for protection from the cold?" I told Mike.

I had a heavy overcoat with me. Mike wore a short jacket, but he had kept a blanket in the car before leaving town just in case. We both had heavy boots on that day, so we were well protected, I thought in the beginning. We turned the ignition switch off and sat in the back seat of the car. Mike was a skinny twenty-year-old fellow. His tolerance to the cold was weak. I thought we were in crisis now. I must take charge to protect him.

"Mike, keep awake do not fall asleep. I heard it is dangerous to fall asleep in such cold weather."

"Okay, I will try not to close my eyes," Mike said. "Boy! My feet are killing me. It's too cold."

"My feet are cold also. We need to constantly move the feet and legs to keep the circulation going," I said. "Even if you are sleepy, don't you close your eyes."

The wind started blowing harder and the snow was whipping sideways. We knew the worst was yet to come, but there was nothing else we could do; just try to keep alive, minute by minute!

I cracked open the windshield on the opposite side of the wind, about one-eighth of an inch to get some oxygen supply. The wind-whipped car rocked from side to side. The snow was so heavy now, within a short while, we were buried in the snowdrift halfway up the windshield. It became increasingly colder. My feet felt so painful and whole body was shaking uncontrollably. We constantly moved our arms and legs but still felt the pain caused by the cold. Gradually our faces became numb and breathing was a struggle. We cupped our hands in front of the noses to trap some heat that was leaving our lungs. We talked about people freezing to death and thought we were lucky that it was not colder.

"I think we are doing the right thing to stay in the car. At least we are not hit by the wind chill effect," Mike said. "The wind must be blowing at thirty miles an hour now and gusting even faster. Just imagine if we were walking outside now," Mike said.

"Well, people would not last very long in such conditions, unless they are wrapped in heavy thermo clothing," I said. Our voices came from our trembling bodies. Each time we talked, a cloud from our mouths was visible, even with just the dim light reflected by the snowy world around. The inside of the windshield formed a white frost layer at least one-sixteenth of an inch thick. At times, Mike would doze off. When I saw his head drop, I would push his shoulders and wake him up.

"Hey! Mike, wake up. Don't fall asleep. You may never wake up again, if you do!" I would yell loudly to his ears.

"Okay! I am awake now," he would say, and soon he fell back to sleep. I would wake him up again and again. I lost track of how many times he fell asleep.

After hours that seemed eternally long, the wind gradually died down and the snow stopped. It was about four thirty in the morning. My whole body felt like it was having thousands of small needles sticking into my flesh at the same time. I knew that we could not last long enough to wait for people to discover us. We must go out and seek help now!

I pushed the door on the roadside open. I dragged Mike out of the car and walked toward a distant light. Mike had lost so much body heat and was unable to talk at that time. I led the way, and he just silently followed. We walked, often losing our balance and falling on the snow. After struggling for one hour, we finally reached a small village. A car repair shop had its lights on. We just pushed the door open, walked toward the big commercial stove, and leaned on it for warmth. The owner of the shop gave us some hot coffee. We drank it down but still felt that bone-chilling cold coming from inside of our bodies. We kept leaning on the stove for another hour or so before we could give the garage owner the descriptions of what had happened to us and where the car might have been. At about eleven o'clock, we felt our life had come back in us. The car was towed in and repair was completed before noon. It was just a broken wire in the alternator that caused the battery to be drained empty.

Mike and I continued the journey. We arrived at Mike's home at three in the afternoon. Briefly, he told his folks about what had happened, and then Mike showed me my room. I took a quick shower and went to bed before eating dinner. I did not wake up until the next morning. Lucky enough for both Mike and me, we did not even catch a cold. I spent an unforgettable Christmas Eve and Christmas Day with the whole Tibbets family. Mike's dad was a very nice, gentle farmer in his early fifties. His mom, a gentle and kind-looking woman in her early fifties, treated me with such warmth and kindness. I thought Mike must have done some selling in front of his parents.

"Richard, please excuse my ignorance. My impression of a Chinese was totally different until I met you. You are just like any of us," his father told me.

"Thank you, Mr. Tibbetts. Mike and I are very good friends. He is so mature and so good. You folks sure have raised him right," I said. "I also had different impressions of Americans before I came over to this country. Now I don't feel there is any difference except the looks."

"I am glad Mike has you as a friend in Menomonie. He is our baby at home—the youngest," his mom told me.

"You ought to be proud of your baby. He is a good man," I told her.

Mike's brothers and sisters asked me a lot of questions about the Orient. We talked and laughed into early morning hours on Christmas Day and had a really good time together.

The day after Christmas, we drove back to the campus. Based on a television news report on Christmas Day, a young couple was frozen to death in the snowstorm about a mile from where their car stalled. They had tried to walk the half-mile distance to their home. It happed only a mile from where our car stalled!

Gosh! That was another close call!

After we returned to the campus, when I thought about what near disaster Mike and I just went through, I could not help but to think about how dangerous it was. The brush of death was very real indeed. It was not less frightening than the .50-caliber machinegun bullet exploding in the stove, the mortar explosion on the beach, and the near drowning in the ocean after the typhoon. I heard that cat has nine lives; did I have more than just one?

In August 1962, Red encountered some serious financial problems. For at least three months, Red had not paid my salary at all. Earlier that year, he had married a strikingly beautiful woman, Coney, with four young children. Coney immediately took over the financial management of his business after a short honeymoon. After she got involved, bills were not paid to vendors and my salary was not paid.

"Coney, my last month's pay is overdue. Can you pay me now?" I asked him.

"Richard, we have a bit of a cash flow crunch. How about just wait for a few more days?" she would say each time I asked her.

In the beginning, she kept everything from Red and told him that things were all right. She just needed some time to work out some glitches in the cash flow. But soon no one would give Red any credit. Debtors were all over Red to get paid. Coney disappeared with the four children without saying good-bye to Red. He had to close the business and went bankrupt. I felt so bad for him and never asked him for my salary in the past.

He took me out for lunch to talk about his broken marriage and cried silently. "Richard, I am sorry to have owed you the three months pay. I do not have any money to pay anybody that I owe money to, since my wife left me and took all I had with her. If you don't mind, I will give you everything—what's left in the store, including the hundred or so broken TVs in the warehouse. I still have three more months on the lease. I will talk to the landlord to let you use the space until he finds a tenant," Red told me.

He was then a broken man. I felt so bad for him. I did not have any alternatives but to accept that offer. There was nothing in the business for me to run. Only the empty store was left for me to use, plus the cash register and the truck; the furniture and the shelving were all taken by the bank or were auctioned off. The only place untouched was the warehouse where the junk television sets were stored. The junk TVs were accumulated by Ray's decision and continued trade-in ones. I requested to restore the phone service and to continue using the same number, and the request was granted. I could take service calls and fix some of the broken TVs for sale.

Since I was finishing my master's degree program by the end of the spring quarter, I had to complete my thesis before the middle of February. I spent a lot of time to repair those old and broken TVs. Most of them were cannibalized for parts in the past. I managed to put about twenty sets to work and put a for-sale sign up in the windows in front of the store—at very low prices. I also took service calls when I was in the store. In the end, I made better than I had anticipated. Just before Christmas, I closed the operation all together and concentrated to get my thesis work done. At the same time, I applied for and was accepted by the graduate program in electrical engineering at Columbia University in New York City. That was where I would be going from here, because my very best friend, Alfred Huang, was studying at Columbia.

The store was formally closed on December 22, 1962. The remainder of junk TV sets in the warehouse was hauled to the city dump. I spent a whole day to clean up the store and then turned the keys over to the landlord. As I finished paying bills and taxes, I figured I had over $300 in my bank account. In addition to making some money, I had learned a great deal about business from this brief run of this aftermath of a bankrupt business. I had bills to pay and I had money to collect. That was something I treated with respect and followed the rules religiously.

I also had to prepare my tax return and pay taxes to the IRS and the state. I did it all on my own to save money from hiring an accountant. Not only I had learned from what happened to Red, but also the management of money and the dealings with creditors and debtors daily. That experience was deeply embedded in my mind.

Jack Gustafson, a graduate student at Stout, came to the store one day to see the old TV sets. We talked about everything from TV to movies. He was very intelligent and personable, and we soon became very good friends. He had a red Chevy convertible sports car, and we took a ride in it while he pushed the speedometer to over one hundred miles per hour. His one hobby was to watch the series *Follow the Sun.* He would stop anything he was doing when the show was on. He had to watch the complete show. Jack was also a pilot. He flew the single-engine Piper aircraft. The flying sure intrigued me, but I never mustered enough courage to climb into his little plane.

"Richard, are you chickening out again?" He always tried to challenge me.

"Jack, I don't know. I just can't go with you this time." I did chicken out every time.

"Okay! I will catch you next time!" he would say.

Jack graduated at the same time as I did. He went back home in Oshkosh, Wisconsin, and I left to the east. We have kept in touch to this day. He retired from a successful teaching career and is enjoying his retirement years with his grandchildren.

CHAPTER 6

DECISION TO STAY IN THE USA

As the graduation date came closer, I wrote to my wife to discuss whether I should go back Taiwan or stay in the United States. If I should stay for another year or longer, I would like my wife and our children to join me here. In letters I had sent her, I described the school, the country, the people, and my friends here in the past. She was very motivated by my suggestion too, at least to visit the United States for a while. At that time, we never thought about immigration. I talked to Mrs. Ott about my wife and children maybe joining me here later.

"I am so happy your wife is going to be here. What is her English name?" she asked me.

"Her Chinese name is Ping-Ping. She does not have a name in English," I answered.

"Really! Let's give her an English name," Mrs. Ott said.

"Sure. What do you think?"

"She is your wife. You think of a good name for her," she said.

"How about Gloria?" I said.

"That's a good name. But it is the same name as my daughter-in-law. You know, Bill's wife." She apparently wanted a different name from her daughter-in-law's!

"All right. How about let's call her Nancy? It's a French name and sounds nice," I suggested.

"Good, let's call her Nancy," Mrs. Ott agreed.

From this day on, we addressed my wife as Nancy. I wrote a letter mentioning this name to her. The response was affirmative. Nancy and I discussed her bringing our children visiting here. She was very much interested in the idea. We also talked about my desire to pursue the advanced degree in the United States. She thought that was also a good idea. If they were here, there would not be any time pressure to work on the advanced degree. We would work toward those two goals before we decided on returning to Taiwan for good.

That discussion and the decisions we made had paved the ground for my wife and children coming to the States in the future. But first, I must have enough money to buy airline tickets, and more importantly, we must obtain the permission from the United States immigration services before they could come. We knew that we still had a long way to go to achieve what we were working toward.

I had heard so much about the great city of New York from friends in the States while I was in Taiwan. My heart was all set for New York City, regardless of many scary tales about the big city. After several going-away parties, I loaded my Cadillac and headed to New York alone in early March 1963. It was still very cold in Wisconsin and in some stretches of road snow and ice were still present. Equipped with a road map, I was very confident about going the right direction. I took a detour to see certain famous cities. I stopped in Chicago, Detroit, Gary, and Cleveland, among other cities. There were no plans on the road or schedules to meet. At night, I would just find a roadside motel to rest. The cost was between five and fourteen dollars per night for a single room. They were just a step above the roach hotels but were much better than the hotels Mom and I had stayed in while escaping the Japanese during the war.

My favorite stop for food was at truck stops where the portions of food were very satisfying for a hungry man. I had not run into any problems in the first two days. After I drove into Pennsylvania, the weather turned a bit warmer. In Pennsylvania, I-94 was very hilly and winding. I had a neat idea to save gas. I thought I could save a lot of gas by gliding down the hills with the ignition off and put the automatic transmission in neutral position. When the car reached the near end of the slope, I just started the engine by putting the shift into the drive position and kick-starting the car. This way, I could save a lot of gas. It worked!

Before leaving Pennsylvania, I heard noises in the rear of the car when I was accelerating and braking. I could hear that knocking metallic sound loud and clear. I knew then that I did something terribly bad to the car. As I kick-started the car, it was extremely hard on the car's transmission and the universal joint. After six or seven hours driving like that, I had ruined the universal joint to bare metal. Fortunately, there were service shops along highway 94. I made a stop at a roadside repair shop to have the universal joint replaced just before I left the Pennsylvania border. It certainly was costing me much more than the gas I had saved.

My car was loaded full in the back seat; that was quite visible from outside. In one of my meal stops, on the Pennsylvania Turnpike, a middle-aged fellow, dressed like a cowboy in long boots and a cowhide jacket, was following me around in the restaurant. I purposefully made turns and stops in the shop in order to drop him from my sight. But I noticed he followed my every move. I stopped at a newsstand and he approached me.

"Hey, mister, are you going to New York?" he asked.

"Yeah," I answered.

He extended his hand, but I refused to shake his hand.

"I know New York very well. I can drive you to New York and take you to the door where you want to go. You know there are a lot of dangerous places in New York City. You don't want to make a wrong turn. There is no charge. Just a free service," he told me.

"No. Thank you," I said.

I walked toward the counter, trying to break away from him. He continued to follow me. I was alarmed and scared. I wondered what he might do next. Did he have accomplices with him? Would they be waiting for me when I left the truck stop? I knew I must stay where there were a lot of people. I wished there was a policeman or a security guard somewhere near us. I walked away from where I stood. He again closely followed me to the coffee table.

"There are a lot of bad guys on the road. You really need someone to protect you," he insisted.

"Leave me alone, or I will call the police!" I yelled at him as loud as I could.

He backed off quickly. I had heard stories of robbers on the road before I left Menomonie. My alarm was switched on immediately when I saw this fellow. I would rather be impolite than sorry. I was still a bit scared of what was to happen next when I walked to my car. I did not wait to finish my meal and just rushed to my car while there were still many truck drivers around. Luckily, the guy was not out there waiting for me. Thank god! I thought, *maybe he thinks I'm still eating my dinner.* Wow! That was so close from being robbed or worse.

I drove into New York City at about one o'clock in the morning and called my good friend, Alfred Huang at Columbia University, to wait for me in his dormitory room that evening. It was quite easy to find the Columbia University dormitory. It was between the Broadway and Holland Avenue. Alfred came down to assist me moving some important items, including two pistols I brought in Wisconsin, my Yashica camera, and some smaller items, to his room, and then I locked the car. Alfred carefully double-checked the locks before we went upstairs.

"This street is so close to Holland Street, you can't be too careful about it," Alfred said.

The car was parked on the street curb right in front of the dormitory entrance. We rested less than four hours that morning. Alfred woke me up.

"Richard, I could not sleep all night. I don't feel comfortable with your property in the car. Let's go down and look before daybreak." Alfred was too nervous.

"This is Columbia University dormitory. You should have some security guards here. Let me have some more sleep." I was very tired from the long drive.

"Come on. Let's look and go back to bed," he insisted.

I reluctantly went down with him to check on my car. From a distance, everything seemed to be fine. But when we got closer, we found the contents in the back seat were gone, except my books. I opened the trunk. Nothing was left in there. The thieves had locked the car up after they had taken most of my belongings. I lost all my clothing, a smaller camera, a hi-fi system, and radios. After going upstairs, I dropped to the bed and slept for another two hours.

At nine o'clock in the morning, I called the New York Police Department to report the theft. "I would like to report a theft and to register my guns," I reported.

At the other end of the phone came this excited voice: "This is Sergeant Miller. My partner and I will be there right away. Give me your name and address."

I gave him my name, phone number, and address and waited. I thought, *Gee! The New York police are really prompt.*

In less than twenty minutes, there was a knock on the door. I opened the door and found the two plain-clothes detectives standing outside. I let them in.

"Where are the guns?" were the first words they said.

"Here they are." I gave the two guns to Miller. Both were collector's items—engraved .22-caliber target pistols. Sergeant Miller looked them over.

"Nice pieces you have. But you know it is against the law to have guns in New York City. You have two choices. You give them to me and forget about them, or you can come to the court to claim them. In that case, I will have to write you up," said Sergeant Miller.

"I was instructed by the police in Wisconsin how to own and register my guns in New York." I tried to explain.

"He did not know what he was talking about. For your own sake, just give up the guns," he said.

I really did not want to have any trouble over the guns. But it pained me to part with my collections. They were very special collector's guns given to me by a friend.

"Sergeant Miller take good care of these guns. They are very accurate shooters. You'll enjoy them. Now can we talk about my lost items?" I knew I could not win. I must give them up.

"Oh! No. We are not the right ones to talk to. You need to report the theft to your university police. However, I do not believe there is any hope for catching the thief or recovering any of your stuff. My advice is, just forget it," he said.

"I will take your advice. Good-bye, Sergeant." I let them out of the door. That was my first encounter with the New York's finest!

The morning after, I got up early at six o'clock to see the city. I walked on Broadway near Columbia's campus. When I saw a gentleman walking toward my direction, I did what everybody would do in Menomonie.

"Good morning," I said to him when he came close to about five feet.

He was startled by me and quickly walked past me. I thought he was impolite and funny, so I turned around to look at him. He also turned around and looked at me with a puzzled look. When I saw Alfred at lunch, I had to find out what was it with me.

"Alfred, do I look like a mugger or someone vicious?"

"Why do you ask me that?"

"Well, I said good-morning to a man this morning on the street. He looked like he had seen a ghost or something. I suspect he thought I was crazy."

"Oh! Richard, this is New York. You just don't want to say anything to strangers," he said, laughing. But I did not feel funny at all. What a pity to live in a place like this!

The next day, after supper, Alfred went to his evening class. I walked alone from the dorm eastward. I crossed Holland Road still going east. The street was full of people, and all of them were African Americans. I was walking and observing the scenes in this new city. No one minded me, and I was just looking around while walking. When it became very dark, I tracked the same street back to the dorm. Nothing had happened to me whatsoever. But when I described where I went to Alfred, he was obviously upset.

"Richard, you were risking your life to walk into Holland. That is the roughest place in New York. Many policemen were killed there in the past. Now even policemen dare not to go into that area alone. Don't do such things again. You really worry me," Alfred said.

"I am sorry! Alfred, I thought it was a street like any street in New York. I will not walk to that direction again," I promised.

After taking a coffee break with Alfred that first morning, I went to Columbia University to talk to the head of the electrical engineering department where I was accepted into the master's degree program. He told me that traditionally there would be no scholarship for any first-year graduate student. I had to prove myself during the first year of study before I could be considered for a grant. The tuition cost at Columbia was so high I would not be able to pay for it, even with all my savings. There would be no school for me for now.

I had to find a job immediately just to sustain myself and feed my family. Reading the want ads from a New York newspaper, I made a few phone calls and made three interviews. I took a job as an electrical engineer in a small electronics firm in Queens. I rented a basement apartment in Flushing from the co-owner, Russ, of the firm and became quite close to Russ and his family. We often dined together at home or went to various restaurants. We were always going Dutch on every meal. It was real news to me to see that Ross and his wife, Betty, counted to a single penny after each meal. Another thing they said that dumfounded me was their relationship with others. They would go their separate ways some evenings to have dates. I first thought it was a poker game for boys or bridal showers for girls where man and woman would not go together. But one day, Ross told me he was going to see his girlfriend and Betty was seeing her boyfriend. What a cultural shock that was!

I was totally shocked and dumbfounded into speechlessness by the Ross family. I could not imagine or comprehend how people could live together like this. Was it that they had total trust to each other? Or was it a total moral breakdown? I talked to some close friends who had been in the United States for a long time. Happily, I learned from them that this was a very unusual situation in the United

States. They had never seen anything like this. What a relief it was to someone who had just fallen in love with this country. I worked for the small company in electronics circuit design and testing from April until I left New York for Wisconsin in August 1963.

After I began to have a steady income, I sent one hundred dollars back home every month. To my family in Taiwan, that was a large amount in the early sixties. It was the equivalent of a five-month salary for me if I was still working in Taiwan. I saved up enough money and bought a used motor scooter and an old hi-fi system for my own entertainment. I thought life was good for us, except the separation from my family, which was very hard for both my wife and me.

As far as I was concerned, life in the United States had been a constant pursuance between studying and working. Days went by rather quickly. The most difficult time was in the evenings when people at school or work began to leave and I would drive alone in the dusk or went back to my apartment alone. My heart was heavy, and a sense of sadness would set in as I drove on the road when the setting sun set the evening cloud on fire. The more the pretty scenes entered my eyes, the deeper the sadness I felt. Where were my wife and our children? What were they doing? How happy would they be if they could just be here to share this moment with me!

My wife was busy with our two children at the ages that required her constant care. I knew how lonely she was after the children were in bed and when there was nothing else to occupy her mind! We resorted to letter writing in those moments in time. We both put many hours on paper and sent our thoughts across the big divide. What held us together were the hopes of a better life in the future. We were committed to trade the short but sharp pain for a brighter future and happiness for years to come.

There were so many things for me to see and to learn in the big city. I also liked the convenience and unlimited resources. A young fellow worker from South America became a good friend of mine and we spent quite a few weekends roaming around famous places in New York City. Our usual pastime was to watch wrestling shows on the television. We also frequented downtown and Forty-Second

Street. We liked to visit the electronics shops, the camera shops, and the factory outlet clothing stores where famous brand clothing was sold at very low prices. My favorite food was the flame steak and the Greek gyro that were sold on the curbsides in Manhattan. In the early sixties, most streets in New York City were relatively clean and safe, if we kept ourselves away from those sleazy places.

I was alone on the street of Times Square one afternoon. After I had watched a movie and bought some little things for my room, I went to the subway token booth and discovered I had only ten cents in my pocket. I thought I had much more than that in my pocket, at least enough to buy a token for twenty-five cents. I searched all over my pockets and wallet. I could not find any extra money. But I did have my checkbook with me. I went to nearby stores to try to buy some things and get change for my token. I told them about my dilemma. I tried at least ten stores, but no one would allow me to write any extra fifteen cents in the check for change for the token. In desperation, I thought about the 1878 silver coin that Mike Tibbetts had given me as a going-away gift. I treasured it very much and carried it with me all the time. Now I had to use it to buy a token. I was very upset about those businesspeople in New York City. Didn't they have any trust in people, or did they have any feelings toward others? I guess not.

The company I worked for was located right on Queens Boulevard, a very busy thoroughfare. I always parked my car on the service road off Queens Boulevard every day. It was about a block from my work place. It was a wide, three-lane street and many cars were parked along the sidewalks. My car was never in anybody's way. One afternoon, after work, I saw the rear quarter of my car was smashed beyond recognition and the car was pushed at least ten feet from where it was parked. I went back and called the police to the site. They recorded the accident and told me it would be hard to find out who did the hit-and-run. I was not happy to see my perfect, luxurious automobile end up like this. I was determined to find out who was the culprit.

I went back to the accident site and searched all around my car. I collected every bit of debris and small piece of paper in the vicinity of the car. As I examined the smashed rear quarter of the Cadillac, I found some red paint high on the rear fender. The impact was such that it could only be hit by a big truck. My first conclusion was that the culprit was a big red truck. I recalled seeing red trucks run by an industrial cleaning outfit that was serving this area daily. Then I concentrated on the pile of debris collected around my car. Through some luck, I found a piece of receipt dated the same day of the accident. It was the receipt of Sam's Cleaning Service. It had all the information of the firm operating the truck, including the address and phone number. I returned to the office and called the company.

"Is this the Sam's Cleaning Service?" I asked.

"Yes. What can I do for you?" A male's voice was on the line.

"May I speak to your manager?" I asked.

"I am the owner here," he said.

"Do you have your trucks painted red?" I asked.

"Yes. What do you want?" He had sensed something wrong.

"I believe one of your trucks hit my car and ran without leaving a note," I told him.

"I don't think so. All our trucks are back here. None had any problems." He was confident.

"Okay! I would like you to check it out and I will call you back later. I want you to know that I have evidence here to report a hit-and-run case. Please be sure your truck was not the one that hit my car." I bluffed a little.

An hour later, I called again. The fellow on the other end of the line was the same man, but he was politer this time.

"Have you done any checking?" I asked.

"Yes. I am afraid you are right. One of my trucks hit a blue Cadillac. Is that your car?" he admitted. "Our insurance company is Travelers Insurance Company. Please give me your phone number. I will have them contact you."

The matter was settled in days. I was paid exactly the amount I paid for the car: $400. The car was still functioning except the left rear end looked awful. It also was making some grinding noises at the rear end. Soon it started smoking badly. Good things must end sometime, but this was too soon. I had not had enough time to enjoy the car in the last few months. But now, I really had enough of the big city. I missed Wisconsin and the people there terribly.

CHAPTER 7

Returning to Wisconsin

Was its mental telepathy or the answers to my informal prayers? Dr. Ray Wigen called me on the phone one August evening. "Richard. How are you?" he said.

"I am fine. How are you and Mrs. Wigen?"

"We are all fine here. Richard. Are you still interested in teaching?" he asked.

"Yes. I am still interested in teaching."

"I have a friend in Racine Technical Institute who needs someone to teach electronics courses. I told him about you. He is very much interested in your background."

"That's great. I have had enough of the big city. I like Wisconsin much better," I said.

"Okay! I will have the head of the institute call you tomorrow. Take care." He hung up.

The next morning, Mr. Jaeger, the dean from Racine Technical Institute, called me. "Mr. Cheng, good morning. I am Earl Jaeger. Dr. Wigen told me I can call you directly," he said.

"Certainly. I talked to him yesterday," I said.

"I am sure he mentioned a teaching position here," he said.

"Yes. He did. Could you tell me a little bit about the school?"

"The State of Wisconsin has funded this new two-year college. It is designed to train technical students for industries. We need someone to establish the new curriculum, the laboratories, and to head the new department," he said.

"I am interested in the position. Please send me the offer letter at your convenience," I told him. That literally was a verbal commitment.

"The letter will be sent out to you today. Nice talking to you," he said.

I wrote a letter to Nancy and described the new job and my moving plan. I told her I was not pleased with the rat race in the big city.

The offer letter arrived in four days. I signed it and sent it back right away. The salary was about $600 per month. It was not high, but I was satisfied with the amount. Now my decision was made, I became anxious to leave the big city. I submitted my resignation to Russ the day after the call.

"What? You are going to accept a job as a teacher?" He was surprised.

"Yes. I always wanted to teach since I was little," I said.

"You are out of your mind! Why do you want to take job that pays so little?" He could not understand there were things more important than just money.

"Well, Ross, teaching has different rewards that you can't buy with money," I told him.

"Okay! It's your life. Good luck," he said. That was it.

A week later, I loaded my old Caddy with much more than I had brought with me to New York just six months ago. Among all the things, I had accumulated a lot of toys for my two boys and a few gifts for my wife. I rented a six-foot-long U-Haul trailer to haul my BMW scooter and some cartons of my own accumulations. After I said good-byes to Russ and other coworkers in the company, I took the Long Island Expressway heading west through the city. When I drove to Manhattan to say good-bye to Alfred, he insisted to go with me at least to the border of Pennsylvania.

"Richard, you are driving this smoky Caddy alone. I don't know it you can make it on the expressway. Why don't you let me accompany you to Wisconsin?" he offered.

"No. I don't want to waste your time. I will make it alone. But thanks just the same," I said.

"Well, maybe I will just go to the border of Pennsylvania. We haven't talked for a long time. How about it?" he insisted.

"Okay! Alfred, you are my true friend." I reluctantly accepted his kind offer.

He was concerned this car would not make it very far from the city. Other than smoking a little, the car ran quite well. I enjoyed Alfred's company all the way to a roadside stop on I-94 inside Pennsylvania. I insisted to take him to a Greyhound bus stop and send him back to New York City.

I continued my journey to Wisconsin on I-94 west. It was an uneventful trip. I did not make any unnecessary stops along the way. It took me only two days to get into the city of Racine. The first night, I settled in a motel just outside the city limits. The first thing I did the next morning was to drive around town to get to know the city and see where the school was located. After lunch, I called several people who had advertised apartments for rent in a newspaper. George was the last one I called.

"Hi! I saw the ad in the paper. You have a room for rent?"

"We sure do," he said.

"May I take a look?"

"Come on over. I will be home all afternoon," he said.

"Are you George? I am Richard. Please give me your address. I will drive right over."

He gave me his address and I drove over to the address given. After I knocked on the door, George, a man in his forties, came to answer the door.

"Hi! I just called for the room," I said.

"The room is rented," he told me.

"I just talked to you a few minutes ago. You said you have a room for rent and asked me to come over. My name is Richard," I said, thinking there was some misunderstanding.

"I told you all rooms are taken," he said impatiently as he shut his door on my face.

I knew what was going on. It was just another ignorant person. I was not upset, but I was quite disappointed with the people in this city that I was going to settle in. That afternoon, I did find an apartment near the school and moved right in. A month later, in a school party, I met George again. He turned out to be the husband of the departmental secretary, Bea. He was quite embarrassed. But I told him, "George, don't feel bad. I understand the feeling of not letting a foreign stranger move into your home. I am sure you would take me in now. Wouldn't you?" I said jokingly.

"Of course, I will take you in now, but I still feel awful about what I did to you," he quietly.

The first day in school, Carl Oscar, an older professor of mathematics, came to my office.

"Richard, the first thing you need to do is to get your retirement plan in place. I will show you how to do it. Come to my office when you have time," he told me.

"Carl, I am only twenty-nine years old. Isn't it too early for me to worry about retirement?" I said. I thought it was quite funny.

"Richard, believe me: time goes fast. Before you know it, you are ready to retire. It is never too early to plan on retirement," he told me.

"Okay. Carl, I will be in your office in ten minutes," I said reluctantly.

He patiently showed me how to get enrolled into the TIAA/CREF program and how to split the coverage between the two groups.

"It is best to split the TIAA and CREF 50/50. You never know how the stock market will be in the future. The TIAA is conservative and your money will be safe there," he told me.

To this day, I often thought about him and his advice and how right he was. Through the past many years, the retirement funds had grown to a substantial amount. Carl passed away many years ago. I never had a chance to thank him for his advice and his kindness.

The technical institute was a small two-year college. It offered associate of science degrees in many technical fields of studies. The first semester, I was assigned to teach six different courses. Not knowing what the normal teaching load was supposed to be, I did not mind taking such a heavy teaching schedule. The six courses ranged from introduction to electricity, mechanical drawing, mathematics, and electronic circuits. I was quite familiar with those subjects and confident that I could handle them without any problems. I devised a plan to prepare for my first-year teaching in the States.

The only thing I was concerned about teaching was my English, both spoken and written. I went to see Earl Yeager, the dean, for his advice.

"Earl, I took the offer to teach courses here. I don't mind working hard, but how I am going to deal with my English deficiencies?" I asked him.

"Richard, I can understand you without any problem. You have some accent and mix up the tenses at times, but the students will understand you. If they give any hard time, just let me know."

"Thank you for your encouragement. I will do my best. If someone complains, please let me know. I will try to correct my errors. If I do poorly by the end of the semester, I will leave the school."

"Don't worry! You will do fine." He was really a very good boss.

I could not fix my English quickly but wanted to do well with my delivery of instructions. I had to do it well. This was my make-or-break for my teaching career in the United States. When I walked into the first class—engineering mathematics—the reception was that of twenty-six pairs of curious eyes.

"Good morning. My name is Richard Cheng," I said. "This class is the engineering mathematics."

The room was awfully quiet. I could almost hear the echoes of my own voice.

"I would like to give you a simple test called the JOP—jumping off point test—to see how you are prepared so I can give you a proper starting level of lecture for this class," I said.

I handed out the prepared test to each student.

"You have fifteen minutes to complete the test," I said, looking at my watch.

The JOP test was purposely made quite difficult. I wanted to be sure that everyone would get zero or very low marks. I then gave the answers immediately following the test. It was designed to make them see how simple the answers were. I used this method in the past to establish authority in the classroom.

"You keep the test and compare with my answers and see how you are doing," I told them.

After fifteen minutes, I told them to stop and I gave the answers to each of the problems.

"Mr. Chin, the answers are so simple!" one of the students said.

"Okay! Anyone get the answers—100 percent? Please raise your hand." No hands were raised.

"Eighty percent or better?" No hands were raised.

"Fifty percent?" Still no hands.

"Ten percent or better?"

"Zero?" Everybody raised hands.

"That is all right. I will try to lower the JOP. I think you will do fine."

It worked here too! They knew who was the boss in the classroom. We had a good start.

In order to prepare myself, each Saturday morning I would drive to the lakeside park and park the car along the beach of Lake Michigan where it was nice, quiet, and beautiful. I would bring some coffee and my favorite donuts with me while I made lesson plans of all six courses for the week. The first week, it took me about two hours to do the lesson plans. The following weeks and on, it took me less than an hour for the entire week's lesson plans.

I had to struggle with my English grammar, pronunciations, and heavy accent, but I could communicate effectively with students through the help of using the blackboard and sometimes hand signs.

My students responded quite well from the start. By the end of the first year, students of the institute elected me the "Teacher of the Year."

Everything was just fine in the school and I enjoyed it very much during the first year. The second year, my course load was reduced to just four courses per semester, and that was the normal load. Earl, the dean, apologized to me. "Richard, we gave you the unusual load of six courses last year because we could not find qualified teachers. You did a first-rate job. I want to thank you for that," Earl said to me.

He gave me a 5 percent raise that year. I thought it was great because in Taiwan a college teacher's salary was the same year after year until one was promoted to a higher rank. Someone told me that as the teacher of the year, I should have received much more than the 5 percent salary raise. The 5 percent was just a raise for average teachers that year. I just did not know better to bargain for more.

Although I was very patient with questions from students, I was quite intolerant to bad behavior in classrooms. One of the students, Ken Olson, was especially naughty. Each time I turned my back to write on the black board, Ken would make funny noises to cause others laughing. When I turned around, he would pretend he was not the guilty one.

"Cut it out. It is not funny," I ordered.

But as soon I turned to the board, he did it again. This time I caught him with an unexpected turning of my head.

"Ken, I would like to talk to you after the class. How about meet me at the gym?"

"Yes, sir. Whatever you say," Ken said.

After the class, I walked to the gym and waited for him. A group of his classmates came along to see what was going on.

"Look. You have been making fun of me in the classes. Now I am going to show you something. If you can wrestle me to the ground, you can do what you have been doing in the class. But if I win, you will stop the foolishness in the class. Do we have a deal?" I was quite confident.

He smiled with confidence that he could overcome a small guy at five feet, seven with his six-foot frame. "Sure, Mr. Cheng, I will do what you say."

I took off my jacket and dress shirt. He also took off his blue shirt. About twenty students were circling the two of us. We used the jumping pads as the platform. Ken was big, but I could tell by his first move that he had never wrestled before. I quickly flipped him flat on the floor and he fell pretty hard.

"Would like to try another round?" I asked.

"No. I think I had enough," Ken said. He apparently was in pain.

I pulled him up and just walked back to my office. Since that time, I was honored with the title "The Chinese Wild Man." When I walked down the crowded hall, a clear path would be opened for me to pass. There were no more funny gestures by anyone else from that day on. As a matter of fact, Ken became one of the best students of mine. He graduated from the institute and went on to get his undergraduate and graduate degrees in a Big Ten university. He stayed in contact with me for many years after I left Racine.

Racine was a relatively small city in Wisconsin. Most of the residents had not seen many people from the Orient. I was often stared at or referred to as the "Chinaman" from a distance. I was not insulted because, at that time, I did not know what the word really meant. It was not unusual to hear friends tell jokes in social gatherings about Chinese immigrants. But they were mostly just being funny. One day, in a party for faculty and dependents, Professor Joe Green said, "I want to tell you a joke about Chinese. I think Richard will appreciate it." He turned to me and said, "Do you mind, Richard, if I tell a joke about Chinese?"

"Go right ahead, as long as it isn't about me," I replied. I was holding my breath and hoping he would not say anything too insulting.

"Okay! There was this professor. He noticed a laundry shop with a sign that says Carl Schultz Hand Laundry Shop. And he was curious. He left home earlier that day, got off the bus near the laundry, and walked into the shop.

"Is Mr. Carl Shultz in?" the professor asked.

"I am Carl Shultz," the elderly man said.

"Do you have a distant ancestor from Germany?"

"No."

"Were you adopted by a German family?"

"No."

"Please tell me how in the world you have a name like that," the professor asked.

"Okay, if you have a minute, I will tell you," said the old man. "I came to this country in 1919. We had to go through the immigration service stations in Ellis Island. I stood in a long line behind a big, burly fellow.

"What's your name?" the officer asked.

"My name is Carl Shultz," the fellow replied.

The official made some notes and processed him through. Then I walked up to the window. "What's your name?" the official asked me.

"Sam Ting," said I.

The officer took a funny look at me and said, "Oh! Same thing." He made some notes on my paper, gave the stack of paper back to me, and waved me through. When I looked at my form I-94, it had the name Carl Shultz on it and I have been stuck with that name ever since." Professor Green concluded the story.

Everybody in the party laughed their heads off. I thought that was very funny too. I had told that joke in many public speeches and private parties. Each time, I made some minor variation in the story. Each time, it was an exploding laughter.

CHAPTER 8

LONG LAST: A FAMILY REUNION

As soon as I reported to work at the school, I learned from the immigration services that if I were to bring my family over here to visit me, I needed a sponsor to back me up. I asked Earl to help me to bring my family over here.

"Earl, I would like to bring my wife and the two boys to join me here. Would you help me out?"

"What do we have to do to help you?" Earl asked.

"I need you to write a letter and sign the form to sponsor a change of my status from the F1 student visa to the first-preference worker status," I answered.

"Does it mean you can stay in this country indefinitely?" Earl asked.

"I don't know about the first-preference status. In order to stay permanently, I would need to get a green card," I said. "For now, I only need the first-preference status to have my family visit me here."

"That's not a problem at all. I will write the letter today and you fill up the form. I will sign it."

Earl drafted a letter for me. The secretary typed the applications forms together with Earl's letter that completed the school's sponsorship for the change of status. The Immigration and Naturalization Services approved the application to change my status to the first-preference work status within a month.

With the new status, I could now apply for my family to visit me in the United States. There would be no restrictions on how much time my family liked to stay in the United States, if I had a job in the field of my training.

I immediately filled out the INS application for my family to join me in the States after the change of status was approved. The Immigration and Naturalization Services approved my application quickly without any problem. I wrote to Nancy and told her the good news. At that point, I had saved enough money for the airline tickets and all moving expenses for my wife and two sons. With my salary of about $600 per month, it took me about four months to save up enough money for the moving expenses.

I sent the money to Nancy for her to arrange the trip to the United States. Again, she had to work through the red tape from the local police department, the city, the Foreign Affairs Ministry, and finally the United States Consulate. It did not take her as much time as I did. She left Taiwan with our two boys on January 23, 1964. At that point, we were not sure how long we were going to stay in this country.

After receiving the telegraph about her traveling schedule, I waited anxiously for that day to come. In the meantime, I started to look for a place for my family to live. The rental apartments were quite abundant on the market in Racine. I rented a second-floor two-bedroom apartment for thirty-five dollars per month. I had been accumulating toys for my boys since I decided to bring them over to this country many months ago. Now they were in boxes piled in a large closet. In order to get a quick start, I also collected a set of furniture, kitchenware, and other necessary items, at least enough for my family's use upon their arrival.

On January 24, my wife and our sons were scheduled to arrive at the Chicago O'Hare International Airport in the evening. I left Racine that early afternoon for O'Hare to wait for them and to bring them back to our new home. I was very excited about this reunion. I was wondering how well they handled the long and tiring trip. How did Nancy take care of the two little boys alone through those twenty hours of flying plus stopovers in Tokyo and Alaska?

Finally, the plane arrived at the terminal. I waited right at the gate. At eleven o'clock at night, I saw a chubby little boy in an oversized coat walk down the ramp all by himself. A beautiful young lady holding another little boy followed. I recognized them immediately and ran forward to greet them. My older boy, a little over three years old, seemed to know who I was. The four of us hugged without saying anything. Finally, we were together after so many years!

"Papa I want to pee" was the first thing the three-year-old said.

I held his hand and led him to the bathroom around the corridor. He seemed very mature at that tender age. The younger one at two years old did not know who I was. When I wanted to embrace my wife, he struggled to defend his mother against this strange intruder. Nancy and I both laughed.

"This is Papa. Do you remember the pictures I showed you?" Nancy asked him.

He nodded his head but was still uncomfortable with this stranger. I finally managed to get them into my waiting car. Soon, curiosity overcame the fear of a stranger; the two boys started to enjoy the gadgetry in this big, old, black Cadillac. They were tuning the radio, moving the antenna up and down. They also found the electric window switch to make it to go up and down. This new world was so much fun for them. They both had so many questions about everything they saw. I tried to explain things to them in Mandarin and found I had not spoken Mandarin for so long, I had forgotten some of the words.

"You talk with a bit of funny accent," Nancy said.

"I guess I have forgotten how to speak in Chinese." I had to agree with her.

"We need to give our boys English names. It is very hard for the Americans to pronounce Chinese names," I told Nancy.

"What do you have in mind?"

"How about we call Su-Ting James?"

"That sounds like a nice name. I like it. Ting, how about people call you Jim?" Nancy asked the three-year-old.

"Okay," said he.

"I suggest we call Su-Ching Raymond, after my mentor, Dr. Ray Wigen."

"Sure, that's a good name too." She agreed.

The new English names would be easier for our American friends to know our sons' names. We talked about what was like at home, including Mom and Dad and others. We had so much to learn from each other. By the time I realized the wrong road sign, I had driven the car over fifty miles in the opposite direction.

James was most curious about the car and asked me questions all the way back to Racine. "Papa, is this your car?" Jim asked. "Can we ride in it every day?" He was afraid I had to return the car to someone else tomorrow.

"This car is ours. It belongs to us. We can use this car every day," I told him. He was relieved.

Jim was satisfied and very happy with the car. Ray was very tired and made some fuzz in the car. I calmed him down by stopping at a gas station and bought three Cokes for them. That was the first Coke for Nancy and the two boys. They really liked it. Soon Ray fell asleep in Nancy's arms.

It was after midnight when we arrived the old apartment. Raymond woke up for a few minutes and fell asleep in his bed quickly, but James managed to turn on the television, glued himself to the screen, and refused to go to bed. There was just one station on at that late hour. Since Nancy and I had so much to catch up with after the long separation, the three of us stayed up until two in the morning.

The next morning the boys found the pile of toys I prepared for them: a battery-powered train set, several battery-powered cars, and all sorts of toy guns. They tried to set up the train tracks before I got up late in the morning. They did such a good job of assembling the tracks that I was truly amazed. All I needed to do was to connect the power through a power supply that plugged into the wall socket. Before the end of the day, the two boys had gone through all the boxes and made a big mess in the living room. It was fun for Nancy and me just to watch them be so happy and totally occupied by those toys.

"I still feel like in a dream. I had dreamed so much of this moment in the past. We are together finally. Look how happy the boys are!" She was a bit emotional.

Taiwan was relatively poor at that time. It was new to Nancy and our children to live in a heated house furnished with a telephone, a refrigerator, and a television set. Back in Taiwan, there were no such commodities in the early sixties. By watching them, I knew they were very happy to be in the States. We took them out to treat them at McDonald's for hamburgers, Coke, and fries. That was the biggest treat they loved.

At that time, a McDonald's hamburger was ten cents. The whole meal for each boy was a little more than a quarter. As a teacher, we felt very happy and rich enough because we could get everything we needed to make a happy living. The old apartment was a great improvement over what we lived in, in Taiwan. There were many parks and playgrounds we could take the boys to play in during the evenings and on the weekends. Nancy and I were very happy with the new country, but at that time, we had not yet decided to make this country our permanent home.

When Nancy first arrived in this country, she knew very little about cooking. The reason was before she was married, her mother wouldn't let the girls get their hands dirty in the kitchen. After she married me, my mom would do all the cooking. Nancy never had a chance to do any cooking in Taiwan. When she moved into our apartment, she did some very simple cooking. That was all she knew what to cook. I had done much more cooking than she did at that time. I started to show her how to make the fried beef, egg dumplings, and sweat-and-sour fish. Before I knew it, she had mastered many new dishes. I decided to retire as the cook of the house soon after she came to the States.

In those days, we could not find our favorite Chinese food, such as Chinese-style sausages, dried chicken, dried ducklings, and ham. Based on the memory of my taste buds, I began to make sausages and dried chicken first. Because the winter in Racine was very dry, the result of my experiment was a big success. Our boys loved the dried food I made. Of course, Nancy's cooking of the dried food had a lot to do with bringing out the taste. My experiment was extended to ham, ducklings, and fish. Since then, we made the dried meat every winter until the import of Chinese goods became common in grocery stores.

Our social life in Racine was very good as well. I became good friends with Kuo-King Wang and his family before Nancy arrived

Racine. They had a girl and a boy at the ages of four and one. The two families frequently drove to parks in Chicago or Milwaukee for the weekends. Kuo-King was a scholarly material scientist working for Walker Industries, a local manufacturer that made mufflers for cars. Cindy, his wife, was a very nice, intelligent lady who took care of their children full time. After Nancy came, we became even closer friends. The Wang children and our boys were friends as well. In addition to the Wang family, we also had Andy Chow and Charlie Lee—both single—as our weekend guests. Together with the Wang couple, we had many bridge games in the evenings and the rainy weekends. We really had some unforgettable good times in Racine.

Our apartment was on the second floor with the front window facing a busy street. James would watch cars going through the street from of the apartment window. He asked me what kind of cars they were, the brand, the models, and so on. Soon afterward, he could recognize most of the brands and models of cars passing by. I suppose car loving was the nature of most boys. Among the toys we later bought for them, more than half were matchbox cars and model cars.

Marie Olson, our neighbor two houses down, came with a box of homemade cookies. She held both Jim and Ray in her arms and said to Nancy and me, "Hug them often, because before you realize it, they will have grown up."

Marie was in her fifties and her four children were all in the thirties. I thought the advice was good, but we were so young and to see our babies growing to adults—that must be a very long time. We did not really understand what she meant but we thanked her for the advice anyway. Our next-door neighbor gave our boys two kittens. The boys kept them in the house and took care of them. One was a tan-colored male; the boys named it Tiger. The other, a pepper-colored female, the boys called Cleo for Cleopatra. Both cats were less than three months old when they were brought in our home. Both cats were very active in the house, climbing all over beds, tables, chairs, and other furniture inside the apartment. They played in the yard only when the weather was good.

One day, James ran into the house, very excited and with tears on his face. At that moment, I had a fellow instructor from the institute visiting me in the living room. I had instructed the boys to speak English only in front of Americans. Apparently in great anxiety, he was trying to tell us in English what had happened.

"Tiger—tree—boom," he said, using his hands to make a top-down motion.

We understood perfectly that Tiger had fallen from a tree. We went outside of the apartment and found Tiger dead from the thirty-five feet fall. Jim told me in Mandarin later that Tiger was chased by a larger male cat and fell from this big tree, hit the concrete pavement, and was killed instantly. That poor cat was less than a year old.

I was not very much attached to the two cats, but I knew how much Tiger meant to our boys. I had my dogs: one lost to a butcher and another bayoneted by a soldier. The emotional impact to a child was difficult for others to understand, unless one had experienced it.

"Jimmy, we will find you another Tiger, okay?" I held him in my arms.

"Papa, I want one just like him," he said, wiping off his tears.

"Sure, we will do just that." I comforted him.

After supper, I would take Jim with me to stores and walk with him on the sidewalks in the neighborhood to familiarize him with the environment. Ray was too young to walk with us on the street at that time.

One day, a neighbor was walking toward our direction while we took a walk on the sidewalk. We greeted each other.

"Is he your boy?" he asked.

"Yes. This is James, my number 1 son. He just came from Taiwan with my wife three days ago," I said proudly.

He looked at both of us with a puzzle in his eyes.

"I thought people in China are starving. How come he is so chubby?" he questioned me.

"Taiwan is not as rich as the States, but it is not as poor as you think. At least people do have enough to eat."

"Oh! I see." He was not totally convinced.

I just laughed and waved good-bye to him. I really did not know where to start to explain to him about what the world was like outside of the States. People here were brainwashed by the media bias and were fed with incomplete information! It was really astonishing to me. Just like the neighbor's impression of people from China was so far from the truth. My own impression of the American people before I came here was just totally incorrect.

On the other hand, all of us must depend on the media to bring information to us. Unless for very serious matters relating directly to him or herself, people would not bother to go to the library to research the true information and just believed in what one received from the press, the newscasts, and motion pictures. My past "knowledge" about American people was mostly from Hollywood movies. I truly felt that I should not have laughed at my neighbor for asking me such ignorant questions.

Another day, I was walking on the main street of Racine. A friendly fellow, whom I had not met before, greeted me and stopped to chat with me.

"Hi! How are you? Are you a Chinese?"

"Yes, I am."

"Oh! Are you a cousin of Mr. Chin of the House of Chin?" he asked curiously.

House of Chin was a Chinese restaurant.

"No, I am not," I answered.

"Are you related to the Tang's Laundry?" He continued to explore this new immigrant.

"No!" I replied. I was a bit annoyed.

"What are you doing for living?" he asked me.

"I teach in a school," I answered.

He seemed to have found the answer.

"Oh! You are teaching the Chinese language," he said with a look of triumph.

I quickly found an excuse to part his company because I did not want to get in a lengthy discussion with a person who always had the answer to everything from his point of view. That was the common perception of Chinese in the United States at that time. The American Chinese had two old major trades: the restaurant business and the laundry business. Although there were hundreds of thousands of Chinese Americans who were professors, scientists, doctors, and engineers, most of the population in the country still had the old impressions from World War II news clips and from Charlie Chan movies.

Owning a home had been my dream since my family moved to town. I had been in friends' houses and seen the basements, attics, and garages. I had dreamed of all sorts of uses of those spaces. That kind of space was something I had not seen in China or Taiwan. I would like a house of our own with a basement workshop and a garage for cars and tools. It would be so handy and so much fun for me to work on mechanical and electronics projects. The attic would be used for storing unused items for the future and just in case we needed them. Nancy was equally enthusiastic about owning a house.

We started looking for a small house to buy. We looked at the for-sale signs along the streets we would like to live on. We also read newspaper ads and called up the owner or the agent for appointments to see houses. Within a month, we bought a three-bedroom brick house in a quiet urban neighborhood. The house had a small lawn in the front and a large fenced yard in the back. To us, it was beyond luxury. Comparing with the old apartment, this house was better by several scales. The cost of the house was $17,000. I was qualified to get 90 percent of loan. All I needed to pay in cash was less than $2,000 down and the house was ours. It could not have happened back in Taiwan at that time. The payment of the mortgage was a little over one hundred dollars a month. With my salary at $640 a month, it was quite affordable. I rented a U-Haul trailer and moved from the apartment the day the house was closed.

"We are the owners of this house. This is all ours!" I told Nancy.

"Not quite! The bank owns more than us," she said jokingly.

"It doesn't matter. We only pay so little money each month to the bank. In thirty years, it will all be paid up," I said. I really thought we might live in that house that long, and I did not mind a bit about that.

After we moved in the house, the basement was quickly made into an electronics workshop. My dream was coming true! It was filled up gradually with surplus electronic components, systems, and old television sets. I repaired these old television sets and then sold them through ads on the newspaper. It was a good supplement to my income. When we needed furniture or appliances, we bought them in garage sales on the weekends. It not only filled our needs, but it was also big fun to drive around town and plow into curious piles of unknown items. The feeling was just like opening Christmas gift boxes.

We felt our life in the United States was quite comfortable. We had everything we wanted and were very content with what we had. The boys were quite happy with the new environment as well. They learned English from watching TV programs and from playing with neighborhood kids. Within a few months, I thought they could speak better English than I could.

We had made many friends in Racine. Most of them were from the school. A few of them were local businesspeople I met in classes I taught. Of the most unforgettable was Stanley Kay. Stanley was a boss of a tool-making factory with about one hundred workers. He was my father's age in the late forties. He attended my evening electronics class and was one of the most outstanding students. He had a curious mind and had a lot of questions. We often went for coffee break together or had a fast food dinner after school. We became very good friends. After my family came to the States, the two families alternately traded picnics and home cooking back and forth. Stanley gave me a tour of the factory that was inherited from his father-in-law about five years ago with only a dozen workers. Stanley took over the management and started to modernize it. He applied many new technologies to the trade. That was why he wanted to learn electronics in his position.

"Richard, as a boss, you must know what your people are doing, so you will not be snowed by them," he told me.

That advice was deeply etched in my mind, and I followed his philosophy of managing people in later days.

In these days, Nancy was at home taking care of the kids' full time.

"How about if I find a job to earn extra money?" Nancy asked me one day.

"Why?" I asked.

"That way you would not have to fix TVs and have some more rest," she said.

"I don't mind fixing TVs after school. I have fun doing it. There is no need for extra rest," I said. "If you find a job, you will need a babysitter to watch our kids during the day. I don't feel good to leave our boys to others to bring up. To care and educate our children far outweighs any amount of additional money you might be making."

"I guess you are right. I also can't leave them to others." She agreed.

"Okay! Before our children grow up, your full-time work is to educate them at home," I said.

Both James and Ray were well-behaving and intelligent boys. There was almost no verbal fight between the two of them, and there was never a fistfight between them. James was big for his age in the kindergarten. He was even tempered and friendly; therefore, he was well accepted by kids in his class from day one.

One day James came into the house crying.

"Jimmy, what has happened?" I asked him.

"Jeff just hit me," he said.

"Jeff is much smaller than you. Did you hit him back?" I asked.

"No. I did not hit him back," he told me.

"James, why didn't you fight back?"

"I don't want to hurt him," he said.

He was always a good-hearted kid. He was crying not from the pain but from the hurt in his heart because someone would hit him. James always acted like a big brother to Ray and Ray's peers, not to bully them but to protect and care for them. When he obtained cookies or candies from us, he would share them with Ray and give Ray the larger portion. Ray knew about his brother's kindness and never forgot how well he was treated. Nancy and I learned about these details only after they had grown up.

Nancy and I were sitting on the bench in a park, watching the boys play. When I saw the obvious happiness in her and the boys, I came up with an idea. "Nancy, what do you think of moving back to Taiwan?" I was testing her.

"I don't know if you can revert back to the living style in Taiwan anymore," she said.

"How about you?"

"When I think about the poor sanitation facilities there, I don't want to go back to Taiwan."

"Okay! If we don't plan to move back to Taiwan, we'd better plan on staying here for good. What do you think?"

"I have no problem with staying here for good. Look! Taiwan is not our homeland. The natives there do not like us. So, we really have only one choice: stay here," she said. We can't go back to the mainland. The Communist is in firm control there.

"Well, in that case, we'd better apply for the permanent-resident status in order to stay here legally. Remind me to call the immigration services tomorrow. I need to find out the specifics," I said.

The information I received from INS was not encouraging. First we needed a school to sponsor us while INS was processing the application. If we should move to another job, we would need the new school to file a petition to support our immigration application. There was a quota to restrict the number of Asian immigrants each year. That meant a long wait.

In order not to lose time, I asked the institute to file a petition for changing my immigration status from first-preference worker to permanent-resident status. The school filed the paper in the fall of 1964. We knew it was a long, long wait before we would hear anything from INS.

CHAPTER 9

Teaching at Stout

I attended a professional society convention in Detroit in the spring of 1966. In the last day of the convention, Dr. Philip Ruehl, my mentor, asked me if I would return to teach at Stout.

"Richard, I have to be careful. I don't want to tear you away from Racine, but I need someone like you at Stout," he said to me.

I was hoping that I had heard him correctly. To teach at Stout was a big step upward in my career.

"Phil, did you say you want to hire me to teach at Stout?" I asked.

"Affirmative. I just have to be careful not to get people in Racine mad at me for asking you to leave there."

"The decision would be mine. I want to work for Stout," I said decisively.

"Okay. Richard, you wait for the offer from the Stout administration before resigning from Racine. I will get the paperwork going as soon as I return to Menomonie." He was happy.

"That is great! Thank you," I said.

"Okay! We have a deal," he said, and we shook hands.

"I am registered to study at Marquette for the summer school. I will move to Menomonie just before the fall quarter starts. Is it okay?" I asked.

"No problem. I know you can handle those courses without much preparation," he said.

"I really appreciate you offered me this opportunity at Stout. I will do a good job for you," I said.

"I am confident you will do well at Stout. I am looking forward to working with you in the fall."

"I will call you when I come in town. Please say hello to Chris, and take care, Phil!"

At the Detroit airport, I called Nancy. "Guess what! We are moving to Menomonie in August. What do you think?" I asked.

"Tell me more about it." She was really surprised.

"I will give you the details when I get home. But Stout is hiring me back to teach there," I said.

"That's wonderful! I can't wait to hear the details from you. Travel safely!"

I went back to Racine, talked all I knew about this job, and waited for the official letter from Stout. Before the letter was sent, Dr. Wigen called me from Stout.

"Congratulations! Richard, the university is offering you the assistant professorship, starting this fall," he told me.

"Thank you, Dr. Wigen. I am so happy to be able to come back to the school. I did not even mind if it was just an instructor position," I said, and truthfully so.

"You deserve better than that. Phil had no problems to get you that position at all. We are looking forward to seeing you back here soon, Richard."

"Nancy and I are excited about moving back there too. Thank you so much for calling me."

The letter and some forms arrived the next day. I accepted the offer by signing the papers and sent the package out the same day. I called Dr. Ruehl about my formal acceptance and thanked him. I went to talk to Earl Jaeger, the head of the institute, about the move I was to make.

"Earl, I was just offered a teaching position at Stout as assistant professor," I told him.

"I don't suppose I can talk you out of leaving us?" he said, and he puffed his big cigar.

"I think I will accept the Stout offer," I said.

"Okay! Richard, that is a step up for you. I wish you good luck! But the world will still go around with or without you here," he muttered.

I supposed he was not very happy about my leaving the institute.

"You and others in the school have been good to me. I feel bad to leave here but teaching at Stout is what I always wanted to do. I will make things easy for Ron to take over my duties," I said.

Ron was a fellow instructor in electronics. The most difficult part with this relocation was to say good-bye to my students. I got to know them well individually. They were my first few classes of students that I taught in the United States. They had left a deep feeling and impression in my heart. We had worked on projects that were not only just instructional but also a lot of fun for students and instructors alike. I advised them to continue their education at Stout for a bachelor's degree in electronics. Many of them did apply and were accepted by Stout upon their graduation.

I wrapped up the semester of teaching in late May and moved to Milwaukee to attend Marquette for the summer program. We locked up the house for the summer and only brought some necessary items for the summer to Milwaukee. After the summer school, I was ready to start my job at Stout State University. The name of the school had been changed from *college* to *university*, and the enrollment had increased from 1,500 when I was there to over 6,000 students. We decided to sell the house in Racine and buy a new one in Menomonie. Without knowing how the transaction should go, I sold our house for the amount I paid, after two years of usage. I thought I was ahead of the deal until I learned that I should have asked at least 10 percent more. I felt like a fool after I learned that houses did appreciate their values in the United States instead of depreciated.

"I am going to look for an apartment to stay in temporarily and then look for a house to buy later," I told Nancy.

"That sounds reasonable. To buy a suitable house takes time," she said.

"I will call you when I get there," I said.

"Drive carefully."

In July 1966, before we closed the deal on the house in Racine, I drove alone to find a place in Menomonie for the family to live in.

I stayed at Dr. Wigen's home that evening. The next morning, I drove to see an apartment that had an ad in the newspaper. As I was driving to the apartment, I passed a "For sale by owner" sign in the front lawn of a ranch house. I stopped the car and walked to the front door. An elderly man came out when he saw me through the living room window. He opened the front door and walked to his front lawn.

"Good morning. What can I do for you?" he asked.

"Are you selling the house?" I asked.

"Yes. I am selling it myself. May I show you around?"

"If it is not too much trouble for you. I am on my way to see an apartment for rental," I told him the truth.

"If you have a minute, I will be glad just to show it to you," he said.

"Okay! Please lead the way."

We walked around the house. He explained that he was moving to Florida. The winter here was too hard for him at the age of seventy. The more I looked at the inside of the house, the more I liked it. The big picture window, the large kitchen, the three bedrooms, the large, clean basement, the one-car garage, and a big backyard with many blue spruces were just what I always wanted. That was all I had hoped for.

"How much do you want for the house?" I asked him.

"I was going to ask $17,000, but if you are interested, I will sell it to you for $16,000," he said.

It was less than I sold my other house for, and it was a bigger and better house.

"Okay. I will buy the house. When can we move in, if we can close the house soon?" I asked.

"I have already found a place down Florida. I guess any time a few days after the closing would be fine with me," he said.

"Is it good if I give you $500 to hold the house while I am arranging a mortgage?"

"Sure thing. I will hold the house for a week for you."

I gave him a $500 check and drove right back to downtown Menomonie. I went to my old bank to talk to the manager about getting a mortgage. He referred me to the manager of the mortgage department. I filed an application for the loan.

"We know you from Stout. Just give us a few days. We should get the loan through," the banker told me.

I called Nancy about the house. She was surprised how fast I decided on such a purchase.

"Did you say you have already bought a house?"

"No. I still need to get the mortgage from the bank," I said. "I need to borrow $16,000 for the house."

"Sixteen thousand dollars? It is less than the house we just sold! Is it a smaller house than the one just sold? Tell me a little more about the house."

"Well, it is bigger house actually. It has three bedrooms and a large kitchen."

"That is good enough for me. You know I always wanted a big kitchen."

"You will be happy with this kitchen. It is much bigger than the one we have now."

She was not too unhappy about me making the decision without even talking to her before the deal was made. But she went along with my decision on the house. However, I heard that could be grounds for divorce to some American couples.

The house was about five miles from the university. It was in the town of North Menomonie. There were several large and small lakes in the area. Lake Tainter, the largest lake in North Menomonie, was within walking distance from the house where largemouth bass and walleyes were abundant in the lakes. It was also convenient to travel out of town. The freeway ramp was only a mile or so from the house.

After I talked with Nancy and filed the applications for the loan, I went back to the house. The for-sale sign was already taken down by the owner. I told him about what I had done in the process. He told me he was flexible about the closing date and time, since they were alone and retired. The mission was completed. I told the Wigens and the Ruehls about the purchase.

"Boy! I have never seen anybody buy a house that quick," said Dr. Wigen.

"I knew. But I didn't know how much better I could do by taking more time to look."

"I agree with Richard. If he likes the place, that is worth every penny of it," Mrs. Wigen said.

I said good-bye to them and drove back to Racine the same afternoon.

In late August, after the summer school, we moved back to Racine and prepared to move to Menomonie. I rented a large twenty-four-foot U-Haul truck and loaded up all our belongings. I was just amazed how much we had accumulated. Humans were just like packrats that accumulated so much stuff that they might never have the chance to use. It was interesting to note that there were more boxes of toys in the truck than any other properties in quantity.

While I drove the big truck, Nancy drove our old Ford LTD. We took the scenic I-94 through Wisconsin Dells and stopped there for a long break. We left Racine in midmorning and arrived in Menomonie at suppertime. We went to our favorite McDonald's for hamburgers, fries, and Cokes before unloading the truck. A few old friends and former classmates came over to help unloading the heavy furniture and boxes. It was less than one hour, and we had moved all the furniture and boxes into the house. The unpacking could wait for a few more days for Nancy and me to do. We had some beers to celebrate the reunion of friends. I really felt like it was my homecoming that day.

The morning after we moved in, I got up at five o'clock and sat on the rocking chair in front of the big picture window in the living room. The predawn cool lights brought out the quiet beauty of the landscape. Looking through the large picture window at the red maple trees lined in front of the house, the gentle autumn breath gently tickled the maple branches and the pair of squirrels played among the trees. It was so peaceful and tranquil in that early morning. I felt a surge of happiness pass through my spine. I thought, *how much happier one could be in the world!* I was so happy that I made the decision to stay in the United States. I was sure that Nancy and our boys were equally happy to have moved into this country.

We often talked about what we should do about the future—stay or not to stay in this country. If we moved back to Taiwan, what would my future look like? I could go back to the Normal University or another university to teach and retire as a professor. The variation of the career path was very limited in Taiwan those days. In this country, the situation was totally different. There were abundant opportunities for people who wanted to enhance themselves with unlimited choices.

We also talked about becoming permanent residents and eventually obtaining the citizenship. Was it so bad to become an American? We thought not. This country was founded and established by immigrants from all over the world almost two centuries ago. More immigrants followed to make this country the strongest and richest and the model of democracy in the world. To become American was totally different from becoming a Japanese, German, or citizen of many such closed societies. We could be part of the forces that contribute to the future growth of this great country.

I was only sad to have left my parents back home in Taiwan. I had not talked to them since I left Taiwan five years ago. My assistant professor's salary was not enough for me to feed a family and make international travel at the same time. There was no telephone at home in Taiwan at that time. I could not even hear their voices through the phone. That was the only thing in our life that I missed in a big way. I wanted to bring them over here someday soon.

Unlike in major universities, teaching instead of researching was the most important task for professors at Stout. It was enhanced to the university status as well. A huge new technology building was built in 1964. My office and laboratories were housed in the technology building. My teaching assignments were from junior to graduate level electronics courses. I was quite familiar with those subject matters. Each Sunday, I spent one hour or so to write course outlines for the week.

When I was a graduate student, I was acquainted with two undergraduate students: James Wilmore and Pat Golden. Jim was an electronics buff. He went to the junkyard for radios and converted them to home radios. His classmate Pat was a locally born fellow. Jim and I visited Pat's farm several times during their senior year. One day both took me out for a pizza lunch.

"Richard, we have joined the army in communications. We are going to Yale for six months and then go to Taiwan for our services," Pat said.

"That's good. Maybe you can visit my folks there," I said. "I'll write their address on a piece of paper. You can go visit them. I am sure my parents will treat you to a good restaurant in Taipei." I wrote the address in Chinese and handed it to Pat.

They went to Yale before my graduation from Stout.

A year after my returning to Stout, Pat and Jim both returned to civilian life and used the GI Bill to pay for their tuition for graduate studies at Stout. Jim married a Chinese girl named Susan. Pat also married a Chinese girl: Jean. We had a very interesting reunion. Both were enrolled in my electronics class as my students. I was still very old-fashioned as a teacher. When Jim wanted to ask me a question, he addressed me as Richard. I immediately told him it was Mr. Cheng to him in the classroom. "Jim, we are friends, but in the classroom, I don't want to be addressed by my first name. It might be old-fashioned. I was brought up this way," I told him.

"Sure, Richard, I understand," Jim said.

We maintained our good friendship until this day. Jim was a brilliant student and became an electrical engineer upon graduation. Pat went to a different state to pursue a teaching career.

Mike Tibbetts also came back to pursue his graduate degree. I was so happy to see him in Menomonie and invited him home to have dinner with us and the Wigens. He acted and talked very oddly. When I got close to him, I discovered that he had been drinking. Further checking on him, I found he had started drinking the first thing in the morning. What had happened to a good young man like him?

"Mike, you are my best friend for years. I beg of you, please stop drinking. It is ruining you," I told him when he was sober.

"I know," he simply said.

"I think you should get some professional help to reduce or stop the habit."

"I tried in the last couple of years. It just made me thirstier after a little while."

Mike left the school one day, and no one seemed to know where he went. Years later, I heard he was teaching near Oshkosh, Wisconsin. I called him at his home one day, but he talked with a slur and made no sense at all. I knew he was still not out of trouble with drinking. Soon I lost contact with him. My heart pained each time when I thought about this very dear friend. I wished I could do something for this friend as he took my car key away before I got my learning permit, but I just didn't know what to do.

At Stout, I enjoyed working with senior students' design projects for their degree requirements. There I saw many creative young people coming up with new and good ideas or new approaches to solve complex problems. I planned the design projects for several classes of students so that the resulting products could be used to equip additional laboratories. In the second semester, we had an open house to exhibit projects from the two senior classes I taught. It was well received by the university and local business as well. Both the school newspaper and the local newspaper wrote several articles complimenting the achievements by faculty and students at Stout.

The US government had a surplus equipment program for colleges. When government equipment surplus was available, colleges and some nonprofit organizations would receive a catalog describing the availability of equipment and location. Normally, it was given at a first come, first serve basis. I found an old radar system available in the air force base in Valdosta, Georgia, that I would consider acquiring.

I selected a three-student team to go with me to inspect the system. If we decided to take it, the four of us would disassemble the system for shipping back to Wisconsin. We signed out a Ford station wagon from the university car pool for the trip. On the logbook it was noted, "Power steering needs to be checked." I went to the supervisor and requested a different car.

"All of the cars are out. The next one available will be tomorrow noon," he told me.

We took the car out for a short spin and did not feel anything wrong with it. We decided just to use this car instead of wasting a day for another car. I was one of the two persons with a driver's license in the group of four. Each of us took a three-hour shift to drive the car. We took highway I-94 going east, connecting Highway 15 to Pennsylvania. It was a bright sunny day. We drove at the speed limit, and the first day was uneventful.

We stayed overnight in a southern Pennsylvania town. The next morning, we switched to I-95 going south. Through Virginia and North Carolina, it was a nice and smooth ride. In North Carolina, we switched to a small county highway to Valdosta, Georgia, in order to save some time. In the early evening after a meal stop, I found the car acting funny; the steering had a delayed reaction and had tended to oversteer. When I turned the steering wheel to the left, the car would not respond at first and then suddenly it would veer sharply toward left. The feeling was quite scary. At the time, we were near the border of South Carolina. All the repair shops were closed at that time.

The highway was dark and slippery. I was behind the wheel that evening. After driving for an hour, I thought I had gotten used to the strange reaction of the bad power steering. The other driver, a twenty-one-year-old junior, was not at all comfortable with that car in addition to the poor road condition. Therefore, I drove the car all that night.

Suddenly, we ran into a section of heavy fog in the middle of a mountain road in a steep descent. I felt like traveling in a thick pea soup, it was so dark; the visibility was less than twenty feet ahead. The road was very narrow; I could not stop on the roadside, even if I wanted to. I could not see cars coming until they were very close. I was sure if anyone in front of me made a sudden stop, I would smash into it. Finally, after more than one hour of frantic and scary driving, we were out in the clear again. I believed that we must have been driving in a tall mountain region that was covered by thick cloud. The three kids were frightened beyond speech. We stopped at a roadside restaurant for a coffee break to catch our breath. My hands and arms were numb from the constant tension.

We arrived at Valdosta after midnight. The next morning, we went to the air force base. The big old system was housed in barracks on the base. After inspection, I decided it was too old and very little use for instructional purposes. Before we returned, we had to wait five hours to get the car repaired in a local Ford dealership. Looking back to that trip, I should not have endangered our lives to take this malfunctioned official car for such a long drive. We could simply wait for a better vehicle that day. But the excitement of going to see a piece of "new" equipment was something those young engineers could not put off for a minute longer. But as an instructor, I should have known better. Another lesson was learned: I was still young and foolish.

CHAPTER 10

Mr. D: A Real Piece of Work!

Our family—Nancy, Jim, Ray, and I—met this unforgettable character. It was unforgettable not because anything he did benefited the human society or anybody else. He was just different from anyone I had met throughout the world. He is still around. I thought I'd better not use his real name because the story was not a flattering one.

Mr. D was a chemical engineering graduate from the National Taiwan University, the most prestigious university in Taiwan. His father and Dad were good friends. When Dad wrote to me about helping Mr. D, I obliged. I assisted Mr. D to gain entrance permit to the University of Wisconsin at Milwaukee in fall of 1966. A month later, Nancy, the children, and I picked him up from Eau Claire Airport and took him home to stay with us for a few days until he could find a place in Milwaukee. Milwaukee was about seventy miles from our home, a little more than a one-hour drive. As he walked down the ramp of the plane, we went forward to meet him for the first time.

"Big brother Cheng, I have brought nothing with me but a whole body of courage" were his first words.

Nancy thought it was a strange introduction. That was fine with us, but our children, not knowing him well enough, were confused by what he had said. On the way to our home, Mr. D talked about his plans in the United States.

"I don't have patience like you and most other people. This country is paved with gold on the ground. I will be rich and famous before you know it," he bragged.

After Mr. D had moved into our house with one bedroom, he thought that was for himself only. The biggest problem was the "bathroom contention" in the mornings. Since ours was a small three-bedroom house that had only one bathroom, Mr. D would use it for a long, long time in the morning. The two older kids were trying to get ready to catch the school bus. We often had to ask Mr. D to use the facility a little faster.

"Mr. D, would you move faster? The kids need to use the bathroom," Nancy would urge him.

"I really enjoy the long shower in the morning. The hot-water system is just great," he would say. And he continued to occupy the bathroom.

"But the children are trying to get ready to go to school in the morning," I joined in.

"Just have them to take their showers at night." He quickly found a solution for me.

I was just speechless and gave up. Soon, I "assisted" Mr. D in finding an apartment in Milwaukee where several of my former schoolmates stayed. I drove him to Milwaukee that afternoon.

On the way, I said, "Mr. D, when you stay with my friends there, be sure to help them out in every way you can. You need all of the friends you can find when you are away from your home."

"I always have many friends. Most people can tell when they first meet me that I can be very helpful to them," he said.

"That's good. I wish you good luck and call me from time to time and tell me how you are doing." I was very concerned about his insensitivity and arrogance.

I introduced Mr. D to my old friends in Milwaukee and asked them to take care of him on my behalf. They were all happy to have one more person to share the rental fee with them.

One day I received a quite angry phone call from Bill Lau, one of Mr. D's apartment mates. "Richard, what kind of friend did you send to us? He is a real jerk!" He was fuming.

"Bill, calm down. Tell me what's going on," I said.

"I have never seen anybody like him in my life."

After he had calmed down a little bit, Bill went on and told me the story about what had happened to them in the Milwaukee apartment recently.

"I just want to tell you before you hear from others. We can't stand to live in the same apartment with Mr. D. You and I are old friends. I don't want any misunderstanding from you." He was still puffing.

"Bill, slow down and tell me what has happened," I said.

"It is a long story, but I will tell you, if you want," he said.

"Please tell me. I feel somewhat responsible because I sent him to you guys."

"Okay! The five of us, including Mr. D, are taking turns to cook dinner each night. One day last week, all five of us were down with a case of bad diarrhea. No one knew what had happened. A few days later, at dinner table, D told us in a very calm voice and a straight face, 'I am a chemical engineer, and I know chemistry well. So, I know exactly what happened the other day. You see, I could not find any sugar in the kitchen when I was making the stir-fried beef, so I cut up a few packs of chewing gum to substitute for the sugar. I believe the rubbery material was not digested well in you,' he said. All of us got so mad at him. We almost threw him out on the street. In addition to that incident, there have been too many things Mr. D did that bothered the hell out of us. This call is to inform you that we want him to find another place to stay."

"I am very sorry about what he has done to you guys. Please tell the others that I apologize to all of you. I will not bother to talk to Mr. D. You do whatever is needed to do with him." I was embarrassed.

One day, we saw Mr. D pulled into our driveway in a beat-up Ford.

"When did you learn how to drive?" I asked him.

"I never took any driving lessons. I just got my driver's license last week," he proudly told me.

"How did you get to pass the driver's road test so fast?" I was astounded. I knew he never learned how to drive and did not have a notion about driving regulations.

"That's simple. Let me tell you how to do it," he said with a hint of a smile. "You just apply for the license, get in the car with the examiner first, then pull from your pocket a pack of cigarettes with just one cigarette in it. I put a five-dollar bill inside the clear foil wrap outside the pack where people can see through it. All you need to do is just to offer the examiner a cigarette. If he takes the packet and puts the whole thing in his pocket, you got your license!"

I was flabbergasted.

"Mr. D, was it how you got your license? You know you may go to jail for that?" I said.

"You have to play it by the ear. If the examiner is clean, he refuses to take the smoke. I did not offer him the money. I just offered him the last cigarette." He smiled—a rare occasion.

Again, I gave up. Mr. D just had it all figured out. He received his master's degree from a college in Milwaukee. It took him less than eighteen months to complete it while he was goofing off on other matters. The degree program required research and a thesis. I congratulated him for his achievement.

"How did you do it so fast to have written the thesis among other business you are involved with?"

"I paid someone fifty dollars to have my thesis written in Taiwan. It would cost me that much just to have the paper typed in Milwaukee," he said with a hint of smile on his face. He was very proud about what he had done.

"Mr. D, I just don't know what to tell you. You are so much ahead of everybody!" I said.

He moved to Chicago after he finished the master's degree. On one of his trips from Chicago, he whipped out a business card from his shirt pocket. "This is my new address and phone number," he told me.

It was clearly printed, "Mr. D, chairman, president, and CEO, MW Enterprises, Ltd."

"Wow! How impressive. You are a big tycoon now. How big is your company?" I said jokingly.

"Well, I am alone now, but I will be hiring people soon," he said.

He never told me what business he was engaged in.

"You will know in time," he told us.

In 1968 we moved to Urbana, Illinois, and lived in the married student housing. It was closer to Chicago than going to Menomonie, so Mr. D came to see us more often than before. He was driving a brand-new Chevy. Apparently, he was successful in moneymaking.

"Richard, I am paying too much tax now. How about letting me adopt a couple of your boys so I can claim tax exemptions for my tax returns?" he asked me with a straight face.

I thought he was kidding or bragging. But he persisted on that request repeatedly.

"Mr. D, first, I do not think I would let you adopt my children. Secondly, how about my own tax exemptions? Thirdly did you mean you would pay for their living costs from your tax exemption?" I tried to make him see the point.

He was still puzzled that I did not go along with him. Another day, I received a phone call at home. It was Mr. D whispering on the line.

"Richard, this is serious. I can't talk on the phone now. Can we meet somewhere quiet?" he whispered.

"Why don't you meet me at the intersection of Green Avenue and Fifth Street near my office on campus at three o'clock," I told him.

I thought he was in trouble or something serious.

"Nancy, Mr. D called me just now. He seems in trouble."

"I would be careful with that screwball. You never know what he might have done!" she said.

I rushed to the street corner to wait for him. He came about fifteen minutes late. In a secretive gesture, he waved for me to follow him to a side street.

"Richard, this is a very big deal. I must be careful because it involves millions of dollars of money. If anybody finds out this, I might be robbed or killed." He was whispering again.

"What in the world are you talking about?" I was worried.

"You know my dad is the head of the commando unit under KMT. That unit left the mainland after the Communists took over. When he left there, he brought a painting that was over six hundred years old by a famous painter. My dad had someone to hand-carry it to this country for me to sell it for him. Because I am well known to too many people, it is dangerous for me to keep it with me. You are just a student. No one will bother you with that." He was whispering to me again.

I was dumbfounded.

"I don't think it is safe to leave that in my apartment. My suggestion to you is to put it in a bank safety deposit box. I will help you to open a box in my bank."

He agreed, and we went to my bank, rented a big box, and put the big scroll in the box. Later, I learned that Mr. D wrote letters to several rich families, such as the Kennedys, Hunts, and Mellons. It did raise some interests and was examined by experts in New York. It was determined to be a fake.

"You see, I am so famous now, the FBI is following me around to protect me," Mr. D told me one day. I was just speechless. From what I could judge, the FBI was tracking him instead of protecting him.

Four years after Mr. D landed in this country, he came to me one day and proudly showed me a diploma of a doctoral degree in sciences with his name on it. I knew he never attended any university for the advanced degree.

"Mr. D, you are joking. Right?" I said.

He admitted to me that he had paid $500 to buy this diploma from a nonregistered outfit in Chicago. Armed with this piece of junk paper, he managed to obtain a high civil service position in Taiwan. He was appointed senior manager in a government-owned plant near Kao-Shiung. Nancy and I were happy that he was out of our hair, for good!

Menomonie was a town surrounded by many large and small lakes. On my way to work, the road was alongside three different lakes. I carried a set of fishing gear in the trunk of my car. When I left school to go home in the afternoon, I would stop and fish at my favorite holes almost daily during the warm seasons. Sometimes, after I returned home, I would take Jim and Ray with me to fish in the lakes. We always caught at least a dozen or more bluegills on each fishing trip. Of course, my assignment was to clean the fish and Nancy would cook them. If I was fishing alone, I would just make a few casts for fun. Unless I caught a larger fish, I just assumed I was going home empty-handed. Because cleaning just one or two fish was a waste of my time, it was not enough to share around the table.

One day, I was fishing on the shore of a small lake. I heard a loud scream coming from behind a large bush.

"Ouch! Ouch! Help me!" the man kept screaming.

I dropped my pole and rushed to see what had happened. A man fully dressed in his business suit and tie was holding the back of his head and screaming his lungs out. I ran closer to check on him and found a big three-pointed hook firmed and deeply anchored to his scalp just above the neck bone. Blood streaked out of his head continuously. I cut the line and tried to help him to remove the hook, but it was too deep. It had to be surgically removed.

"Your wound is pretty bad. Let me take you to the hospital. Come with me."

"Thank you." He was in great pain.

I helped him into my car and drove the five miles to the county hospital emergency room. It took a surgeon half an hour to take the hook out and sew him back. After he was discharged from the hospital, I drove him back to his car.

"I really appreciate your help," the salesman said.

"Don't mention it. I hope you recover quickly," I said. "Are you from this area?"

"I am from North Carolina. I am selling firecrackers to retailers," he said. "I would like to give you a pack of firecrackers for your trouble."

"No. You don't have to do that. It was not any trouble for me at all. Besides, firecrackers are not allowed in this area."

"Well, let me thank you again. I am going to St. Paul now. If you do need any firecrackers for the Fourth of July, please give me a call," he said as he handed me a business card.

We shook hands. He continued his journey to the west. What a freak and painful accident for the unfortunate fellow!

CHAPTER 11

Near-Fatal Penicillin Reaction

In the spring of 1966, I started having cold symptoms. I was sneezing and felt cold all the time. I went to my doctor. He prescribed all sorts of antibiotics for me to try out once a week just to see the result. I must have tried over ten different antibiotics. None of them worked for me.

"Richard, you must have hay fever. Try to drink the mix of warm honey and vinegar," a university custodian told me.

"I don't think so, because I have no fever," I told the old guy.

I kept going back to the same doctor. One day, he said he would try something new. "Richard, have you had penicillin shots in the past?"

"Yes, I had penicillin shots many times in the past."

"Okay! I think you need a strong dose to cure the problems you have," he told me.

"Sure, Doctor, give me a shot," I agreed.

"You need to come back in two days for a follow-up shot."

That was a Monday morning; he gave me a strong dose of penicillin shot. The material he gave me looked as thick as toothpaste. I felt better in the next couple of days. Then, on Wednesday, I went back in the morning and received my second penicillin shot. There were no unusual symptoms that morning after the shot. I taught a class at eleven o'clock in the morning and then went home for lunch.

Before my two o'clock lecture, Raymond saw a snake in our backyard. We were afraid of snakes. I took my .22 rifle, found the snake, and shot it dead in the head. It was a snake I could not identify. I picked it up with my fingers and put it in a plastic bag before I threw it into the garbage can.

During my afternoon lecture, my fingertips on my left hand were very itchy. I kept scratching the fingers with my right hand. Soon after, I had to scratch my fingers on both hands while I was giving the lecture. After the class, I thought I might have some allergy to the snakeskin I had touched earlier. I used rubbing alcohol from the first aid kit to clean my fingers to no avail. I went home that day still trying to get rid of the itching problem. After dinner, I felt very tired and went to sleep early.

By one o'clock, I was awakened by the intense itch throughout my body. I got up and saw my fingers had swollen to twice the normal size. I woke Nancy up. She almost fainted when saw my face, which was swollen to as big as a hog head. Nancy called my doctor at home and reported the situation. He was sleepy and grouchy.

"Tell Richard to take couple of aspirins and go back to sleep," he instructed Nancy.

I took two aspirins and still could not sleep, so I sat there and waited until six o'clock.

"I will take you to the emergency room. Your doctor is not reliable," Nancy told me.

She drove me to the emergency room of the hospital without bothering my doctor again. The duty doctor in the emergency room checked me out. "Mrs. Cheng, I am glad you took him in here. If there were any more delay, it might be fatal," the doctor told Nancy.

He immediately administered several shots of adrenaline, antihistamine, and other unknown drugs. The doctor and a nurse stood beside me and monitored the treatment and the progress for more than two hours before the doctor went on to attend other patients. It was not until noon that day the doctor declared the danger was over.

"Richard, you had a really bad reaction to penicillin. Don't use it again," the duty doctor told me.

"How bad was it?" I knew it was bad.

"It could have been fatal in a matter of hours if you didn't come in," the doctor said.

"Wow! I didn't know it could be so serious."

"When your windpipe closes up by the swelling, you would die," he said.

I was lucky to be alive. In the same week, a *Life* magazine article described the penicillin-induced near-death experience by a *Time* magazine reporter. The story was very much like what had happened to me, except that the swelling of the tissues had not constricted my windpipe—not yet. Life and death had such a narrow divide that no one could predict how and when the divide was crossed. Just in my own case, I could recall a few very close calls in the past.

I lost my faith in my regular doctor and decided it was time to get a new family doctor. The new doctor found that ragweed's pollen and molds had caused my cold symptoms. He gave me a dose of antihistamine and it took care of the cold symptoms right away. From that point on, I had to take antihistamine to get through both the day and the night during hay fever season. I wished I had listened to the custodian at Stout instead of the doctor.

Before Nancy conceived our third child, she had lost one baby in her second month of pregnancy. That was in 1964 when we lived in Racine.

"The doctor told me the Rh-negative factor in my blood was the problem," she told me after she came home from the hospital.

"How did it happen to you? How did you get the Rh-negative factor?" I was ignorant of the medical term.

"The Rh-negative factor was caused by my prior pregnancies, the doctor told me."

We did not pursue such medical theory any further at that time. Now we really wanted to prevent any problem of this pregnancy; we wanted a bigger family.

"We need to protect this baby from the Rh-negative factor. Can you talk to the doctor and see if he can do something about it?"

"I will try when I see him next week," she said.

Nancy's physician, Dr. Schlepper in Racine, learned about her history of the aborted pregnancy, he prescribed a medication to Nancy that would prevent abortion caused by the Rh-negative factor. Nancy was very careful to follow instructions from Dr. Schlepper during the entire pregnancy. We moved away from Racine in June 1966, but we went back to Dr. Schlepper regularly. Only when the term of pregnancy was going into the ninth month was when we knew the medication did work and our third child was saved from being aborted or premature delivery. At that time, the doctors were not able to pinpoint the date of delivery. Dr. Tweeten, in Menomonie, could only tell us it would be sometime in November. Therefore, from early November, I was on alert twenty-four hours a day.

I knew that I had to be prepared to take Nancy to the hospital at any moment's notice. But my old car was my biggest concern. I had had a lot of problems with the air ride of this old 1958 Cadillac. After several repair jobs done by a local auto repair shop, it was still unpredictable as to when the air bag or air bags would collapse. Often it broke down at the worst moment and place. We knew our baby was due anytime soon. I filled up the gas tank of the car and checked the engine and transmission oil levels and the air pressure in all tires. The only thing I could not do anything about was the air ride bags. All I could do was to see if they were good before I went to bed and kept my fingers crossed.

That night, I was tired and went to bed early. At three o'clock in the morning, Nancy woke me up and told me the contractions had started; the baby was on its way. I woke up Jim and Ray and got them into the Cadillac. That was the time we found one of the four air bags had collapsed in the night. There was no other alternative for me but to drive this slanted car all the way to the hospital. Fortunately, there was absolutely no traffic at that early hour in Menomonie. After

Nancy was admitted, we all waited downstairs in a small room. Both Jim and Ray fell asleep on the chairs.

The doctor came out to the waiting room at seven o'clock. "Congratulations! It's a boy," the doctor said to me.

"Boys, you just have a new little brother," I told the boys.

I first took Ray to Dr. Wigen's house for the day, because Dr. Wigen liked Ray very much. "You call him Ray. You must have named him after me. Ha! Ha!" he would jokingly say.

"It is quite possible," I told him.

"He is smart, like a little wizard. We have a lot of fun together," he would say. "I will babysit for you any time you want me to."

"Well, I will take your offer sometime later," I told him.

When we arrived at their home, Mrs. Wigen already prepared a cup of hot chocolate for Ray.

After I took James to school, I returned to the hospital to see Nancy and the baby. Nancy looked fine in the hospital bed. A nurse brought the baby in to show us. He was a healthy-looking, seven-pound baby. I held him for a few minutes and returned him to the nurse. The doctor ordered Nancy to stay in the hospital overnight for observation before discharging her. I stayed in the hospital most of the day and went home with the two older boys around suppertime. I treated Jim and Ray at a local pizza shop. They were very excited about their new baby brother.

Nancy came home with our third boy on November 21, 1966. Jim and Ray set up some decorations in the home to welcome Nancy and the baby. We named the baby William and nicknamed him Billy. Baby Billy was very beautiful and energetic. Immediately after he entered the home, he became the center of the universe for the whole family. My mind was on him at work and I was anxious to go home to see him. Each morning when I woke up, the first thing was also to look at the baby.

Nancy took care of the baby day and night. I normally did not wake up until the next morning, so I really did not know what had happened during the night. Nancy told me the baby seldom made any fuss at night. I used the old camera, the one I brought from Japan, and took numerous photos of the baby. The two older brothers adored him. I did not detect any trace of jealousy by the two older brothers. He sure had brought instant joy to the house since the minute Nancy took him home. Billy was very bright and expressive from just two or three months old. While he did not know how to say the words, he could communicate with others using hand motions and some peculiar sounds. He was very effective to get his message through to us.

Jim and Ray had been very well behaved and intelligent boys. When we moved to Menomonie, Jim was in the second grade and Ray was just being accepted to the first grade. Both boys brought home report cards with excellent grades. Jim was an A student and Ray was a straight A+ student. Nancy and I never had to push them to study or to do homework. They did the homework themselves and then watched television or played with neighborhood kids. There was not even one thing about them that would have caused us to be concerned at that time. Nancy and I seldom or never had to discipline them. At that young age, we could see early-age development that might be indicative of their future interests and careers in our children. As a young teacher, I paid very keen interest in observing the process of development in our children.

Automobiles and fire trucks amused Jim while Ray was interested in drawing dinosaurs. I found the boys were so different in their interests and characters. "Jim, what do you want to do when you grow up?" I asked.

"I want to be a fireman," he said without hesitation.

I knew that Jim was very much amused by fire trucks.

"How about you, Ray?"

"I want to be a mailman," Ray said after thinking for a moment.

Nancy and I laughed about their choices of professions. Not that there was anything wrong with the professions; we just knew what they liked now might not be the same after they grew up. Jim told me later that Ray had been accompanying our mailman almost daily around our block.

"What kind of girl are you going to marry? A blonde with blue eyes or someone with black hair and brown eyes?" Nancy jokingly asked them one day.

"Black hair and brown eyes," Jim said quickly.

"I like blonde hair and blue eyes," Ray immediately followed.

Well, who could tell what lay ahead, but it was interesting to see what their thoughts were and what the future would be.

Starting in the eighth month, Billy's daily active pattern changed some. He was so lovely when he was awake, but when he was sleeping at night, he began crying a lot. We did not know what the cause was and thought some babies just cried more than others.

CHAPTER 12

The Doctoral Degree

In the summer of 1967, I was granted a National Science Foundation fellowship in "Electronic Circuit Design" from Colorado State University at Fort Collins. That meant two months of separation from my family. But it was to my greatest interest to study in that program. It was important to my teaching job at Stout as well. Nancy encouraged me to go because she knew I really wanted to advance my studies. After packing up a small suitcase with just what I needed for the summer, Nancy took me to the bus station where I'd gotten off the bus almost six years earlier. It was a solid two-day ride on the Greyhound bus to the school. The whole trip was uneventful. Before I reached Colorado, I was already missing my family. I wondered how I could get through these three years when I left my family in Taiwan a few years back.

Fort Collins is a city on top of a mountain. It is a very pretty city, but Colorado is quite different from Wisconsin. It reminded me the wild-wild west and the cowboys. In Fort Collins, everywhere I went, I saw cowboy hats and high boots. Pancake houses were very popular places for people to congregate. The university was very strong in electrical engineering and with a very strong faculty body. I enjoyed the classes and befriended with several classmates. My dorm mate who shared the bathroom between the two bedrooms was Ray Dignan from McGill University in Canada. Another close friend was Bob Seawall from Pennsylvania State University. The three of us attended classes together and went to lunch and dinner at the same table all through the summer.

All three of us were assistant professors. Ray was from England and was a very sophisticated and elegant English gentleman. He was very peculiar about table manners. He was most unhappy to see the casual table manner of both Bob and me. One day during lunch, he could not bear us anymore. "You should never turn your fork tip upward," he said unhappily.

"How do you eat the peas with the fork upside down?" I protested.

"Of course, you can." Ray showed us with the fork down how he scooped up some chopped vegetables.

"See? This is the way to do it." He showed me and said.

"I don't see what's so important about using the fork in such an unnatural way." I was not convinced.

"That's the dumb Brits' way of doing things," Bob said.

Ray got so mad he left before finishing his lunch.

"You two are quite uncivilized and unreasonable. I don't like to eat on the same table with you," he told Bob and me. And he just walked away. However, at dinnertime, Ray joined us again as if nothing had been said. Bob and I were just happy that Ray was not angry with us.

Another day at dinnertime, we were discussing the drug situation in the United States. "The source of the illicit drugs is China. Do you know that, Richard?" Ray said.

That really touched my nerve!

"Ray, if anybody complains about the drug trade, I would accept that, but from an English gentleman, it is a bit hypocritical. Have you forgotten the Opium War?" I was surprised of how cool he was when he said that.

"What was the Opium War? I had not ever heard anything about it," said Ray.

He was astonished to hear my strong statement. I turned to Bob.

"Bob, do you know the Opium War?"

"Of course, I do. It's in our history text. It was in late nineteenth century when England forced China to buy opium. The Chinese government seized the opium from British merchants and burned the opium, so the war broke out," Bob said.

"You are kidding me, aren't you, I have never learned anything like that from our history books," Ray said.

"You see, Ray, if the Chinese are the drug culprits, they are just trying to unload the opium that was forced on them by your ancestors," I said, using this opportunity to give him a hard time.

Ray sank into deep silence. Bob changed the topic into what movie we planned to see that weekend.

"How about let's go see *You Only Live Twice* with 007?" I suggested.

"Let's go in my Mustang," Bob said.

Ray never again talked about the drug trade throughout the summer.

The three of us frequented the pancake house right across the street from the engineering building. We were not serious drinkers of alcoholic beverages. The most we drank was one or two beers a week. Most of the other classmates liked to consume hard liquors. We decided that was not the crowd we wanted to mix with. Bob had a red 1966 Mustang and he drove Ray and me to Colorado Mountains where people skied in the summer. As we approached the top of the mountain, the air started thinning; at that level we all experienced light-headed sensations.

"You'd better drive us down the mountain now before you faint," Ray told Bob.

Bob agreed not to go up any farther and took a U-turn down the mountain. After summer school, Ray went back to teach at the same university. We kept in touch by exchanging Christmas cards and occasional phone calls. Bob went back to Pennsylvania. Neither Ray nor I ever heard from him after we said good-bye.

About halfway through the school, I saw an ad in the local paper. "For sale by owner—1961 Mercedes-Benz Diesel—$800." The brand name and the price combination caught my attention. I called the owner and asked him to take the car to the campus to show it to me. The owner was a middle-aged man who drove the car to the parking lot right in front of my dorm. It was a vintage 1961 Mercedes diesel model 190. The paint was fading into a light gray. Several places on the car had dents, but there was no rust on any part of the car.

I had heard a lot of praise about the quality of Mercedes-Benz and it was a high-priced car. Now the price was affordable to me. I instantly fell in love with this old, beat-up car, although it had over 100,000 miles on the odometer. I paid the man a deposit and called Nancy to wire the balance to me. I bought the car and that was the beginning of a stream of used Mercedes I owned in the future years. I loved the Mercedes-Benz not just the fame and the high cost, but I admired the craftsmanship and the quality of its mechanical sophistication. Every part in the car seemed to fit so perfectly, and no labor was spared for details in the most inconspicuous places. That was the dream car for any mechanical buff. Never in my wildest dream did I think that I could own such a beautiful car when I was just turned thirty-two and had been in this country for just less than five years! I was then truly a proud owner of this old clunker.

When I told this news to my good friend Al Huang in Wisconsin, he told me he would fly to Fort Collins and accompanying me to drive the old car home. He was genuinely worried for his old pal. I tried to talk him out of it to no avail. Alfred did come after the summer school was over in late August. We drove this old diesel through Nebraska, Iowa, and Minnesota all the way to Wisconsin. Where could one find another loyal friend like Alfred?

There was not a bit of problem with the old car on the road for the thousand-mile trip. Diesel cars were almost unheard of in the sixties; we had a hard time to convince people at truck stops to sell diesel fuel to us. The diesel fuel was not available from regular gas stations, so we had to go to special gas pumps to buy diesel that was restricted to farm vehicles. With some begging and reasoning, we were able to get the tank filled up at sixteen cents per gallon. Due to the high gas mileage, we did not need to make many fuel stops.

On the road, we particularly enjoyed the big steaks, in Nebraska's steak houses. It was the best steak I had ever had. Not only the portion was four or five times as big as a regular steak but also the way it was prepared. It was very tender and tasty without adding any salt and pepper. Alfred and I consumed our one-and-a-half-inch-thick and twelve-inch-wide steaks completely.

When we drove the old, beat-up car into Menomonie, I was surprised to find out how many people knew the good brand, but no one had heard of a diesel car. I insisted to have Alfred stay with us for a day before going back home. After I sent Alfred to the airport in Eau Clair, I took the car to a body shop and had it cosmetically overhauled. After a week, I was proudly driving this shining blue-gray old Mercedes. Since that was the only Mercedes in town, many people turned their heads when it roared through the streets of Menomonie. Was it because of the beauty of the car or was it because of the noisy diesel engine? I would never know.

Teaching college had been my lifelong dream. After I had taught college for more than five years, I found that not having a doctoral degree was not only a handicap but also a disaster to one's career, regardless of one's teaching ability or knowledge in subject matters. First, promotion would be difficult if not impossible for faculty without a doctoral degree. Second, people without a doctorate on the faculty had very little voice to any major decision-making process on campus. An associate professor in the same field of electronics with a doctorate who was not well versed in his professional field was assigned to major committees while I was on minor committees. He had a small teaching load and had many more privileges than those without a doctorate.

Since I really wanted to stay on teaching at colleges, I had to have a Ph.D. degree. I contemplated to apply for admission to a major university for the doctoral degree program. I consulted with Nancy and talked to our children.

"If I would stay teaching in a college, I must have a doctoral in order to have any future," I told Nancy one day.

"Well, while you are still young, why don't you do it now?" Nancy asked.

"You know our lifestyle will be downgraded to a student's life. It would be hard for you and the boys," I told her.

"I know. But for your future and for all of us, I think it is worth the sacrifice of lifestyle."

"Do you mind having hamburgers for dinner every night for the next three years? Whether I would receive my doctorate degree or fail to get a degree, three years will be my limit," I said.

"If you want to get the doctoral degree, I will eat just hamburgers with you for however long it takes," Nancy said.

"We will be living in the student housing and have very little money to have fun in the next three years. Do you mind?" I told the boys.

"We like hamburgers," Jim and Ray both said.

They did not quite understand between eight and ten years of age, but it did not really bother them any. However, Nancy and I knew we must sacrifice the living standard for a better future.

"I want to do it right away, before I become too old to go to school," I told her.

"You are not too old, but I agree you might just well to get started right away," Nancy said.

I started to search for a university for my doctoral degree the next days. Basically, I liked the Midwest's Big Ten schools. I had been living in Wisconsin for five years and we all liked the environment. Since I attended the summer institute at the University of Illinois in 1965 and found the university was on the top of major national universities, I was hoping to be accepted to it. But admission was very strict and many of my friends had washed out from their doctoral programs. It was a difficult choice for me: should I choose a less tough school to attend or should I attend the best? My choice was to attend the best university in the field. The University of Illinois was my primary choice.

I sent my application to University of Illinois at Champaign-Urbana. At the same time, I also sent an application to the National

Science Foundation for a fellowship given to a limited number of selected college faculty members. The National Science Foundation fellowship was granted, about two months after I sent in my application. I was still waiting to hear from the university. When I forwarded the National Science Foundation offer letter to the university, the reply came quickly to accept me into the college of engineering. The starting date was in the fall of 1968.

I was very happy that I finally got the chance to attend a school I had admired for years. We knew that we would be away for at least three years. After the study, we did not know where we would be going. I talked to Nancy about the house.

"I don't know where I will get a job three years later, whether I get the degree or not. What would you like to do with house? We can rent it out or sell it," I said.

"Aren't you coming back to Stout?"

"I don't think so. I would be in a different field of study when I get through the program I want to take. Stout does not have it," I said.

"Well, whatever you decide to do with the house is fine with me," Nancy said.

"Let's sell this house now and buy another one when we leave Illinois. What do you think?"

"I heard a lot of horror stories about renting the house out to someone we don't know. It might be very messy. I agree to sell the house before we move down south," Nancy said.

"I want to sell the house by myself. If I pass the 6 percent fee from a real estate firm to the buyer, I can sell the house faster," I said.

"That makes sense to me," Nancy agreed.

I made a small sign and placed it in the middle of the lawn in front of the house.

Someone came in town, drove by the street, and saw the sign. He came and knocked on the door. I was home to answer the door.

"Are you selling the house?" he asked me.

"Yes. It is for sale," I answered.

"What is the price?" he asked.

I thought I would like to increase the cost by 10 percent, which brought the price to $17,500.

"I am asking $17,500 for the house," I told him.

He did not even ask me to show him the house.

"I want to buy the house. If I paid you $500 now, do you give me a week to get the deal through the bank?" he asked me.

"Sure. I will hold it for you for a week," I said.

He paid me $500 cash. The deal was closed in a week. We sold the house the same day I put the sign in the front of the house. I thought I was lucky, but Nancy thought the price I asked was too low, which was why the man bought it so fast. I learned later that she was right. The local houses had appreciated much more than 10 percent in the last two years. I should have had it appraised by a professional for the correct price. On the other hand, if I asked the right amount, it might take me many more months to sell the house. I had no regrets.

This house must have been blessed by some super beings. It was bought by me at first sight and sold by me the first day it was on the market. Was it the house or the price or both? Looking back, it was one of the best deals I had made. There was no time wasted, no tension caused by haggling, and we did get our money back when it was sold. What deal could beat that?

I submitted my resignation to the department head, Dr. Phil Ruehl. He encouraged me to pursue the advanced degree.

"Richard, we knew from the beginning we could not keep you long, as I have talked to our administration. Stout is a small pond for a big fish. I am certain that you will go far and beyond Stout. I am glad for you to be accepted at Illinois. It's an excellent school. We will miss you here, but the doctoral degree is important for you to stay in academic world. I am truly happy for you," he told me. What a difference between Phil and Earl!

"You have been my mentor ever since I first got here. I really appreciate everything you have done for me. I don't know how I can thank you enough. I will do my best at school and keep you posted on my progress at Illinois," I told him.

After the school was over in mid-May, I drove six hours from Menomonie to Urbana to arrange for living quarters. The university had a student-housing complex on campus called the Orchard

Downs. I rented a two-bedroom apartment on the second floor. Nancy was happy with the description I gave her about the married student housing arrangement. After we got rid of all furniture and garage equipment, the number of things still had increased quite a bit since we moved two years ago. The weight of the boxes totaled over 1,000 pounds. I towed the trailer home and packed everything into the trailer with help from friends and students.

Nancy drove the old Mercedes with Billy and Ray riding in her car. I drove the old Ford LTD with Jim next to me, towing the large U-Haul trailer. We took the I-94 freeway down south. I had told Alfred in Madison that we would stop by to see them. The five of us stayed overnight in their Eagle Heights apartment, which was University of Wisconsin married student housing. Al and El had been married for four years and did not want any children. As a very close friend, I stuck my neck out and tried to persuade them about starting a family.

"Alfred, you and El have been married for five years now. How come you don't have any children? Is there any problem?"

"We just don't want children so early. There is no problem with us," he said.

"You are three years older than me. You are close to forty, right? If you don't start your family now, you might not have enough time to see them grow up," I said.

"Richard, I think you are right. We want children, but we have been putting it off. Let me talk to El later and we will consider starting the family sooner," Al told me.

"I can assure you that you will not regret that," I said.

They both agreed that they would have a serious discussion about when to start the family. We talked about our past and future and forgot the time. Next morning, Nancy and I left Alfred and Eleanor with our three sons early to beat the rush hour traffic. We drove straight into Champaign-Urbana and moved right into the married student housing on the edge of the campus.

The married student-housing complex had over a dozen of two-story buildings. Each building had eight unit's upstairs and eight unit's downstairs. We were assigned to an upstairs end unit. It was not fancy but was quite equitable to a student family's lifestyle. It was fully furnished, so we did not have to buy any furniture at all. My fellowship paid $575 a month and the rent were less than one hundred dollars. I had to drive to classes because the campus was too large to walk from one end to the other. A campus bus came around to the housing complex every half hour, but it was not as quick and as convenient as driving the car right to the engineering building complex.

As a full-time student at the age of thirty-five, I found most of my classmates were about six to ten years younger than I was. Our children were from two years to eight years old while most other children in the housing complex were infants and toddlers. At Illinois, the foreign student population was very large. There were at least 350 Chinese students on campus; most of them were from Taiwan and just a handful of them were from mainland China.

There were many political factions within the Chinese student community. The mainlanders rivaled Taiwanese groups constantly. The Taiwanese group was divided into three groups: the native Taiwanese, the Taiwan independence group, and the "out of province" people who moved to Taiwan with Chiang Kai-Shek's government from the mainland—like my mom and dad. The slogan of the Taiwan independence group was to "push the mainlanders into the ocean with a bulldozer."

The Taiwan independence group was divided into radical and moderate factions. There were constant arguments among these factions. There had been verbal and paper wars but there had never been a violent act while I was attending the university. At that time, the radical Taiwanese independence faction was the smallest minority group on campus but was also the loudest one. I decided to keep out of politics and concentrate on my schoolwork. After all, I had to get out of the campus within three years, as I'd promised Nancy.

Three doctoral students from Taiwan were politically active. All three of them grew up in Taiwan but were born on the mainland. They majored in social science and political science, so I never had a chance to know them. In 1970, they went to Beijing to offer their services to Deng Hsiao Ping, the prime minister. The Chinese leader refused to accept their offer. Upon returning to the campus, their thesis advisors disliked what they did and dropped them from the degree program. That was one of the twists in the complex political environment among the Chinese student community and the university.

In the first semester, I took a full load in electrical engineering, and at the same time worked on the engineering education certificate program. Besides schoolwork, I also worked with a radio shop to repair CB radios. My family life had not suffered a bit from my intense schoolwork and the radio repair job. Nancy and I took the boys to the park at least twice a week. We decided that she should stay home taking care of the children full time. Although we needed extra income, we understood the parental care for our young was much more important than any amount of money for us.

I also worked as a freelance photo equipment repairman for photo studios because I liked photography. The extra money was more than enough for the five of us to enjoy a very decent living. As a matter of fact, we ate much better food than just hamburgers.

Jim was a born entrepreneur. At eight, through his own initiative, he applied for and was offered a newspaper route at Orchard Downs, all by himself. He often shared light duty with Ray and paid Ray handsomely. With the money he earned, he bought a nice three-speed small bike and some toys for his brothers. I had a collection of hand tools for my repair work. I discovered one day I was losing diagnose pliers one after another. It turned out Jim was using them to cut the newspaper ropes that bundled the papers and the pliers were left on the curbside after use. I was glad to supply the diagnose pliers for the little businessman. As a solution, I bought several low-cost diagnose pliers to replenish my toolbox.

After two semesters, in May 1969, I completed my master's degree in electrical engineering, and received the certificate for engineering education. I was so glad that I did not have to compete with other students for ranking in a class for my degree. I found most of them were razor sharp and very dedicated young people. Those were the cream of the crop among graduate students in the country. Some of them were so excellent in their research fields I knew they would contribute significantly to America's lead in the world of technology. I was committed to my promise of the three-year limit. My focus was to finish my degree work instead of devoting to research.

Now I needed to decide which doctoral degree program to pursue. I consulted several faculty members and people working in the industry, and the answers were totally different depending on whom I talked to. I had to make up my own mind what to do next. I certainly wanted to pursue my interest, but it must also be employable after graduation. My choice was between the electrical engineering and the computer science programs. It was the summer of 1969. At that time, the electrical engineering employment level was hit very hard by government's cutting back on research and development. I decided to pursue my doctorate in computer science, which was a new department that had grown from the electrical engineering department. Many faculty members were transferred from the electrical engineering, mathematics, or physics department. Since the field of study was so new, not a single professor in the department of computer science had a degree in the field of computer science.

To pursue the doctorate degree in computer science, I had to find a research project sponsor. I went to see Dr. Wolfgang Poppelbaum and asked him about the possibility of studying under him. I prepared a set of documents, including all my transcripts and recommendation letters to show him. After a fifteen-minute conversation, as he flipped through my papers, he accepted me to work under him. He promised me a research scholarship right away. The funding of my scholarship was under research granted to the university by the Atomic Energy Commission.

Ted, as Dr. Poppelbaum insisted his student address him, was a renowned researcher in the computer hardware field. He was a visionary in the advancement of computer technology and was supported by numerous US government agencies. He selectively chose over two dozen computer and electrical engineering graduate students by providing research or assistant scholarships to us. Each of the graduate assistants under Ted was given office space and a private laboratory workspace. A group of technicians was available to do bench work for the assistants. I felt much more supported there as a student than when I was teaching in a smaller university.

Several junior faculty members assisted Ted to supervise research work for about twenty-five master's and doctoral students. My junior advisor was Dr. Bill Kubitz, a fresh electrical engineering Ph.D. graduate who studied under Ted. Bill was a brilliant and friendly person. He was also helping Ted advise two other graduate students. The hardware laboratories in the Digital Computer Laboratory (DCL) were very modern and very well equipped. I picked a research project to work on as soon as I entered the program and luckily the project was later qualified for my doctoral thesis.

As I turned thirty-five, I was a senior citizen among my peer group. Most of the students on the campus were under thirty. Although there was the age gap, we got alone quite well. Nancy cooked good Chinese dishes for different groups of friends during the weekends. We also spent many evenings and weekends with fellow students in picnics and playing bridge games.

In one of the groups, we had the Rouchs from Ireland, the Semars from West Germany, and the Gohs from New Zealand. This group had dinner and picnic together about once a month. The other group was mainly students from Taiwan. This was the dinner and bridge group on weekends. In the three years on campus, the Taiwan group had many more activities that included Nancy and me or the children than the multinational group. We had parties at different apartment at least once a week. At that time, I had not met anyone from mainland China. Because of ideology differences between the two main groups on campus, I preferred not to get involved in the constant arguments.

Currently, Jim and Ray were in a university-sponsored grade school. Both were good students with excellent report cards. Nancy and I never had to worry about their schoolwork. Billy was very happy there with so many kids about similar age. One thing that bothered us was that Billy at three still cried a lot at night. But during the day, he was the loveliest toddler we had ever seen. We consulted with doctors but without any diagnosis. We thought he would grow out of it and did not pay too much attention to his nightly crying.

I had so much pressure to finish the doctoral degree in the self-imposed deadline that I had to devote my total attention to course work and the research project. I enjoyed the coffee prepared for research assistants in the laboratory by an elderly technician. The coffee was very thick and strong. I added a large amount of sugar and cream; it tasted great. I drank at least five or six mugs a day.

"Nancy, I feel awful. My heart stops beating occasionally. That is a horrible sinking sensation." I complained to her after it had happened for a few weeks and was getting worse.

"Maybe you should have some rest. I think you should take a few days off," she said.

"I can't take a break. I feel fine other than that craze feeling. I don't feel weak, so I don't think I have a heart problem," I said.

"Well, I think you should see a doctor right away, even if it is not your heart," she said.

"I hate to see a doctor and make a fool of myself," I said.

"Rather be a fool than sorry, I think you should see your doctor right away," she insisted.

"Okay! I will go tomorrow," I promised.

"Not tomorrow. Now! I will take you to the clinic." She was serious.

We drove to the university clinic.

"Doctor, I feel my heart is skipping some beats. I feel awful," I told the doctor.

The doctor listened to my chest and ordered an EKG test.

"Richard, your heart is fine. It does have the premature heartbeat though," he told me.

"Is it a serious problem?" I was worried.

"It could be. What do you drink each day?" he asked.

"I drink about five or six cups of coffee," I replied.

"Strong coffee?"

"Very strong," I said.

"Ah! Stop drinking any coffee or tea. I assure you, you will not drop dead from the symptoms you have. See me in three weeks," the doctor ordered.

After just a week without the thick and good-tasting coffee, the symptoms disappeared. They never came back to bother me.

During the second and the third years at Illinois, I was working part time for several radio shops to repair CB radios and hi-fi equipment. I was also maintaining the intercom and TV distribution system for the local hospital. With course studies, research work, part-time jobs, family life with three young children, and social activities, my life on campus was full and with no dull moment. When one was busy, time seemed to go by much faster. I was busy, but I was not stressed out or overwhelmed by all the activities. However, life was not always that smooth. I had a big problem with the hay fever.

I started to realize the problem when I was in Menomonie. But in Illinois, it became much more severe. Because of the flat terrain in middle Illinois, together with the vast crop fields and grassland, the pollen count was extremely high during late summer and late fall. I was allergic to many kinds of allergens and was particularly sensitive to the ragweed pollen. In the beginning, I just took some over-the-counter drugs. Soon after, nothing I bought from the drugstore would have any effect except they made me drowsy.

I could not sleep at night because my nose was plugged up. Even with the air-conditioning on and doors closed tight, it was not enough to thin down the pollen in the house. I resorted to using a nasal mask in the house, which helped a lot but was very uncomfortable. I had to go to classes every day; the nasal mask did not work for me outdoors. I finally found an active charcoal poison mask like the ones used in war movies. I had to wear that strange-looking thing while driving and to classes.

"What in the world are you putting the gas mask on for?" Bill asked me the first time I wore the gas mask to the laboratory.

"I have to use this in order to breathe. It filters out all of the pollen," I explained.

"It sure looked funny on you. Can't you find something more conventional like a surgical mask?"

"It does not work well. I have tried it. It only works in a room that is air-conditioned well," I told him.

"How about take things like Allerest and Ornade? My neighbor takes them quite effectively."

"I did take them, but they made me sleepy. I can't afford to be sleepy when I take courses," I said.

"I did not know you had so much trouble. Oh! Well, you just have to do what must be done for yourself, I guess." He sighed.

I could imagine how other people would jump to the conclusion that I was crazy or worse to wear that gas mask in the car and in a public place.

The doctor in the university clinic recommended that I should see an allergy specialist. I called one near the university through the Yellow Pages and made an appointment to see him. The allergist suggested giving me shots of allergens.

"The shots are the most effective way to cure hay fever, but it progresses very slowly," he told me.

"How long would it take?"

"It depends on the individuals. I'd say from five to ten years or more," he said.

"Well, I want to get started right away."

"It is not without any risks. You must follow the instructions and watch out for your reactions to the shot," he told me.

First, I had to take a test for substances I was sensitive to. The procedure was quite simple. A grid of ten lines by ten lines was drawn on my back. A small amount of liquid containing ragweed pollen, house dust, cat hair, and so on was injected at each of the cross point of the grid. The test result showed that I was allergic to twenty-three of the allergens that included all flower pollens, ragweed pollens, tree pollens, and house molds but not cat or dog hairs.

The injection started after the allergen mix was prescribed and delivered to the clinic. In the beginning, a very diluted mix was injected once a week and the strength were increased every month. Even at the minute doses, I would get a red bump on my arm as big as a golf ball for three days. I had several severe reactions to the shots and the doctor had to give me antidotes to prevent my windpipe from closing. The hay fever symptoms reduced noticeably with each injection. Since then, I continued the treatment everywhere I moved. This treatment lasted over ten years before I was 99 percent cured.

I finished the doctoral course work in about one year and passed the qualifying examinations. I was fortunate to have a research project that was good for a doctoral thesis. That had saved time as much as one year to several years. Some students could not even nail down a research topic for several years. I wrote the thesis under the guidance of both Ted and Bill. I submitted my thesis in May 1971. The final defense was scheduled in June. A panel of professors from computer science, mathematics, and electrical engineering was selected. I passed the final thesis defense without any serious challenges. In July 1971, I was formally granted the doctoral degree. That was exactly three years for both degrees, as I had promised Nancy.

Although I enjoyed the school and the research environment, due to my age and the desire for a normal family life, I did not spend the extra years on the campus as most of my fellow students did. As I rushed to finish my degree, I did not bother to submit research papers for publications as required to establish myself in the technical field. I would have better opportunity to do research on campus because of the research environment and people I could consult with. I aimed to quickly finish my degree and find a job. My plan for my career was to devote to education instead of research.

I started looking for a teaching job just before my thesis defense in June 1971. I knew I probably had passed the prime of being a dedicated researcher. Teaching was my primary interest, and I thought I could do a better job in teaching than research. I decided to write to the second-tier universities instead of top research institutions.

"How come you don't send applications to the Big Ten universities?" Nancy asked me when I wrote the application letters.

"Well, the main reason is that I don't like the pressure to write research papers just for the sake of publications," I said. "I have enjoyed teaching, so I am going to schools that emphasis teaching."

"As long you are happy, I am happy," she told me.

At that time, most of the campuses did not have a computer science program. Many did not even know what computer science was about. There were several offers of teaching positions from various universities.

Alfred and Eleanor had moved to Urbana to pursue his doctoral degree in special education. They had two small, lovely boys: Bryan and Bradley. I consulted him regularly on my job search. After I received an offer, I would check with Alfred before I pursued any farther. Several universities had shown interest in me and wanted to have an interview with me. One of the universities that invited me was Old Dominion University in Norfolk, Virginia.

"Al, what do you think of Norfolk in Virginia? I have an offer from there," I asked Huang. "I wouldn't go there. Norfolk is a sleazy naval town full of sailors," Alfred told me.

"How do you know?" I asked.

"I was there to visit the beach two years ago. I have a very bad impression of the town."

"In that case, I am not going to consider the school there." I decided to drop it.

Another university was the Whitewater campus of the University of Wisconsin.

"Al, how about Whitewater?"

"That's a nice little town, and it is close to Madison campus and Milwaukee. I heard good things about that school. Why don't you go look?"

The interview went well, and the offer was quite good. I decided to take a position as assistant professor in the department of mathematics at the University of Wisconsin-Whitewater, where they planned to offer a new computer science program.

CHAPTER 13

U.S. Citizenship

Whitewater, Wisconsin, was only three and a half hours by car from Urbana, Illinois. I towed the Mercedes behind the twenty-four-foot U-Haul truck while Nancy drove the Ford LTD. The three boys rode in the cab of the big truck with me. The cab of the truck was so high above the road it was truly an interesting experience for the boys and me.

"Dad, I feel like we are flying an airplane," Jim said.

"Look at those cars. They are so small!" Ray said.

Billy extended his arms and pretended he was an airplane. I enjoyed driving the big machine. It was clumsy but very sturdy and stable. We rented a three-bedroom house from the math department secretary, Mary. The old house was prepared for rental. We moved into this readily and fully furnished house as soon as we drove into the town of Whitewater.

Two days after we moved in, we saw a board that read, "Puppies for good homes," as we drove home from the grocery store. I thought it was a good time to get a puppy for our children.

"Hey! Boys, would you like a dog?" I asked.

"Yeah! We want a puppy!" all three boys yelled in excitement.

I turned around and doubled back to the house with the board. The owner saw us pull into the driveway and came out of the house to greet us.

"Howdy! Looking for a puppy?" he asked.

"Can we see the puppies?" Jim asked as he jumped out of the car.

The old guy took us to the side of the house. He had a pan about five feet across. In the pan, the mother dog looked like a mutt, with six fat little puppies of different colors. The old man randomly picked up a tan puppy and handed it to Billy. Billy just held the puppy tightly onto his chest and would not let go of it. The two older brothers were trying to select another one, but Bill had already made the decision for the family. We thanked the old man and took the puppy home.

"What do we call the dog?" Billy asked his brothers.

"She is a female. She is like a princess to us," Ray said.

"Okay! That's a good name. Let's call her Princess," Jim agreed.

Princess grew quickly into another yellowish mutt like her mother. She was a very smart and playful dog and brought a lot of laughter and extra work for the boys. She was a very gentle and friendly dog. We saw our neighbor's cat often sleep on top of Princess's back. In May 1972, Princess gave birth to five of the cutest little puppies. It was time for us to put a sign up to give our puppies away. All of them were taken within two weeks.

The University of Wisconsin at Whitewater was a campus of about 11,000 students. The mathematics department was one of the largest academic units on campus. I was hired to establish a new computer science program in the department. To design a curriculum and teach advanced courses were the key tasks for my job. I was well prepared for both curriculum design and teaching from my past teaching experience. I designed the curriculum in just three weeks and started to implement the degree program in computer science right away.

Many second-year students with majors from mathematics, biology, and others applied fields had transferred to the new program.

I worked with each of the forty or more transfer students to get their program adjusted.

"Why are you changing your major?" I always asked the student doing the transfer.

"I don't think there is any job for me after I get my math degree. I heard the computer science is the choice of the future." How right they were!

My new job was very busy but interesting work. I taught all the advanced courses while assisting several mathematics faculty members getting started to teach programming and basic computer science courses, such as data structure and logical design. They became the core faculty of the new computer science program at Whitewater.

In the early seventies, there were very few computer science Ph.D. degree holders in the United States. I was the only one who graduated from my class of doctoral graduates from Illinois in the summer of 1971. At that time, very few computer science Ph.D. degree holders took a teaching job. Most of my colleagues were hired into industries. I suppose the salary differential was the main reason.

The computer science program grew at a rapid rate at Whitewater. By the beginning of the second semester, the declared majors in computer science surpassed the first two years of mathematics majors. Some of the junior and senior math majors declared a minor in computer science. The program was a stunning success at the university. That was great news for the university. The enrollment had been declining gradually from 17,000 in 1967 to 11,000 in 1971. Worse, the university had built the campus to house 22,000 students in anticipation of further growth in 1968. Now it was very empty. The surge of computer science majors and course takers provided recruiters with good stories to tell potential applicants throughout the state. There were hopes that the enrollment would increase in the future. Nevertheless, it was depressing to see all those deserted dormitory buildings and empty office spaces.

We changed our visa to immigration status after University of Wisconsin-Stout sponsored us for citizenship in 1966. The decision to become the United States permanent residents was made in 1966 after Nancy and I had decided this would be the country we wanted to live and grow old together in. At that time, there was a small quota for people from Asia. A waiting list lasting seven to ten years was common. That did not really bother us. If I could pursue my career and had our children well educated, permanent residence or not had no impact on us.

In early 1966, when Congress signed into law to change the immigration quota system, we were granted permanent-resident status shortly after our application was submitted. Five years later, in the summer of 1971, Nancy and I were eligible to apply for the citizenship. I applied immediately after the five-year requirement in the United States was fulfilled. An interview was scheduled with an immigration officer for Nancy and me. The questions asked in the test were very simple. We passed the English language and the portion about the government. In July 1971, we went to Milwaukee to swear in as citizens of this great nation. Although the citizenship did not impact us in our daily lives, we were very happy and proud to be a member of this country.

"Do you think people back home might say that we are abandoning our motherland by becoming American citizens?" Nancy asked me after the fact.

"I don't think so. The United States is a melting pot of people from continents all over the world. People who were not afraid of difficulties and were determined to work hard to pursue their dreams came since hundreds of years ago and made this a great nation. Like those came here from Europe and elsewhere," I said, "We are pioneers of our family to come here, work hard with our heads and hands, to realize our dreams in this land. There is nothing wrong with it, and to heck with what people back home might say."

"Wow! That is a long speech. But I do agree with what you just said though," she told me.

"As pioneers, we did not ask for any help from anyone. We have worked for everything that could be called our own. I think we should be proud of what we have done this far instead worrying about what others back home might say," I said.

"I am quite comfortable with ourselves, and I believe we have made the right decision," she said.

"Yeah! In America, the sky is the limit, as people say. We still have a long way to go to reach our sky. We just have to try to climb one step at a time and be content with what we have at this moment of life." I was so long-winded. I was too excited that day.

Halfway into the teaching contractual year, I was approached by Hunter College of New York City. They also planned to establish a new computer science program within their mathematics department. Someone had passed my name to Dr. Andrew Weil, the dean of sciences at the college.

The chairperson of mathematics department, Dr. Mary Dolcciani, called me one day from New York. "Dr. Cheng, would you like to visit New York City and have lunch with us at Hunter College?" she asked me.

"Thank you for calling me. What do you folks have in mind?" I asked.

"We are hoping you would consider teaching at Hunter College," she said.

"Well, that is nice of you. May I call you back in a few days? I need to talk to my wife," I told her.

I was taken by surprise, but I knew they were anxious to get the computer science program started. I had heard of Hunter College as an elite school with a good reputation for excellence in academic programs. Although she did not say a word about any specifies, I understood that the intention was to see me in person before they decided to talk about an offer of a position.

I was concerned about the program at Whitewater that had just gotten underway and the interest was very high among faculty and students. I really did not want to leave Whitewater at that time, but I thought it would be good for Nancy and the boys to experience the famous New York City. And Hunter College was a well-known elite school and Dr. Weil was a renowned scientist in the world. Dr. Dolcciani was the author of a popular calculus text. The more I thought about it, the more I became inclined toward going to Hunter College. I call Dr. Dolcciani back a few days later.

"Dr. Dolcciani, I would like to visit Hunter College. When would you like me to come?"

"How about next Wednesday? Dean Weil would like to join us for lunch," she said.

"Next Wednesday is good for me," I said.

"I will send the round-trip airline tickets to you. Do you plan to stay overnight?"

"No. Thanks. I need to teach the next day," I replied.

"Okay, we are looking forward to seeing you next week. Goodbye," she said.

I went to New York to meet Dean Weil, Dr. Dolcciani, and several faculty members of the math department. I was quite impressed by the quality of the faculty I met that day. They apparently liked what they had seen. After lunch, we had a private meeting with the dean and the chairperson.

"We would like to offer you an assistant professorship in charge of the computer science program at Hunter College. If you would consider it, please let me know. The formal offer will be sent to you within a day," Dr. Dolcciani said to me.

"I am very impressed with your school here, but this is a big decision for my family. Please let me talk to my wife. I will give you my answer in a few days," I said.

I flew back to Whitewater the same evening.

"Nancy, what do you think about living in New York City?"

"It is an exciting place to visit, but I don't know about living there," said Nancy.

"Well, you know my bad experiences in New York. Maybe we will just try to live there for a while. If we don't like it, we can always move away," I said.

"I don't mind being in New York for a year or two. I think it might be fun," she agreed.

I called Dr. Dolcciani back four days later. "I have conferred with Nancy. She doesn't mind moving from here," I told her.

"That is great! I will send the offer letter to you today," she promised me.

"By the way, I have not asked about the compensations," I said.

"It is all in the offer letter. But I can tell you the salary is 24,000 for the nine months. We will pay all of your moving expenses," she said.

"That is very generous of you. I am looking forward to receiving the offer letter. Thank you!"

The letter came two days after the call was made. The salary offer was exactly doubling my salary at Whitewater. I thought I could learn a great deal from the outstanding faculty at Hunter. Nancy liked the move because she thought I would be happier in New York.

I called Dr. Dolcciani and informed her I accepted the offer and signed the paper. I went to see my boss, Dr. Carroll Flannigan, and told him my decision to go to New York. He was not happy to see me leaving. But he realized that the computer science program at Whitewater was up and running and the faculty could continue to develop it. In a sense, my job was done there. A going-away party was given to send me off to New York at the end of the spring semester.

Right after final examination papers were graded, I flew to New York and spent two days to look for a place to live. Manhattan was out of question because of the high cost in good neighborhoods and crime problems in the lesser neighborhoods. I decided to live in the Bronx, where I knew that I needed to do a bit more of traveling, but it had an old and good neighborhood. A longtime friend, Captain Lin-Chia Li, the one who sent Mom and me from pier twelve in Fu-Chow, had retired from the army as a colonel and was now an acclaimed painter with substantial fame in the artists' world. They lived in a Bronx high-rise condominium with their three daughters and two sons. When I called him from Whitewater, he told me that there was a vacant space right next door to his apartment. Nancy and I were thrilled to be close to them. Nancy did meet Mr. and Mrs. Li when she was in Taiwan. Mr. Li was working with Dad in the Republic of China army headquarters in Taipei at that time.

I took a train to the 241 Street Station and walked up the two hundred or more steps to reach the street level of Riverdale, a subdivision of the Bronx. It was a nice, old, and quiet upper-middle class neighborhood. Mrs. Li prepared a nice dinner for the family and me. I had not seen them since I left Taiwan in 1961. Both had aged so much. We talked a lot about the States and Taiwan but not the mainland. The pair went out to participate in art exhibitions regularly throughout the nation.

After touring the apartment, I put down a deposit and had accomplished my mission to New York. The rent was four times the rent we paid in Whitewater and the place was old in every aspect. The water heaters stuck on the walls were ugly. The bathtub was very old without a shower, but it was very large. The kitchen had cockroaches crawling around. This was old town New York established many, many years ago. What a change of living it was from Wisconsin! I wondered what Nancy and the boys would say when they saw this.

It was time to move again. This year in Whitewater, we had accumulated more than ever. Nancy suggested we should sell some items since we were going to move to a much smaller space. We decided to have a garage sale just before we moved out of town. Nancy and I cleaned the garage, set up three mess hall tables, and started to choose things we would not be using in New York, such as the lawn mower and garden tools. In three days, we had filled up the one car garage for the sale. It consisted of things from clothing to television sets. We marked the prices very low in order to move things faster. Within two days of a weekend, we sold most of the items displayed. The leftover items were hauled to Goodwill Industries. Because the college was paying for the moving, we hired a professional mover to pack and move for us. They even put the old Mercedes inside the truck together with everything of the household.

Our apartment was seven miles from Hunter College. Driving to work was not feasible because there was no place to park the car, to begin with. I did try driving to work a couple of times, and each time, my car was towed away. I had to spend time and money to reclaim my car. After my car was towed the second time, I never drove to work again. My only option was to take subway trains and make two transfers to get to Hunter campus in Midtown Manhattan. The trip from home to work took me at least forty minutes each way. The apartment building was situated on top of a hill while the subway station was just at the foot of the hill. A steep walkway of more than two hundred steps was the main path between the apartment and the subway station. I needed to walk down those steps to catch the train in the morning and then climb back these steps at night when I was tired. Many times, when I was struggling up hills at night, I wished it were the other way around.

Mr. Li liked Ray very much, because he was such a fast learner. Mr. Li taught ray to paint. Not knowing Ray was left-handed, he made Ray paint with the right hand. Ray did it very well. Mr. Li never found out Ray was left-handed. Mr. Li's children were much older than our sons. Therefore, they never played together. After a short while, Nancy became very close friend with Mrs. Li. Since Mr. and Mrs. Li did not learn how to drive, I served as the driver for them when I had free time.

"Tien-Ren, how about take me to Williamsport this weekend? I want to see the baseball game," Mr. Li asked me.

"Sure. What baseball?" I asked.

"The junior baseball. Taiwan's team might get the world championship this year again," he said.

"I want to see that too. Is Mrs. Li going?"

"No. Just you, me, and David," he said. David was his eldest son at twenty-six years of age.

"Great! I will get the car ready. We will leave around ten in the morning," I said.

We went to Williamsport that weekend and did see the Taiwan youth team win the final game to win the world baseball junior title.

At Hunter, I did much the same work as I did at Whitewater. The only problems I had were with living in the big city and with new policies toward the low standard of some the students. Before the new open enrollment policy took effect in 1970, Hunter was one of the most elite liberal arts colleges in the nation. After that, the quality difference between the junior/senior and the freshman/sophomore was astounding. For the junior and senior classes I taught, the students' quality was just superb. On the other hand, many of the sophomore class students' qualifications were totally unacceptable.

In the second week of classes, I was giving a lesson in Assembly Language about the radix conversion. When I divided a number by another number using the longhand method, a student was quite confused, showing his displeasure while sitting in the class.

"Hey! Teach, what are you doing on the board?" he asked me.

"I am dividing a number using longhand division." Surprised by such a question, I told him.

"I never did that."

"How do you perform division?"

"I have no need to do it," he replied.

"What is your major? And what year are you in?" I was petrified.

"I am a sophomore in mathematics," he said.

"How many of you have the same problem?" I asked the whole class.

No one raised their hand. Although he was the only one like that, I was totally demoralized by such an incredible situation. How could someone like that be allowed in the class? The subject of longhand division was taught in the second or third grades in elementary schools! It was hard for me to believe a second-year mathematics major could be so underprepared.

After the class, I went to the department head's office. "Berry, you will not believe what I found in my class today," I fumed.

"Surprise me," Berry said.

"I have a second-year math major in my class who does not know how to divide numbers by longhand. Besides, his attitude was very bad," I told him.

"That is sad," he said.

"What are you going to do about it? At least you can remove this guy from my class," I pushed.

"Okay. Richard, listen! Let me tell you something. It is just impossible to remove any student from a class. If you remove him from the class, you can be sure of a protest," he told me.

"What protest?" I asked.

"There would be a bunch of students sitting and blocking you from entering your office," he said.

"I will call the security to chase them away," I said.

"No way. The security simply dares not do such a thing," he said.

I was very sad and unhappy to hear that.

"Berry, I like you and Hunter College, but please consider this is my resignation. I will complete my contract for the nine months and I am leaving Hunter," I told him.

I just walked out of his office in disgust. I was not unhappy with Berry, but I was sad for the students. The politicians in New York who had promoted the open-enrollment policy had ruined a great institution of higher learning.

"I have verbally resigned from the school," I told Nancy.

"You just got here," Nancy said.

"The politics in the city has ruined Hunter and other colleges, I am sure. Some of the students are very poor and the school can't do anything about it. So, I told Beery I quit by the end of the year."

"Good! I don't like the big city that much anyway," she said. "Where do we go from here?"

"I am not sure. We still have a few months to find a place to go," I said.

I was glad to have decided to leave New York City. The problem with student quality was the main reason, but I was very unhappy with the unsafe streets and subways in the city as well. Both Jim and Ray were robbed when they were either delivering newspapers or walking to convenience stores near the apartment. The apartment was supposedly located in a clean and safe neighborhood. I had two close calls of being robbed on the train, if not for the luck that policemen just happened to come by at the critical time.

One night, I worked late at school and left for home by subway. It was after ten at night. I boarded an empty section of the train at the Times Square station heading north. Just as I sat down, two big African American fellows walked from another section and sat on each side of me. They started to make remarks of my eyes, hair, and clothing. I just ignored them. One guy tried to grab my briefcase from my hands. I tried to hold on tightly. Very scared, my heart was jumping out of my throat. I thought the two big, bad guys were too much for me to deal with. They might kill me for just that. At this very critical moment, a black police officer opened the door and walked into this section of the train. While the two bad guys let go of me, I jumped up from the seat and followed the cop until the train arrived at the 241 Street Station in the Bronx. I got off the train and looked around to make sure that the two characters were not following me. After I was sure that there was no one following me, I quickly walked home from the station. I was still shaking after I arrived home.

"You wouldn't believe what I just came through," I told Nancy.

"What has happened to you? You look very pale." She was concerned.

"I was almost robbed by two big, black men on the train, if that black police officer had not come in at the right time," I said.

"This is the thing I am worrying about living in New York City. I am also worried for our three small children when they go to school here," she said.

A similar event happened a few months after that horrific incident, on the same subway route. Except this time, the rescuers were a group of five young passengers walking through the section of the train; I followed them away from the two potential assailants. At this point, I was very anxious to leave the city.

As for the college, I worked very hard to get the computer science degree program designed, proposed, and accepted by the dean and his committees. I assisted in recruiting new faculty members and set up a microcomputer laboratory. In the second semester, I taught junior and senior courses only and to avoid teaching courses that might have those underprepared students in the class. The department head went out of his way to arrange such a teaching schedule for me. The student that did not know how to do longhand division was still on Hunter's campus when I was in the school for the last time. I did not follow up on him afterward. But I supposed that he would get his degree in time because no one could *politically correctly* flunk him out.

The only communication I had with my parents was through letter writing back and forth between Taiwan and the United States. I had not seen them since I'd left Taiwan eleven years ago. There was no telephone in an average home and my parents did not have one. I could not call and talk to them in so many years. As a new graduate, my income was not enough to make any transoceanic flights. Instead of spending money on my ticket, we could get my parents to live in the States with us.

"Nancy, it cost me just as much to go back to see Mom and Dad. We could get them to live with us in the States. What do you think?" I asked.

"I think it's a great idea. We have not seen them for a few years, and they have not seen Billy yet. I hope they will like it here," she said.

"Okay! I will start to apply to the immigration services right away." I was excited about this idea, and I really missed them terribly.

Nancy and I started the preparation for moving my parents to live with us. Dad had just retired as an army general from the Republic of China. Both of my parents were in their late fifties. Our letter was responded to quickly, and they agreed to come live with us in the States. I was particularly happy that they agreed to our invitation.

The process for parents to visit children with citizenship in the United Stated was very simple and fast. It took less than a week to get the visas for my parents. We bought two one-way tickets and they were in the country within three weeks. All five of us went to the airport to greet them. It was an emotional and exciting reunion at John F. Kennedy International Airport in January 1973.

"Son, I am so happy to see you. I see you have a few gray hairs already. Ping, you still look so young and beautiful," Mama said. "Oh! This is Billy. What a handsome boy! And the two babies I saw last time, you are big boys now," Mama said with big smiles.

"We have waited for a long time to this day that we are all together." Baba was very happy.

The kids were excited to see Grandpa and Grandma. We squeezed all seven members of the family into the old Ford with Ray and Billy on their grandparents' laps. We talked all the way home, or more accurately, we listened all the way home as Baba talked 99 percent of the time. Mama did not even have a chance to say a word. When she started to say something, Baba would speak for her or shut her up.

"Ren, I want—" Mama tried to say something to me.

"Wait! Let me talk to him about this first. I have not talked to him for such a long time. Just don't interrupt me. Okay!" Baba would take over the conversation again.

Nancy and I moved out of the master bedroom for my parents to live in, and we used the smaller bedroom. A screen divider was used to divide up the living room and make part of it into two bedrooms for the children. We had not seen one another for eleven years. Suddenly I found they had aged so much since the last time I had seen them in Taipei. We had so much to catch up on. At home, Baba could not stop talking and Mama did not get a chance to cut in, even for one sentence throughout the first day. Neither the children nor the two of us had much opportunity to converse with Baba or Mama. It was just a one-way stream of talk; there was hardly any conversation at all. Nancy and I both sensed the potential difficulties that were head of us.

There were several gaps between my parents and us after eleven years of separation. First was the generation gap between any two generations. It existed even in the best of circumstances everywhere in the world. The second gap was the cultural gap. Nancy and I had been in the United States for over ten years, so our ways of thinking and lifestyle were conformed to Western societies, which was quite different from that of China. The third gap was the time gap. After so many years, we had all grown older and changed with time. Things were just different from many years ago. We all had aged and experienced different things in those long years; thus, our mind-sets were different.

In Taiwan, when three generations lived together, the grandfather would be the head of the household and the grandmother would handle every household matter. Because the ways of doing things were so different from in Taiwan, Nancy was handling the money and making household decisions. Mom went along well and was happy with just being with us. The first sign of problems was whenever we gathered. Baba always dominated all conversations and Mama and all of us never had a chance to talk. Mama was sent by Baba to tell us what to do in a very manipulative way. We thought things would be better after a little while and just went along with what was coming to us.

When Nancy and I did something that we did not even give a thought about, we might be called to the carpet and be lectured for hours. That was tough because we all had day-to-day chores to do. Sometimes, I would be called to the carpet in the morning, before I went to work. I could not be excused to leave because Baba said it was more important to listen to him. That caused some problems with Nancy after I fell and injured my leg when I rushed to catch the train. Nancy was very upset and confronted Baba about that incident.

"Baba, you don't have to lecture him in the morning. He rushed to the train this morning, fell on the ground, and injured his leg. If you don't care about him, I do. Our children depend on him," Nancy said in great distress. That only made Baba angrier toward Nancy.

The most frequent causes for being called to the carpet were just minor misunderstandings. When I walked home late at night and bone-tired or had too many things in my mind, my greeting to Mama and Baba might be less pleasant or not smiling. The next thing we knew was the talk between Mama and Baba in the master bedroom with the door closed. Soon we would hear Mama crying. At first, we did not know what was happening. Only during the lectures, we knew it was because of our "bad attitude" toward them. We tried to explain that I was just too tired at night and too much was in my mind.

"Baba, I was tired. I did not mean not smiling to you," I explained.

"I know you did that on purpose," Baba would say. "You two want to show that we are not welcome here so you just try to make me feel bad," he would say.

"No! Baba, we just invited you over here. There is no reason for us to do that. Please ignore what we may have done wrong. I want to assure you Ping and I will never do things deliberately to offend you and Mama," I tried to assure him. Not only would he not accept any explanations we gave him, but he would lecture us on how bad it was when children were treating their parents badly.

"What do you mean you would not deliberately offend me? You did all those little hints and trying to control the two of us. In Han dynasty, the Wang..." He would start his lecture without giving me any break. He would not want to hear any explaining from us.

Whatever he thought led to a conclusion that would be the only truth.

He would recite historical examples from 3,000 years ago for hours. When Baba was in a bad mood, Mama was the first to be scolded. It was always a one-way fight. Baba was a total "Never forget" and "Never forgive" person. He would repeatedly drag up past things when he thought he was wronged by anyone. He would fume and complain for hours, often exploding in rage or loud swearing. All Mama could do was just cry, since Baba did not want to listen to anybody for any explanation. As his only child, all I could do was hope for miracles.

We were treading on a minefield and never knew when the explosion might occur. The children were petrified and did not know what to do. The mental stress on Nancy and me was close to the breaking point. I always tried to think about how much they loved me and how kind they were when I was little back home. I spoke to Nancy and asked her to be patient. I said that the situation would improve as time went by. She was very supportive to me and agreed to my pleas, but I knew how much pressure she was under.

Baba and Mr. Li were very happy to see each other. They had been colleagues for over twenty years. Now that they became neighbors again in the foreign land, the old friends became almost inseparable in the first few weeks. They talked of the past, often excitedly. Baba must have complained to Mr. Li about Nancy and me, among other things in the States, because we were not conforming with the lessons given by saints from 3,000 year ago.

"You are coming to the States. Y**ou** should do like people do here. You are not going to make people do the way people did in China 3,000 years ago," Mr. Li said to Baba. Mrs. Li told this conversation to Nancy but never gave her any specifics about his complaints.

Tragically, death struck the Li family soon after we moved out of the apartment. Mr. and Mrs. Li died of a car crash after a painting exhibit in Orlando, Florida. Mrs. Li was driving with a newly acquired license. When she pulled the car into the expressway, a big truck hit them from the rear left and killed them instantly.

They were only fifty-two years old. There was no will and they had hidden their treasures, money, and good paintings in a bank vault. Their children had no clue where things were stored. The younger girls were only eighteen and sixteen. Fortunately, the older brothers and sisters were working with decent jobs and they chipped in to raise the younger ones.

CHAPTER 14

Rochester Institute of Technology

In March 1973, I went to Detroit to attend a computer science professional conference. The conference was for technical information exchange and for job-hunting purposes. Many schools were sending representatives to scout for new faculty and administrators. I was assigned to chair a technical presentation session for ACM. During a midmorning break, I met Dr. John Gunter from the Rochester Institute of Technology (RIT). After exchanging some school and personal information, John and I went to take a coffee break.

"Are you interested in leaving New York City and working in Rochester?" he asked me directly.

"Do you mean working for RIT?" I asked.

"Yes."

"I will be delighted to learn more about the school and the job," I replied.

In the Office of RIT

This must be a godsend, I thought. I was trying to get out of the Big Apple at that time. John and I then decided to have lunch together and talk more about the job.

"I am the director of the computer center at RIT. I also have a staff to handle the programming courses for the colleges. The provost, Dr. Bullard, wanted to have a formal computer science program established at RIT. I heard your name from a friend and thought I will talk to you about it," he said.

"That is very interesting because I am tired of the big city and the city politics there," I said.

"We are not just looking for a teacher; we are looking for a head of the new department. Are you interested in administrative work?" he asked me.

"I have no administrative experience, but I am interested in the type of work," I said.

"Great! How about come to RIT to have an interview with the provost? He wanted to make the selection himself. I have not seen him doing any interview of a faculty in the past. This is a very special event," he told me.

"I will fly to Rochester after I talk to my wife. How about if I call you next Monday?"

Two days after I returned to New York, I received a call at home from a RIT official representative inviting me to Rochester for a two-day interview. I promptly agreed. I flew to Rochester, New York, and took a taxi to the Hilton Hotel on campus. I was quite impressed by the well-designed campus architecture and fine manicured landscape.

The first day, I met with all the instructors and staff at the computer center. John Gunter and two lead instructors, Dr. Roy Czernocowsky and Rodger Baker, conducted formal interviews with me. There was a group discussion about computer science curriculum with me and the other instructors. The next day, the provost, Dr. Todd Bullard, scheduled an early-morning interview with me. This was quite unusual, because none of the deans of any college was involved in this interview. It was even rarer for the provost to interview a new faculty member. I sensed that some importance was put to this interview, but I had no clue what that might be.

Dr. Bullard was a tall and heavyset person with a deep voice. "Dr. Cheng, I am pleased to have you here today. I have read your résumé and found it very impressive. Tell me: can you handle a bunch of professors in a department?" He was very straightforward.

"Dr. Bullard, I have not been a department head before, but I believe I can work with them to get the teaching job done," I said confidently.

"Do you mind if we appoint you the acting chairman of a new department that is to be established and see how it goes?" he asked.

"I don't mind that at all," I replied.

"Can we count on you to start the program in the fall? If you could, I would like you to start your job here on June 1, for you to put the department together," he said.

"I like that very much. You can be assured that I will get you a first-rate program at RIT," I said.

He was very forthright and apparently a sincere person. I found him indeed a respectable and impressive leader of RIT. I was very impressed by him, although I was the one under scrutiny. After the interview, I went back to the hotel on campus. The next morning, I went to see John Gunter and was ready to leave the RIT campus.

"We have decided to hire you," John told me.

I was surprised, because normally the offer would come in the mail.

"Oh, that's nice. Could you tell me a little more about the offer?"

"Of course," he said with a smile on his face. He took me to his office. "We have a proposition for you. Dr. Bullard would like to offer you the acting department chair. If you can establish a new computer science department and run with it, then your position will be made permanent."

"I would like that very much. But to whom do I report to?" I asked. I was in minor shock.

"The provost himself," he replied.

"Wow! This is very unusual. I am used to reporting to a department head. I had never had too much to do even with a dean before. Now directly reporting the provost?"

"You will get used to him. He is tough but very fair. If he supports you, you can get all the resources you need to do the job," he said.

"How about my rank?" I asked.

"Since you are assistant professor at Hunter College now, the best we could do is to offer you a promotion to associate professorship without the immediate tenure," he replied.

"Okay. I have no problem with that. But how about my salary?" I asked.

"We will match your salary at Hunter College. You know it is high for this area. But Dr. Bullard is willing to offer you that," he said.

"You folks are very good to me. I will try my best to do a good job for RIT. But how about moving and starting dates?" I said, very happy with this unexpected interview.

"We will start you June 1, and the institute will pay all of your moving expenses, including hotel stay before you find a house," he said.

I was elated. No other school had treated me so well in the past. I agreed to report to work on June 1, 1973. I called Nancy after returning to my hotel room and told her what was taking place.

"Wow! That sounds good. We will be moving again, but I don't mind that a bit," she said with apparent elation.

I went to Rochester alone by the end of May and lived in the hotel on campus. I knew I had a lot of work to do to take on such a challenging assignment. RIT is a private school. It enrolled about 12,000 students in 1973. It had five colleges and an independent two-year college: the federally funded National Technical Institute for the Deaf. The computer science department was not excited when I reported to work. I proposed the structure of the computer science department in a week and was approved quickly by the administration. However, it had no college to attach to. I reported directly to the provost.

There were nine instructors on the job when I started in June. My first task was to make a three-year development plan for the department. I laid out the undergraduate and graduate curricula, faculty growth plan, equipment, and laboratories plan. Before the fall semester started, I had completed all the curriculum design and the five-year plans for the computer science degree program. All six new faculty positions were approved and filled after I had interviewed more than twenty candidates from a list of over one hundred applicants.

I also proposed a new building for the department. I knew it was a long shot, but we really needed that. Although there was a shortage of people and space, we started the operation. I proposed a bold plan to offer three tracks in computer science instead of the traditional one. The computer science faculty and the institute's administration accepted the proposal without any challenges.

Among the tracks, two were pragmatic and tailored for future industrial and other applications. My plans were accepted by our faculty and approved by the provost in total. Before the fall of 1973, I hired five more new faculty members to join the department. The department enrollment was two hundred or so computer science majors and about five hundred non-major students during the first year of operation.

During weekends in Rochester, I went house hunting. I learned about a good subdivision called the Pittsford. I found one house in a very nice new neighborhood. The owner was transferred to a new location. I called Nancy about what I had found.

"Go ahead and make the decision to buy or not. I trust your judgment on houses," she told me.

"I know what your concern is in houses. How about one with a big kitchen?"

"That is all I need," she would say.

The next day, I made a down payment and bought this two-year-old, four-bedroom house for $38,000. It was near the top of a mountain with great valley views. Nancy let me make all the decisions for the house. She was very easygoing on those matters. Before fall, I went back to New York to move my family to Rochester. Again, the school paid for all the moving expenses. Nancy and I each drove a car. It was only a four-hour drive from New York to Rochester. We arrived at the new house about one hour before the truck pulled in the driveway. Moving into the house took about three hours to complete. My parents were happy to move into this quiet neighborhood. The children were happy to see the large yard and much more spacious place to live. There was a finished basement for a playroom and for shop work.

As an Asian American, to be the new boss of fifteen younger, freethinking, liberal professors were not as easy as "a piece of cake." They would come to my office to make demands for good or poor reasons, questioning some of my plans and decisions or checking out my professional knowledge. Since I had anticipated all these possible behaviors, I was not upset by any of that. I was fair with their demands, including going to the provost to request salary adjustments when I felt their demands were justified. I was also patient with them and answered any personal or professional questions without any trace of hesitation or emotion. Within a month, we were working as a team in harmony. My personal secretary, Jenny Miller, was a young and talented but no-nonsense type of a person who was quite upset about the behavior of some faculty in the beginning.

"Dr. Cheng. How come you are so calm and put up with all that nonsense?" she asked me.

"I know I am right. So, I am not upset. Only time will tell if my way of things doing will work or not. Please be patient and treat them professionally, would you?" I told her.

"Yes, sir, I will try my best," she promised me.

My demands for their job performance were also very high. I made sure that my promises to anybody were absolutely carried out. I dismissed an assistant professor for lack of classroom preparation in the first semester and called several of them on the carpet in the first three months. I forgot I was just an acting chairman, or I really did not think there ought to be any different ways of doing my job. Anyway, I was called into the provost's office four months into my new job in the fall semester.

"I have heard a lot about you and there were some complaints about you too. However, I was glad to have heard those complaints against you—the type of complaints one would get only when you pushed people to perform their jobs. I want to make you the permanent chairman effective immediately. Do you accept it?" Dr. Bullard asked me.

"I accept your appointment, Dr. Bullard. I am happy to have your trust. I promise you I will do my best to be a good chairman for the computer science department," I told him.

When I first reported to work, my office was a small room next to a programmer of the computer center. My secretary had to sit two rooms down the hall from me. All existing instructors were originally reporting to the computer center director. The office spaces were all mixed together by the two groups. The computer science faculty realized the new organization was an academic unit equal to that of the computer center. But the computer center folks still treated computer science faculty as if they were part of the center but second-class citizens.

At that time, the new director was Mr. Richard Bagby. I was introduced to him in a social function but not in a formal situation. One day in the summer of 1973, about two weeks into my job, my secretary Jenny came to my office. "Mr. Bagby would like to see you at ten o'clock in his office," she said.

I thought it was funny to call me into his office. "If he wants to see me, ask him to come to my office," I told Jenny.

"Yes, sir, I will tell Betty that," Jenny said. Betty was Mr. Bagby's executive assistant.

A few minutes later, Jenny came again. "Betty said Mr. Bagby's office is more comfortable," Jenny said.

"Tell Betty that it is my principle. I will visit him in his office, if I want to see him. But if he wants to see me, he must see me in my office," I told Jenny.

Jenny called Betty back about my demand. After five minutes, Jenny received a call from Betty. "Dr. Cheng, Betty has made an appointment for Mr. Bagby to see you here at three o'clock," she said.

Mr. Bagby came to my small office that afternoon. We just exchanged a few nice words and he left. There was not a thing he needed to see me about that morning. The story went out quickly. That had changed the way computer science faculty members were treated by the computer center staff. Dick and I later became very good friends. That simple gesture worked well. Soon the story was spread to people in other departments and colleges. A new identity was firmly established in the minds of computer science faculty and the staff of the computer center that we were independent academically and not a part of the computer center.

Equipment for the computer science program was the most important part of the curricula. However, there was nothing available for the department in the beginning except the computer time provided by the computer center to students to do programming assignments only. Since we missed the budget cycle, there was no funding for computer science laboratories in the budget. We had to have some equipment for certain courses. In order to get equipment right away, I solicited some donations of old computers from local industries and led a few interested students to repair these. We repaired some older computers, such as the IBM1620, IBM1401, and IBM360/40, and used them for instructional purposes. The provost approved my funding request for computers during the first semester. With the funding, we established a microcomputer laboratory with new and updated microcomputers. There was enough equipment for teaching and research work in the department starting in the beginning of the second semester. My electronics hobby starting from picking up debris from crashed planes to the junkyard in Taipei again helped me on my new job in a big way. To me, the computer repair was a simple matter, but soon the entire school knew that the chairman had repaired computers for his students.

As the program was put in place at the school, we needed to inform potential new students. All new program announcements were sent to high schools and two-year colleges in the state of New York. In order to promote the new program, I had to drive throughout the state and talk to faculty and students. It would be a long-term commitment on my part to the program.

"Nancy, I have to be on the road at least three days per week for a while," I told Nancy.

"What are you doing on the road?" she asked. "Did someone in the school ask you to do that?" She was not too happy with me driving so much on the road.

"No. Nancy, I want to do it myself. It is not part of my job, but I need to do it. You see, if we have a good program here but no one knows about it, then we may not have enough students here," I said.

"Where will be you be going?"

"All of the good high schools and two-year colleges."

"Most of them are out in the nowhere. I am worried about you driving alone in those country roads. Do you want me to go along to keep company?"

"No, don't worry. I will be careful. Remember this is not New York City," I said.

"Well, you must be careful on the road." She reluctantly went along with my plan.

I began to visit schools in the fall of 1973. The response was very encouraging. I made friends with faculty in many schools and invited them to RIT seminars as often as I could. As a result, new applicants to the freshman class and transfer students to junior class had increased dramatically. In the second year of operation, the enrollment of computer science majors had more than doubled.

In the fall of 1974, Dr. Bullard called me to his office. "Richard, I noticed you have done a good job in the department. I am very pleased. I have requested the president to promote you to full professorship and grant you the tenure," he said with a typical broad smile.

"Wow! That is very kind of you to give me the promotion. I want to thank you, because without your support, I wouldn't be able to get any of the work done. You have been instrumental for the success of the new program." I was truly moved. That was the record time to be promoted to a full professor from associate professor.

At RIT, co-op is a mandatory program. That meant all students had to fulfill the course work and industrial work experience alternatively between academic quarters in order to receive their undergraduate degree. Therefore, I had to sell this program to industries for our students to find a co-op job. Because of the need to recruit, I was out of the campus at least one solid week per month.

I still had my old diesel car with over 150,000 miles on that. Driving alone in New York State from west to east and up down the country roads, I had problems finding diesel stations in all parts of the state. On the expressway, it was not difficult to find a truck stop to fill up my tank. But away from the expressway, it was impossible to find a diesel station. New York is a vast state. But sometimes, I was the only one driving on the country roads for hours, not seeing any people or cars.

Some schools were in the remote countryside that could be a hundred miles from any expressway. I carried a five-gallon spare tank, but it lasted only a little less than a hundred miles on such hilly roads. More than once on the road, I had to knock on the door of a farmer's house to ask to buy some kerosene to keep the car going. Due to the hard driving on steep, hilly roads and the bad fuels used at times, the engine was overloaded and carbonized. Soon the car was trailed by a streak of thick, black smoke.

I must credit the success of the computer science program to the quality of our faculty, the direct support from the provost, the good curriculum, and the intensive effort in recruitment. The enrollment in the department grew at a phenomenal rate. The computer science enrollment doubled or tripled each year. Within two years, the computer science enrollment surpassed that of some smaller colleges at RIT. By 1975, the third year, there were over eight hundred computer science majors and more than 2,000 course takers. I prepared a proposal to elevate the computer science department to the school of computer science and technology with three undergraduate departments and a graduate program. Dr. Roy Satre, the dean of Institute College that was a new college established in January 1975, to house the new programs.

I reported to Roy administratively, but for major decisions, I still went directly to the provost for resources. This arrangement caused some tension between Roy and me from time to time. Roy was such a nice and gentle person. He had tolerated me going around him, but it was under Dr. Bullard's advice. Nevertheless, he supported my new proposal immediately after I presented the proposal to him. The school of computer science and technology was established in May 1975. I was appointed the director of the school. There were three new chairmen and a director of graduate programs in the school. We did not search for new department heads. All new positions were filled with current faculty members. New faculty positions were filled during the years. By the fourth year, the department had over 1,000 major students and twenty-seven full-time faculty members.

Dr. Bullard was the most powerful, respected, and feared figure at RIT. President Paul Miller delegated all academic affairs and administrative matters to Todd, so the president could devote his full time to deal with industries, the government, and fund-raising. Dr. Bullard's reputation and physical appearance were so dominating that almost every senior academic and administrative head would tremble in front of him. But I saw him differently. He had a very important but difficult job to do, and he handled it very fairly and effectively. He was also very forthright about what he had in mind to say and never gave an inch to any political pressures. I also found him treating people quite kindly but very firmly.

In the summer of 1974, after I gave recommendations for faculty salary raises, he called me into his office. "Richard, why did you give Evelyn such a high salary increment? Not because she is young and good-looking, I hope!" He looked straight into my eyes.

"Absolutely not. I recommended the highest increment for her because she is doing well in teaching. Secondly, she was so underpaid. I want to bring her salary at par with male faculty in the department," I answered in a very definitive tone.

"I thought so, but I just have to make sure by asking you. I support what you are doing to reward the excellence and make it fair for your faculty," he said as he smiled to me.

"I thank you for your support, and I do appreciate that you bring any of your doubts in the open."

On the RIT campus, academic unit heads were always competing for resources. The final say was always by Dr. Bullard. The computer science department was always in need of more space, more staff, and more money to buy equipment and have activities, because of its rapid growth. Dr. Bullard required all the heads to give a presentation to justify our cases in front of him and answer his sharp questions. My contenders were all deans of colleges. I always prepared my requests with all sorts of analysis and backup documents and I had never prepared to take no for an answer. Almost nine times out ten when I was competing with other deans, I would win the approval. To me, that seemed to be the only logical result.

In one of those cases, he was so upset with a dean. With the two competing parties present, he literally yelled and cussed at this dean like a grade school boy for presenting such an ill-prepared argument for resources that I also wanted.

One day, Dr. Bullard, Dr. Satre, and I had lunch in a restaurant. "I knew Richard was strong, so I hired him as the department head, but I didn't know he is *that* strong. He wants to win all of the resources in contention with other college deans in my office," Dr. Bullard told Dr. Satre, and they laughed.

"I am glad that I am not the one to make those decisions," Dr. Satre said, and that was the truth.

We all laughed. If Dr. Satre were in the same position, I seriously doubt that the result of the computer science program would be as successful.

CHAPTER 15

The Long-Lost Relative

When Nancy first came to the United States in 1964, she mentioned to me that she had a close cousin that she had not heard from for over twenty years and he might be in this country. I soon forgot about what she had said to me. This is a big country; how could someone be found without any further information? We never pursued that subject after the brief mentioning by her. The first day in the fall quarter of 1973, I went to the school cafeteria for breakfast. After I picked up and paid for the food, I was looking for a place to sit. It was a very large mess hall with more than one hundred tables. Most of the tables were empty at that early hour. I spotted an Asian man in the early sixties eating alone at a table. I approached him at the table.

"May I sit here and keep you company?" I asked.

"Please sit down and eat with me. My name is Kenneth Chiang," he said as he smiled at me. "I am a professor of economics."

"I am Richard Cheng from the computer science department," I said. "Are you a Chinese American?"

"Yes," he answered.

"Do you speak Mandarin?" I asked again.

"Yes. But I speak English more often than Mandarin," he said.

"Your family name in Chinese is Chiang like Prime Minister Chiang?" I asked.

"Yes," said he.

I detected his heavy accent from Tse-Kiang Province, where Nancy's parents came from.

"Are you a native of Tse-Kiang Province?" I followed up.

"Yes," he answered.

"Did you live in Chungking during World War II?" I kept my questioning.

"I did," he said.

"Did you work for the Twenty-Sixth Ordnance factory at that time?" I asked.

"Yes," he said.

By now, he looked quite anxious.

"My wife's father is Pen Yu Chiang. Do you happen to know him?" I asked.

It was a long shot, I thought. His face turned pale and he got up from the bench.

"Sorry. I must leave now. Someone is waiting for me in my office," he said. He took his tray while walking away from the table.

I knew I had said something to cause the panic in him, but I did not know what it was. When I went home that night, I talked to Nancy about the incident.

"Nancy, I had a real strange feeling this morning when I met this guy. I think I have found your lost cousin."

"You are kidding me! How do you know that's him?" she said.

"Well, the way he acted. I thought he should be happy, but he was scared as if I were a secret agent or something like that. Does he have anything to hide?"

"I don't know, but I don't think so," Nancy said. "You acted like a detective probing right into the man's past. What do you expect him to react?"

"Maybe I was too pushy," I said. "There are too many coincidences. I believe he must be your lost cousin. There is no doubt he is the one. Ask your dad if his name is Yu-Kan."

"If that's the case, it is wonderful. Maybe I should call my parents and let them know."

"Don't tell your parents yet until it is confirmed," I said. "Why don't you wait for a while and let me find out more about him to be sure. I don't want you to raise their hopes up too high."

Two weeks later, Kenneth called me in my office and told me on the phone in Chinese, "I think your wife is my cousin," he said.

"Ken, I already had a hunch about you. I am so happy to have found you for them," I told Ken.

Nancy called her parents in Canada. They were thrilled. Soon after, we had a family reunion with Nancy's parents and her siblings at our house. Everybody was happy about this long-awaited gathering, but nothing was said about the past and the missing years. Ken was married to Helen, a very bright and nice lady. They had two daughters about the same age as our boys. Both were extremely smart. Shirley graduated from Harvard and Berkeley with a doctoral in physics. The younger daughter, Carol, obtained a doctoral degree in electrical engineering from MIT. We got together often, but Ken avoided any mentioning about his past. We could only speculate why he did so, but Nancy and I just played dumb about his past, especially in front of his family. Ken passed away in 1998 at an advanced age.

Rochester was a unique city for my family. In the metropolitan area of Rochester, many Chinese American scientists and engineers at Xerox and Kodak were graduates from Taiwan universities. I found at least two old friends from Kaoshiung high school years. They were all well educated and successful in their professional fields. Among them, there were nationally renowned physicians, professors, chemists, and engineers. A group of them—twelve families—was the core of our particularly close-knit friends. I was thirty-nine years old at that time. The youngest was thirty-four, and the oldest was fifty-five years old. I was a latecomer to be included in the group soon after I arrived in 1973. Although people in this group were all successful, none was super rich. There was only one business executive in the group, and there were no business owners. I chose this group as my closest friends not because of their fame or successes but because this was the most fun group to be with.

In the summer of 1973, I received a phone call. "Dr. Cheng, there is a Mr. Liang on the phone asking for you. Would you take it?" Jenny asked.

"Okay! I will take it," I said.

"Good morning, Mr. Liang," I said, not knowing who that was.

"Ha! Ha! Ha! Mr. Liang! Can you tell who I am?" The person on the line spoke in Chinese.

"Tell me, please." I was lost.

"Tien-Ren, I am Kai Liang. Do you remember now?" he said.

"Kai, you son of a gun! How did you find me?" I asked.

I was dumbfounded. I had not heard from him since he went to the university in 1953. He was my basketball buddy in Si-Tze Bay and we grew up as toddlers and as neighbors during both wars.

"I saw your picture in the newspaper this morning with our chairman side by side. I did not recognize your name, but I could tell it was you," he said.

"Where are you? What are you doing?"

"I have been in Rochester for over ten years now. I am working for Kodak as a senior scientist," he said to me.

"I am married with three boys. How about you?"

"I am married, but we have no children," he said.

"Where do you live?" I asked.

"We live in Penfield up in the north. Where do you live?"

"We live in Pittsford," I said.

"What is your address? I will pick you up tonight and introduce you to my friends here," he said.

I gave him our address. He picked us up and drove to his home. There were ten other families at his house.

"I want to introduce my old buddy, Richard. We grew up together. He is the chairman of computer science department at RIT," he said.

That was the beginning of the long association with the rest of the gang. Every weekend, starting Friday evening, a family would host a dinner followed by two tables of poker games. Saturday games were follow-ups for the Friday games but would start early in the afternoon. Sunday was the day of rest, only sometimes. We played on most Sundays but ended early at night, say midnight. The Friday and Saturday games often lasted until two or three in the morning. Christmas and New Year's Eve, we always played until daybreak. No one would suggest quitting the games for various reasons. The antes were small. It ranged from five cents to a quarter per bet. The highest winner and the biggest loser were under one hundred dollars per night. Most of the time, the swing was in the tens of dollars.

On the poker table, we all acted like high school kids. During the parties, we forgot about the stresses and tensions at our jobs and daily lives.

"This is the best therapy for the heart. You forget the stress during the workdays, and laughter is the best medicine, as *Reader's Digest* claims," said the physician Paul Yu.

"I believe it. I feel much better since I've played poker with you guys," said Joe, the executive.

"You know, we play small amounts. Everybody can afford it. It is really a low-cost entertainment that money can buy," said another physician, Donald.

"Okay, stop yakking. Let's play some cards." Ben got impatient with the stalled game.

The group started such social functions a few years before I moved to Rochester. The frequency of activity increased over the next few years; by 1978, there would be three parties per weekend. That was a marathon from Friday evening to Monday morning. We all had to recuperate during the weekdays and get ready for the weekends. Social activities with other groups were almost reduced to zero, except for official functions at work that could not be excused. Even at that, we would leave the official parties and rush to the poker games later.

It was interesting to read and to know more about people in poker games. They were so different from how you knew them from usual contact in the office or at a party. Most people's personal traits could be easily detected in poker games when they let their guard down or became "desperate" to save face. People in this group were all extremely smart and sharp. It was very interesting to watch how they were making decisions, bluffing, and reacting to losing or winning.

There were the calculated ones that only risked when the odds were greatly in their favor. There were the conservative ones that threw away cards with any presence of real or imaginary threats of losing. There were some opportunists or daredevils who would throw in chips regardless of the situation and then regretfully watch the winner scoop their chips away. There were the poor losers who would make gestures or remarks to win back some of their lost faces. A few squabbles did occur; it was the face not the money they were trying to save. The fun, the challenge at the tables, and the friendship were unparalleled in anywhere we had experienced. They were the most enjoyable years Nancy and I ever had.

My interest in Mercedes was for its precision mechanical work and its fine craftsmanship. I loved the old diesel car that I had put another 200,000 miles on in the last eight years. It worked as well as when I first bought it in 1967. However, the winter in Rochester had taken its tolls. The heavy salted roads had caused the car to rust. The first part rusting was the fenders, and then the door panels. I took it to a body shop. The estimate was too high for my budget. Instead of getting rid of the rusty car, I thought I would fix it myself.

I went to a body shop and observed what they did and then I bought all the compounds, sanding tools, and painting equipment from Sears. I began to experiment on just one spot on the door panel. It came out beautifully. I spent a week working at nights after school to finish the whole car. I was amazed how easy it was. After that, I bought and refinished four more salt-damaged Mercedes and sold them at good profits. I spent a year to restore a sport coupe I'd bought with all the metal on the body rusted out. By the time it was finished, I was the proud owner of a Mercedes sport coupe. I kept it and used it only when the weather was perfect. Jimmy liked to work on cars too. He had been my key assistant to get the work done in our garage. On the other hand, Ray did not even know what a wrench was.

Rochester is in the so called the "snow belt" for the large amount of snowfall during the winter season in the Great Lakes region. I had experienced snowfall as early as October 1 and snowstorm at the end of April. On April 24, 1974, I had an engagement to interview a highly qualified faculty candidate for the department. When he flew in from Texas, the institute was closed due to a big snowstorm. He struggled to reach the campus to meet with me. He liked the program and the school but was discouraged by the weather conditions in Rochester.

One night I picked Ken up to play poker in a friend's house. After the game was over at one o'clock in the morning, I drove Ken home from about five miles away. After I turned off from the main highway into the country road, I suddenly found there was no trace of the road anymore. The fresh two feet of snow had covered everything like a white blanket in front of me. I recalled there were some ditches around there, so we decided just to abandon the car and walk the half mile home. The snow was way above our knees and in places was waist deep. Fortunately, it was not very cold that night and the snow was loose. I stayed at his house that night.

One evening, I received a call from Nancy. "I am in trouble. I just had an accident," she said.

"Where are you?"

"I am in someone's house on Farmhouse Road right across from the fresh food stand. My car is in a ditch," she said.

"What has happened? Are you all right?"

"I am fine, just a little dizzy. The snow had covered the road. I was driving too close to the roadside and my car just lost control."

"Okay! Just stay put. I will be right over," I said to her.

I picked Nancy up from the farmer's house and she took me to her car. That was the old Ford LTD we had had for a few years. I called the tow truck to take it to a dealer. It was all bent up and the frame was damaged beyond repair. It was time to look for another used car.

Nancy and I also experienced the best time in our life with our children. In the years we lived in Rochester, we had seen Jim and Ray growing from small grade school boys to high school junior and senior. Billy had grown from a toddler to a grade school student. The school system in Pittsford where we lived was one of the best in New York State. We never had to watch over the shoulders of our children for their schoolwork. Each one came home with report cards that any parent would be happy with.

Both Jim and Ray were involved with the school music band. Jim played the tuba and Ray the trumpet. Neither of them took any formal lessons, but they were selected to the band. Ray was especially talented in his trumpet and was the first trumpet in the school band. None of the boys had any behavioral problems at school. We talked about drug abuse and how to avoid being hooked by drug distributors.

"How is the drug situation in your schools?" I asked the three of them together.

"Pretty bad and getting worse," Jim said.

"Tell us something you know at school," Nancy told them.

"There are bad guys putting drugs in Coca-Cola and offered it to kids in school," Jim told us.

"How do you handle that?" Nancy asked the three of them.

"I just stay away from them and I don't take any offers," Jim said.

"Good boy. That's the way to do it," I told Jim.

"I know some of my friends took the bait, but I knew better," Ray said.

"My teacher watch over our shoulders like a hawk. No drug problems in my class that I know of," Billy said.

Nancy and I felt quite relieved from the way the boys talked. We have such open conversations frequently, but we did not detect any problems with any of our three sons.

Dr. Ivan Trombley was my doctor in Rochester. He called me one day after my annual physical. "Richard, I need you to see me right away," he told me.

"I will be in your office right away," I said, my heart sinking. What in the world was wrong with me? I was only forty years old.

"Doctor, what is the problem?"

"I found blood cells in your urine. I want to check further," he said. "Do you feel any pain?" he asked while chopping on my lower back. "You have a kidney stone. I am sending you to the hospital to get the X-ray," he told me.

"Okay, Doctor!" I felt like a defeated man.

After the X-ray was examined, it did not show any stones. I went to see another doctor: Katherine Lee. She checked me out and said it was inflammation of the tissue in the urinal track. She prescribed a red pill for me to take. A month later, the result was the same: a presence of red blood cells. I went back to Dr. Trombley and told him what I had done.

"I will use the bladder scope to look. It is a simple matter," he said.

He called the nurse in to get me prepared. After the examination, there was still no clue.

"I can't find anything inside the bladder. I don't know what to tell you. Come back a week later and let me check you at that time."

I went home uncertain what was going on with my condition. One day, I received a package of twelve bottles of a difficult-to-find medicine called Yu-Nan White Medicine. Nancy and I did not know where it was from. I recalled Baba mentioned often during the war that the powdery medicine could stop bleeding if wounded. I took half a teaspoon of the powder just to try it out. It was so bitter and hot my tongue was numb for at least two hours. I decided I did not want to take it again. Two weeks later, I went for another checkup by Dr. Trombley.

"Richard, what did you do? The bleeding has stopped," he asked.

"I had not done anything since I saw you two weeks ago," I told him. I totally forgot taking the Chinese medicine.

The matter was over. To this day, I never found out what did cure my urinal bleeding. Nor did I find out who did send us the Yu-nan White Medicine.

The situation at home with Mama and Baba had not improved any. Baba was constantly unhappy, and Mama was crying frequently. Baba would call me to talk. "The grandchildren are not close to us. I believe they don't like your mama and me living in here with you," he told me.

"Baba, the grandchildren love you, but they have their own companions, so they can't spend too much time with you," I said.

"It must have been Ping, or you instructed them not to come near us," he said.

"We never instructed them not to come near you, Baba."

"Yes, you did." He started fuming.

Such was one of the minor incidents.

At that time, the boys were old enough, so Nancy found a job as the shoe department manager at the local Woolworth store. During the day, only Mama and Baba stayed home. In the evening, everybody was at the house. Baba was writing his *I-Ching book,* but Mama was very lonely. She did not watch TV because she did not know any English. Again, when we came home late and tired, we would lie down for a while before we had the strength to say anything. We would be blamed for showing them our displeasure by not greeting them.

The mental stress was so intense it was like putting clamps on both sides of our temples. We were in constant fear of not knowing what we might do wrong next and step into a minefield. Many times, it turned into unhappiness between Nancy and me. We were fighting or not speaking to each other for no reason at times. When I tried to talk to Baba about the problem, he would not explode right away but then Mama would be crying, or Baba refused to eat dinner with us. The whole thing just drove us crazy. For the sake of my own sanity and the future of my family, I had to do something I never thought I would do. I decided to talk to Baba that he might want to go back to Taiwan where he had many friends and students. Both Mama and Baba had just turned sixty years old. Staying home with no one to accompany them might have been one of the reasons they were so unhappy here.

"Baba, I have something to talk to you about. Please don't take it the wrong way," I said.

"Go ahead and say it," he told me.

"Baba, I know you and Mama are not happy here. Your friends and students are all in Taiwan. There is no way we can be with you during the day or serve you like the book says. You are still strong and full of energy. Keeping you in the house is the main reason that you are not happy. It might be better for you and Mama to go back to Taiwan and wait until you are too old to work. We will bring you back here with us at that time," I said.

"If we go back to Taiwan, we will never be back here again. You have pulled us from our roots. Now we don't have a root in Taiwan, but you are kicking us out of your house." He began to get upset.

"Baba, please! We are not kicking you out of our house. You still have the house there. I have money in my saving account of $7,000. I will give it all to you to refurbish the house in Taipei," I said. "I am very sorry to make you so unhappy here. I wished I never made such suggestions."

"Well, you did. We will go back to Taipei as soon as possible," he said.

He agreed with me to move back but was extremely upset. Not because he was leaving us to Taiwan, but he interpreted that we were kicking them out of our house. In June 1975, we sent Mama and Baba to the airport in Rochester. Before boarding, Dad turned his head and told Nancy, "I am going to avenge this," he said.

We did not understand what he really meant. I felt so bad. After we went back home, I cried alone in the bedroom for the first time in many, many years. Later I found several sheets of paper Baba had written describing how disappointed and how sad he was. They made me feel guilty for causing all that had happened. I often asked myself, "What could we do differently, so Baba would be happier?" I never found the answer. After all of this, my love to Mama and Baba had not changed. I often recall the good times and good things we had when I was very young.

It was a great relief for the family. Our lives were gradually returned to normal.

"Baba will never be happy here, even though we did everything exactly as he wanted—the 3,000-year-old way—because he couldn't shake off his hate to his mom and her sister. He still fumed for no reason when he sat alone in his chair," Nancy told me. She knew I felt so guilty for asking them to leave.

I wrote a letter to Mama and Baba just as they arrived in Taipei to further explain our intentions. Baba wrote several angry letters to us. That really made me feel rotten. With the extra money, they installed a phone in the house. I called them often, but only Mom would talk to me. I did go back there to visit them almost once or twice a year after 1978. Baba gradually turned around and made peace with me. Since he went back, he published several books in *I-Ching* and was very active in teaching and research.

Dr. John Humphrey, dean of students at RIT, thought a trip to Taiwan and visit these colleges that had graduates taking graduate degree program on RIT campus.

"Richard, what do you think if you and I go together to visit Taiwan?" John said to me.

"Yeah! That's a good idea. I guess that's your department. You go ahead and get the travel plan approved by the administration. I'll go," I told him.

"How about if I write the proposal and you take it to Bullard for approval?"

"No! You should go, because it is your responsibility for student affairs," I said.

"Richard, you know I am scared of him."

"Why? I don't think he will bite you. The worst is a big no from him."

"Seriously, Richard, how about you go with me?"

"Okay! You write the proposal and I will go with you to see Bullard," I agreed.

Dr. Bullard gave us the approval without any questions. We made plans to visit Taiwan colleges in the winter of 1978, when the weather was more desirable in this subtropical island. When we arrived in Taipei, several groups were at the airport to greet us. Mama and Baba were among them. I asked a friend to get John settled in a hotel and I went home with Mama and Baba. The house they lived in was the same one I used to live in, but it was needed repair. I stayed home for the first night instead of the hotel. Baba had a lot to say to me, and I made a real effort to make him happy. Mama was very happy to see me but said very little. I gave Mama some more money and asked her to eat well and not worry about money.

Taiwan had taken a great transformation since I left there seventeen years ago. The central city had the same big, old buildings, but in the old rice fields, multistory high-rise buildings had sprung up in every direction. The streets I used to ride my bike to school on were all changed to wide speedways. All the landmarks I knew had all but disappeared. There were very few cars and buses in 1961, but now the streets were full of cars, motor scooters, motorcycles, trucks, and buses. The small, quite village in the suburb of Taipei was now a city of its own. The mountainsides where Nancy and I used to walk, and climb were filled up with all types of buildings.

I used to like the clean air and blue skies in Taipei. It was so polluted by the automobiles' exhaust and the smoke from industrial power plants. I was very disappointed to return to Taipei and find everything was ruined by the so-called progress. However, economically, Taiwan had done wonders. When I taught college in Taiwan, my monthly salary was twenty dollars a month. Now the same position paid over $600 per month. Of course, prices on food and everything went up proportionally too. I used to be able to buy a bowl of beef noodle from the street vendor for about ten cents in 1961; now the same noodle was sold for three dollars.

Taiwan progressed and caught up with the Western standards of livings, but it had lost its cleanness, the quietness, the natural beauty, and its innocence. After the seventeen-year absence, Taipei was no longer the same city I had in my mind. John had a ball in Taipei. Different schools treated John and me with banquets at noon and at night every day. While we were in Taipei, I went home every evening after the dinner to see Mama and Baba for the entire week. Baba had been patient with me. There was no displeasure in him while I was there. We talked about participation in a governmental subsidized housing project for retired military officers. I promised Mama and Baba that I would fund the project in its entirety. Again, it was a difficult good-bye for me. I could not stand the thought of them being old and alone there.

Taiwan Normal University was enhanced from provincial to national university. The campus was unchanged but many of my professors had retired or passed away. The head of the industrial education department was a student of mine from University of Wisconsin-Stout. Most of the faculty members were my underclassmen or my students. I could not help but feel age had caught up with my generation. The laboratory I set up nineteen years ago was still functioning except the equipment wore the age marks as well as the building.

John and I visited colleges in Tai-Chung and Kaoshiung. After official business, I took John to see where I used to live in Kao-Shiung. There was no armed soldier guarding the tunnel any longer. We just told the taxi driver to go through the tunnel into the Si-Tze Bay. The change was dramatic. The beautiful and quiet natural beauty had turned into a busy business resort area. People were everywhere in the entire area. Many commercial and residential houses filled up the mountainsides and the beach strip. Our old living complex was replaced by several high-rise buildings. If this was the progress, I'd rather it stayed primitive.

When we traveled south to Kao-Shiung, I had a chance to call my old friend on the phone. Before I knew it, my room was full of my old buddies. Won-Sun Yuan, the one who introduced me to Nancy, was a general in the ordnance command. Chen-Chi Fan, the newspaper delivery boy, was head of a hospital. Shin-Yen Wu, the tall basketball center, was a successful dentist.

"Where is our old principal now?" I asked.

"He is at home nowadays," Shin-Yen said. "I just checked his dentures last week."

"How about let's go see him?" I suggested.

"Let's go. We can walk. It's not far from here," Wen-Sun said.

We went to visit Mr. Gia-Gee Wang, the former principal of Kaoshiung Provincial High School, at his home. He was eighty years old but still could recognize me and several other fellow students. After we introduced ourselves, each of us told him what we were doing. I went to talk to Mr. Wang.

"Mr. Wang, do you remember me?" I did not think he really recalled that much.

"I remember you." He smiled. "You were the one who almost got kicked out of the school for calling that poor teacher names."

"Ilasaii!" Wen-Sen said.

"Ha! Ha! Ha! Ilasaii!" Several others remembered the teacher and joined in laughing.

My old classmates and I laughed when we recalled the funny way that teacher walked. I thought perhaps we were too cruel to that poor fellow!

After Kao-Shiung, John and went to Hong Kong to visit Hong Kong University and the Chinese University. From there we flew home. The entire trip was sixteen days.

CHAPTER 16

The Largest CS Program in the United States

By the fall of 1977, the school of computer science and technology had enrollment exceeding 1,200 major students. The school had become one of largest academic units of computer science in the nation. In addition to the 1,200 majors, there were course takers per year. Since we had been "borrowing" spaces from other colleges all over the campus, it was time to build a dedicated building just for computer science and technology. My proposal of a building in 1973 was approved for construction. I designed the conceptual building facet, room layouts, and detailed application specifications and then turned them over to the architects.

The building took about one year to complete. We moved into the new building in the fall of 1978. Our new computer science tracks worked out very well for industrial employers. Demands for co-op students and graduates was extremely high. I was invited to professional symposiums and conferences to present papers or talks regarding the new multitrack approaches. I also hosted a few computer science conferences on RIT campus to exchange ideas of how to enhance computer science research and education. As the director of the school of computer science and technology, I was less involved with the day-to-day academic work but more with administrative hassles. Life was not as challenging as it had been. We were just waiting for the weekends to go to poker parties. I enjoyed the fun but knew I was wasting my life away without achieving anything other than what I had done for the school. With all said and done, I began to feel a bit restless.

Dr. Tom Wallace, the dean of the college of sciences at RIT, went to Old Dominion University in Virginia in 1978 to assume the dean of sciences and health professions. Tom and I were the two big rivals of acquiring academic resources at RIT. He witnessed the fights I had won in the past few years. Now that he took a position with ODU as the dean of the largest college, he remembered the battles I had fought and won at RIT. In the winter of 1978, Tom took Dr. Stan Weinstein and Dr. Ann Savage to visit the school of computer science at RIT. Stan was the chairmen of applied mathematics department and Ann was the director of distant learning. I hosted them all day to see our facilities and had our faculty present our programs. I did not give a thought what else they had in mind.

A week after their visit, which was in January 1979, I received a call from Tom that he needed some help at ODU. "Do you have time to do some consulting at ODU?" he asked me.

"If the price is right," I said jokingly.

"I am serious. We need your advice on how to get our computer science program going," he said. "I am not teaching any courses. Any time is fine with me," I said.

"How about next Monday? I will make all necessary arrangement for you to fly down here," he said.

"Okay! I will see you down there."

I recalled the invitation for an interview when I graduated from Illinois in 1971. Alfred told me Norfolk was a bad place to live. But I was just doing a short consulting work; no harm would be done. The name Old Dominion was so close to Old Dominican, I mistakenly thought it was a Catholic school, although it really did not matter any.

Tom sent me a letter formally and hired me to come down to Norfolk as a consultant to ODU. My first trip down Norfolk was in January 1979. It was a cold and miserable day in Rochester. But Norfolk was sunny and unusually warm that day. I wore a heavy coat when I stepped off the plane and saw local people dressed in short sleeves. I took note of the weather here seriously. After a lunch cruise in the harbor, Tom started testing me a little.

"Have you ever thought about moving down south?" Tom asked me.

"No. That had never crossed my mind," I said.

"How was the weather up there?" Tom asked.

"Lousy as usual. It was snowy and cold when I left there."

"I wonder why people would want to live in such a snowbound country?" he said.

"Yeah! Like me?"

"I wonder if you would consider heading the computer science department at ODU, if we give an offer you can't refuse."

I noted how good the weather was down here, and the university was comparable to RIT. Better yet, they offered many doctoral programs at ODU.

"I have not thought about this. Give me a detailed offer in writing, and I will consider it seriously," I told him.

A week after I returned to Rochester, the offer came. ODU was offering me the title of eminent professor of computer science and associate dean of the college of sciences and health professions. The salary was more than double that at RIT. My duty would be to oversee the graduate programs in the college and develop a new computer science program into a department in the college. I talked with Nancy about the offer.

"You have just established the program here. It's time for you to enjoy the reward of success," Nancy said.

She was talking about my best reward of seeing the success of my students.

"I am a bit bored. I have no challenges here. What's waiting for me here is the retirement. I feel I am still young enough to venture once more," I said.

"What about our friends here? We will miss them terribly, I am sure," she said.

"I have thought a lot about that. The flip side of it is the time wasted on poker tables. I don't want our life limited to poker parties and waiting for retirement," I said.

"I feel the same way. Now you said better. What do you think of the offer?" she asked.

"Well, the eminent professorship is a big honor. There are just a few people with such titles in the whole state of Virginia. It is the first one in computer science. I am not impressed with the associate dean part of the offer. I will be struggling like when I first came to RIT to get the computer science going. That part excites me," I said.

"Since Jim is in his last semester here, and Ray is going to be a senior next fall, I think we should stay here until next year," she said.

"That makes sense. I can commute for the year. That is not a problem for me," I said.

As a teacher, there was no money in the job, and there was no power in the trade. The only thing I could hope for was higher recognition in the academic world. The eminent professor title was an attraction to me. The negative points about moving down south were several. I had to start from scratch to establish myself both in the school and the community. This part did not bother me too much. I was anxious to meet the challenges. Overall, there were more merits to move than stay in Rochester, so we decided to make the move. I signed the offer and started preparing to start my new job. I went to see Dr. Bullard and told him me decision.

"Todd, I believe I have completed the mission you hired me to do," I said.

"Indeed, I think you have done a first-rate job for us, and don't tell me you are leaving us," Dr. Bullard said. He was sharp in his observation.

"I am afraid that was what I came to see you for, to thank you for all of those years of support. It is time for me to move on," I said after I had pumped up enough courage.

"Where are you going? What can we do to change your mind?" Dr. Bullard asked me.

"I am grateful for your kindness, but I want to move on for new challenges. ODU offers doctoral degrees. I would like to establish one there. As you know, the trustees at RIT would never allow any doctoral programs at RIT," I said.

Dr. Bullard saw that my mind was made. "Richard, I am very sorry to see you leave. But if there is any reason you change your mind, please come and see me. We'd really like to keep you here," he said.

I thanked him again and felt bad when I left his office. For I knew Dr. Bullard had never tried to convince anyone to stay after they had requested to leave the job.

After an institute-wide going-away party hosted by the president, I immediately went home to load a few clothing items into the car and drove alone to Norfolk. At that time, I drove a newer diesel car, a 1974 Mercedes 240D, which I bought used. The car had AM/FM radio but no tape unit. It was a long haul through stretches of country roads and some sections of expressways. Normally it took twelve hours to drive each way. I would leave Norfolk after work on Friday, at around three o'clock, and arrive home early the next morning. I attended parties on Saturdays and Sundays from noon on. I would participate in the parties and play poker on Sundays and leave for Norfolk around five o'clock. This long travel and lack of rest every weekend did not bother me at that time. I listened to radio with the preset button; when the first city faded out, I set to the next city. That had made the long drive more bearable. However, in the long six months before my family moved down south, there were several minor mishaps and at least one scary event on the road.

On my third trip to Norfolk, it was a sunny autumn day when I left Rochester at about five o'clock. The traffic on Highway 15 was very light and so was Expressway I-81 that afternoon. It was uneventful all the way to the end of Highway 17. I was driving my blue Mercedes diesel and wore a ranger's hat. The hat was used to block the sunbeam in the afternoon, but I just kept it on my head. At about four o'clock, I thought I was turning on to Highway 64 at the junction but instead drove into an area I did not remember seeing before. I kept going the same direction; I thought I was too tired to recognize the landmarks.

Suddenly I discovered I was at a military gate. I slowed down and was waiting to be checked out, but the armed guards saluted me and waved me through. I was totally puzzled about what in the world was going on. As I drove on the unlit road, I saw tanks and missiles on both sides of the road. I knew I was in a wrong place. The road was so narrow I could not make a U-turn to go back to the gate, so I just backed up slowly all the way toward the gate. Before I knew it, four armed soldiers converged on me. One used a flashlight shining the beam on my face.

"How did you pass the gate?" he asked.

"The soldiers saluted me and waved me in. I am trying to go to Norfolk," I said.

"His car looked like the general's car and his ranger hat looked like the general's as well. I think whoever was waving him in must've mistaken him as the general," a sergeant with many stripes on his sleeve said to the few soldiers standing near my car.

"You are a lucky man. If we caught you farther down the road, you may have to be put behind bars," the sergeant said.

"Now you need to back the car all the way out the gate and make a U-turn back on the highway," he told me. "You just follow the road to the first traffic light and turn left. That will get you to Highway 64."

"How far am I from I-64?"

"It's about five miles," the sergeant said.

I had made the turn too early that early morning. I was very tired. Thanks to the excitement, that woke me up completely.

One other clear Sunday evening in October, around seven in the afternoon, I stopped at a roadside fast food restaurant on Highway 301 south of Washington, DC. After dinner, it was about seven thirty when I returned to my car in the parking lot. I discovered the battery was too low; the starter motor rotated slowly, and the car could not be started. Someone from the restaurant helped me to get it started with a jumper cable.

Without giving any thought of why the battery went so low, I went back on Highway 301 and later connected to Highway 17 southeast toward Norfolk. Highway 17 was a narrow two-way country road in 1979. Very few cars were on that road on Sunday night. After thirty minutes of driving, I found my instrument panel indicator lights became quite dim. I knew, right away, I was in big trouble—the battery was near empty. I was losing the headlight beams. Since the diesel engine does not need electricity to keep the engine going, it could go indefinitely without any battery if there was fuel in the tank. I knew I would not have any problem running the car until the fuel in the tank was used up. The problem was that I could not see the road without the headlight beams in that dark night.

All roadside gas stations were closed on Sunday night. I could not find any place to charge up or to replace the battery. It was a night with clear sky and a budding new moon. Under the faint moonlight, I could barely see the white paint line on the road to guide my driving. When sections of the roads were covered by roadside trees, it blocked the moonlight, so I had to drive slowly in the dark. Many stretches of Highway 301 and Highway 17 were tree lined. I could not see the road more than half of the time. I was going seventy-five miles per hour when there was some visibility and slowed down to a crawl when I ran into these pitch-black shadows of the trees.

At that moment, I was hoping a cop would catch me and guide me to a place to get me out of my current situation. But throughout the entire two hundred miles of driving, not single police were in sight. There were very few cars on the road that night. I guess there was no need for police to patrol that road.

On a stretch of Highway 17, a fast-going car passed me. I stepped hard on the gas pedal and followed the car, using its taillights as my guiding lights. Suddenly, the car slowed down, pulled behind my car, and then turned off its headlights. The car followed me for a few seconds and then sped away. I was wondering whether I had spooked him, or he was just trying to tell me that my lights were not on.

Finally, it seemed eternally long before I reached Newport News. The roads were brightly lit, and my real problem was over. Twenty minutes later, I arrived at my destination in Norfolk after fifteen hours of driving. Looking back, I was lucky to be back there without any accident that night. It was indeed a nerve-racking experience and a good story to tell my poker pals when I returned Rochester next week. The car had the same alternator problem, a broken wire, exactly like when I rode with Mike Tibbetts in his Chevy back in 1963 when we almost froze to death in Wisconsin.

I started my job at ODU in June 1979 on a full-time basis. I worked on the five-year plan for the computer science programs from the bachelor's degree level to the Ph.D. degree. The curricula, faculty, space, equipment, and budget were all carefully planned out in stages of development. The entire development plan was completed in two solid months and was submitted for approval by the administration. I found myself getting back to the same situation as those days when I was at RIT in the summer of 1973—working fourteen hours a day. But I thoroughly enjoyed the work and the challenge. Especially when I had to present and sell the ideas to several levels of management in the university. I welcomed and anticipated their questions and had real satisfaction when I convinced them with my answers.

During the first three months at ODU, I had to work in a classroom-converted office. My secretary, Kathy Warfield, shared the same large room with some simple desks and working tables. A temporary wall divided the large room into two parts. That was the humble beginning of the computer science department. Kathy was a very efficient typist and office manager that had made possible for all my plans and proposals rushing out of the office. Three months after I reported to work, the university decided to convert the classroom into a formal office for me. The workers came, divided the rooms, and replaced the furniture with my choice. The curtains were several years old and faded so I requested they be replaced. The man in charge did the measurements and gave me a sample. I did not like the sample. The next thing I knew, the vice president of administration, Dr. Allen Clark, came to my office.

"Dr. Cheng, we have bent over for you to get you new curtains, but you wanted the expensive ones. I don't think the president would approve the request," he told me, in no term for negotiation.

"Dr. Clark, please tell the president if he wanted me to build a first-rate computer science department, he needs to furnish me with the first-rate curtains," I told him.

He went to Tom Wallace and complained about my choice of curtains. "I don't know where you found this hot-shot fellow. I don't think I will go along with his request on the curtains," Clark said.

"Well, you know we have spent a great deal of money just to get him down here. You mean to upset him for a few bucks on the curtains?" Tom was upset with Clark.

The curtains, as I specified were installed within a week. However, I knew Clark was still unhappy with anyone he thought was overcompensated. To many of the academic people's eyes, he was just a high-ranking clerk with no vision for the institution.

My normal working hours were from eight in the morning to about ten at night. The only time I was away from the campus was to go back to the hotel or eat in a nearby restaurant. After five o'clock, when everybody left the building, I worked alone in the office until ten.

In order to save time, I just heated up some canned food and hot dogs for dinner. I did so to save me at least half an hour each day. My temporary office became my main living quarters, except for sleeping. My checkbooks and much of my personal things were put in my desk and credenza drawers.

One day the campus police came to my office. "Dr. Cheng, did you lose anything?" the sergeant asked.

"No. I don't think so. Why do you ask me that?"

"Someone was trying to cash a check of yours for a large amount of money," the officer said.

"Did you say someone tried to use my check to cash money?" I asked. I was confused.

"Yes," he said.

I opened my desk drawer and took my checkbook out and examined it. I found two checks were torn off from the check and the two stubs were also missing.

"I lost checks numbered 106 and 107," I said.

He wrote the numbers on his notepad and filed a report. Within three days, he called and told me the person was apprehended and I should not have any loss from my account. From that day on, I knew the office was an open book to everyone. I moved my personal items out to my hotel room.

CHAPTER 17

The Saudi Programs

In spring of 1980, I received a letter from the director general of the National Information Center of the Ministry of Interior of Saudi Arabia, Dr. Abdulaziz Al-Sagr. He had visited me at RIT in 1978 when he just finished his doctoral degree in computer science from the Texas A&M University. In the letter, he asked me if I was interested in a consulting job for the Ministry of Interior. The National Information Center was a branch under the ministry. I was very curious about the myths of the Middle East countries and would like to know more about the culture, so I responded affirmatively. Within a month, a formal consulting agreement was sent to me to appoint me as a senior consultant to the Ministry of Interior, reporting to the vice minister. I signed the agreement and returned it to the ministry.

With My Saudi Friends in 1982

The main purpose was to evaluate and monitor the progress of the $360 million project designed to establish the computer center and the computer network for the ministry. The center would be the nerve center for vital information the ministry needed to maintain the nation's data on national security among other important functions. Dr. Sagr was oversaw the project. His predecessor signed the contract with a US contractor two years earlier, but there were a lot of holes in the contract. There were major problems with the execution of the contract on both sides.

In the beginning, three consultants were hired to assist Dr. Sagr to sort out the problems and see to the completion of the critically important project. Among the consultants, Dr. Dick Simons was a professor from Texas A&M and Dr. John Kruger was from Arizona University. Both them were old friends of Dr. Sagr when he was a graduate student. Dr. Simons had supervised Dr. Sagr in his research work just a few years ago.

A week after I signed the agreement, Dr. Sagr called me in my office. "Hi! Dr. Cheng, how are you? This is Abdulaziz Al-Sagr. I am calling from Washington, DC."

"Good morning! Dr. Sagr, I am fine. How are you?" I asked.

"Can you come to Washington to meet with us and the two other consultants?" he asked.

"Certainly. When do you want me to come?"

"How about meeting us for dinner tonight?"

"Okay! Where do you stay?"

"We all stay in the Marriott in Roselyn. Do you know where that is?"

"I sure do. I will see you tonight," I said.

The three of the consultants met with Dr. Sagr's group from Saudi Arabia in Washington, DC, that night. We had a banquet hosted by Dr. Sagr.

"How long are we going to be here?" I asked during the dinner.

"I hope we can finish the audit work in a week," Dr. Sage said. I was almost shocked because I had brought one night's clothing. Well, I had to get Nancy to send more clothing to me by UPS.

Each of the three consultants was assigned a specific area to focus on. I was designated to lead the auditing of the hardware part of the project. That included the cost of computer mainframes, peripherals, testing and acceptance, communications, and networking equipment. The other two consultants were working on the software part and the management part of the project.

The first night in Washington, Dr. Sagr and the three of us went down the restaurant for a drink after dinner. After a few drinks of beer, Dr. Sagr became very relaxed and we started to tell jokes. The one that I felt was worth noting was the joke Dr. Sagr made on his consultants.

"I want to tell you a joke about consultants, since you are all consultants to me and the ministry."

"Okay, let's hear it," Dick said.

"There was a large farm somewhere down south. It was fenced in with wired grids from its neighboring farm. On one spring morning, a beautiful young cow in the farm met a young bull from the neighbor's farm through the fence grids. They hit it off well.

"'You are very pretty,' the bull said to the cow.

"'You are so strong and so handsome.' The cow said. They kissed each other through the hole in the fence.

"'Why don't you come over?' the cow said.

"'How can I do that?' the bull said.

"'You can jump over. I really think you can do it,' the cow said.

"The bull knew that cow was in heat and he was also uncontrollably in love with this cow. 'I will come over now,' the bull said.

"The bull backed up from the fence about twenty feet and rushed toward the fence, using the momentum to jump up. It came just a bit short. His front feet went over the top and hung on the top of the fence.

"'You came very close. Next time you need to back away farther. You will make it,' the cow said.

"The bull got off the fence and backed off thirty-five feet from the fence. By now, he was very excited and anxious to jump over. He kicked up a storm of dust and rushed toward the fence at a high rate of speed. He flew up over the fence with both of his front and rear feet, but they heard a loud snapping sound as he was over the fence and the bull cried painfully. When he landed, he knew exactly what had happened. He was bleeding, in great pain, and most of all, he was greatly depressed. The cow came over to comfort him.

"'Don't be sad. Although you have lost your tool, you still can be my consultant,' she said.

"I hope you guys haven't lost your tools. Ha! Ha!"

"I hope you will not become a consultant someday!" Dick Simmons said. We all laughed.

The system procurement was completed before Dr. Sagr took over as the director general. At the time the contract was signed, the economy in Saudi Arabia was booming. Money was not a subject in buying high-tech products. In order to simplify the cost accounting, both sides agreed to a deal that the CIF prices were set at 250 percent of the published list prices. In other words, any piece of equipment sold in the United States for $100 would be charged $250 to the Saudis. That was a very good deal for the US contractor indeed.

I took the one-foot-thick document back to my hotel room and read it through. I was quite familiar with computer hardware prices at that time because of the recent setting up of laboratories and computer centers at both at RIT and ODU. I quickly spotted several serious discrepancies in the invoices. Several items were charged over ten times of their list prices. I called these manufacturers representatives to verify the current prices, and I was right. The Saudis were overcharged in a big way. That afternoon, in a meeting with the program manager of the US contractor, I brought up the question about the discrepancies.

"Dr. Sagr, do you want me to check the deal by the book or just a formality?" I asked.

"I want to see if they really abide by the purchasing contract. I heard there are some questionable charges. The stakes are very high. I will support your judgments," he told me.

The first day of the meeting, we sat in a large conference room on a long table. The Saudis and the consultant sat on one side and the contractor on the opposite side. After Dr. Sagr gave a brief introduction, we started to go through some basic briefings by the contractor. In the afternoon, the Saudi staff asked a few questions. Then it was my turn to ask questions.

"I have found some items with much higher prices. Might there be some errors? Could you invite your staff in charge of costing to verify the prices?" I said to the contractor representative.

"I stand by our procurement standards and accounting staff. I don't believe there is any mistake in the costing," he said. The program manager of the contractor denied the whole notion.

He was very rude to me and was quite upset that anybody was challenging the invoices. The Saudis had never questioned the contractors in the past. I knew by that point this was not a simple case of clerical error.

"Look at the equipment racks. They cost around $1,500 each. The price to the ministry should be $3,750 each. But you can see the charge is $14,500 each." I pointed at the specifics.

"We are selling only the best items to the ministry. I think you are comparing apples with oranges," the manager said, his face turning bright red.

"Okay! Let's find out what is the brand of these racks you have procured and sold to the ministry. Would you please get your staff to show us the list price of the racks? I am not asking you for the price you paid, just the list prices," I said.

He was angry at that point. He got up, walked out the door, and slammed the door hard behind him. Dr. Sagr and other Saudi attendees in the meeting were quite upset by the contractor representative's behavior. Dr. Sagr called the president of the contractor.

"If your people do not cooperate with us, we will not pay the bills. You can protest to the minister, but I am the one in charge of the project," he said.

We all left the conference room and returned to the hotel. I assumed they did try to call the minister of interior, but they did not get the support they wanted from the ministry. A day later, the contractor's program manager came back like a different person—very polite, humble, and cooperative. They produced all the documents I requested and recalculated the bills. Just including the part, I had checked, the invoice was reduced by several million dollars. We finished our work in six days. The Saudi team in Washington, DC, was elated. Dr. Sagr hosted a big banquet for all of us working on the project. We said good-bye and departed for home.

A month later, I was invited to Riyadh, Saudi Arabia, to visit the ministry and to meet the minister. My consulting appointment was extended to a three-year term and renewable at the end of three years. The consulting contract with the Saudi government continued for more than fifteen years.

Before I traveled to Saudi Arabia, I had a lot of curiosities about the land and the people there. I heard they were very wealthy, and I had met a few government officials from there, but I knew very little of the customs and living conditions. I asked my friend Dick Bagby (the computer center director at RIT in 1974) who had lived there for a year.

"Dick, can you tell me anything about Saudi Arabia?" I asked him during a lunch.

Dick grabbed a piece of paper and drew a rectangle on the sheet. He said, "This is Riyadh." He then flipped the paper over with nothing on it and said, "This is Riyadh after a sand storm."

I knew he was kidding me a little bit, but he was also expressing the image of the place. When I arrived Riyadh, I was pleasantly surprised to see well-built high-rise buildings, wide streets, tree-lined sidewalks, and a few flower gardens.

I went to Riyadh at least once a year from 1981 onward. It was always in late January, leaving before the end of February. The weather there was very cool at night, down to the fifties. During the day, the average high temperature in January and February was in the low eighties. My first impression of Saudi Arabia was that it was quite different from anywhere I had been before. The air was so dry that the first few days staying there I was so dehydrated and thirsty all the time. My lips started to break up a little. Everywhere I went, including big office building with tightly sealed windows, had a layer of very fine sand dust covering everything. The green trees and small flower gardens in the city were all covered with a layer of fine dust.

Most of the city buildings were congregated in groups. There was unused land and sand dunes placed right in the middle of modern buildings. All the home dwellings were walled in. The walls were as high as eight feet tall. Some walls were topped with broken glasses to discourage thieves from climbing over them. Private homes were very well built. Stones and marbles were the most common materials used, to make the homes cooler in the summer. The few homes I visited were decorated beautifully and luxuriously. Gold color was most popular on furniture and toiletry. Together with marbles floors, marble walls, and huge and small crystal chandeliers, I felt I was in the world of *One Thousand and One Nights.*

The Saudi people were very cordial and polite. Everywhere I went, Arabic tea was served. There was the Arabic traditional green tea that was served with a small cup about one-inch deep and one-inch round. The green tea had a special taste that took me a while to get used to. Another tea was the black tea that tasted like the common Lipton tea but was always loaded with sugar. It was like drinking sugar paste. A server was standing by; as soon as one finished the cup, it would be refilled immediately.

The ministry required all the consultants to fly first-class, which I was not really accustomed to. I was wondering why the Saudi government paid the much higher cost of flying first-class while we did not ask for it, until I had the experienced sitting in the coach class once. The first trip to Saudi Arabia, the plane arrived in Riyadh late at night. My luggage had not yet arrived. I was told that it would be delivered to the hotel a day later. A ministry official, Hakim, was at the gate to greet me. He took me to Marriott Hotel in downtown Riyadh.

Just as I was ready for a quick shower, Hakim called. "We are taking a flight to the eastern shore to visit the University of Petroleum and Minerals at six o'clock in the morning," he told me.

"Oh no, Hakim! You are kidding me, right? It is one thirty in the morning now. I need to have some sleep," I said.

"I am not kidding. You have a meeting with the president and the chairmen of several departments at nine o'clock there," he said.

"My luggage is not here yet, and I have only casual wear on me. How about changing the meeting to a later time?" I requested.

"I am afraid it is not possible. Dr. Sage had worked on the schedule of this meeting several weeks ago. It would not be possible to get this group of people together any time soon," Hakim told me.

I had no choice but trying to get a few hours of rest before leaving. It seemed like I had just dozed off for a few minutes when Hakim was pounding on my door. I quickly readied myself and followed him to a waiting car that sped toward the airport. After we entered the aircraft, Hakim was walking toward the rear while I had a first-class seat. I felt bad about it, since Hakim was a high-level official.

"Let us sit together," I told Hakim.

"You go ahead and sit in the first-class section. I can only travel coach," he told me.

I insisted to go to the coach section. Luckily his next seat was open. We sat down and chatted about the new information center. When I felt tired, I pushed the seat backward to rest. Just as the seat was settled in position, I felt a tremendous kick from behind. A young fellow was angrily cussing some Arabic words I could not understand. I quickly straightened my seat.

"This is why our government requires you to sit in the first-class section. We have too many uneducated foreigners working here, and they are very rude," Hakim told me.

That was my last time to sit in a coach section when I traveled to the Middle East and inside Saudi Arabia.

In 1982, under the request of Dr. Sagr, I proposed a computer science and engineering college to the Saudi government. The proposal included the organization, administration, programs, standards, curricula, faculty qualifications, laboratory, and laboratory equipment. It was approved within two months by the Saudi government. I was invited to assist the program implementation with the college of engineering faculty at King Saud University in Riyadh. The new program was to offer computer science and computer engineering undergraduate and master's degree programs. An undergraduate management information system program for women was also established but was to be located at the old campus of King Saud University in downtown Riyadh. The university had a huge, brand-new beautiful campus in the suburb of Riyadh that was completed in 1983.

In Saudi Arabia, all Saudi men enjoyed free education from kindergarten to college. A stipend was also given to young people who enrolled in a college. Because the Saudi economic condition was booming, most Saudi nationals were very well-to-do; therefore, the need to work and go to school to earn a living was not a priority for Saudi young men. Saudi women were not supposed to work in any event. Because there were only a few universities in the kingdom, at that time, the enrollment at King Saud University was very high—about 15,000. The new program was a big success in Riyadh. The enrollment grew at a rapid rate and the graduates were 100 percent placed upon graduation. Many computer science and engineering graduates from that program went to the United States to complete their master's or doctoral degrees in later years.

The new information center office was a six-story modern building on a city block-sized lot and was equipped with an underground parking garage. I was assigned to an office on the sixth floor, adjacent to the director general. The offices were very handsomely furnished with top-grade office furniture imported from the United States and elsewhere. The hotel I stayed in was within walking distance to my office, but they provided a driver to shuttle me around. Looking from the top floor, I could see construction cranes like forests all around me. There were a few sand dunes spotting the city landscape amid those tall office buildings. Other than that, the city looked just like other cities in the Western world.

I was invited to Talal's parents' house for dinner one day. It was a magnificent ranch-style building surrounded by eight-foot-high stone walls. The floor and the interior walls were made of imported Italian marbles. Talal's father asked me after we were introduced, "What would you like to drink?"

I heard that liquor was forbidden at homes, so I joked, "Whiskey will be fine."

His dad clapped his hands. The male servant came into the room. The old man said some Arabic words to him. In a few seconds, the servant pushed a gold cart into the room. On top of the cart were all sorts of liquor bottles, looking very fancy. I normally drank only one beer a day maximum. Facing the challenge of hard liquor that I asked for, the only way out was to talk to Talal and ask him to instruct the servant to pour just a little bit of whiskey for me.

Before dinner, Talal, his father, several male relatives, and I were chatting in the living room. I could hear women's and children's voice from the kitchen. They never showed their face in front of guests. At dinner, we all sat in a circle with other male family members on a large rug. Food was placed at the center of the rug. At the center of many dishes was this whole roasted lamb. Talal's dad pulled out the tongue and offered it to me as a gesture of respect to the main guest.

"Would you like the tongue?" his father said in Arabic, translated by Talal.

When I saw the dripping blood, I begged Talal to excuse me from taking the offer. "Thank you! Talal, please tell your dad I don't eat lamb tongue," I begged.

Talal said something to his dad and the senior dug the eyeball out with a large spoon and offered it to me.

At that point, I used my hand to grab a chunk of meat from the lamb's shoulder.

"I really like the shoulder meat," I said.

Talal translated to his father what I said. The old man was not at all offended. I tried the lamb shoulder meat. It was the best lamb meat I had ever had in my life. It was tasty, tender, and had no smell whatsoever. The problem was that I ate too much good food that evening and suffered a little stomach discomfort for a day or two.

In Saudi Arabia, people were the same as people everywhere else in the world. But each region of the world has its own local characteristics. I found all the Saudi nationals to be faithfully religious and devout Moslems. Each morning at six o'clock sharp, the loud speakers would start chanting the Koran. People had to pray toward Mecca on a carpet. For people on the road, they had to use portable small carpets to kneel and pray. Each day, people had to pray five times, whether in the house, on the roadside, or in the airplane. Of course, the most desirable place to pray was in a mosque.

In Saudi Arabia, the moral standards were very high and were strictly reinforced. Each Saudi woman had to wear a veil to cover her face. Otherwise, the religious police would seek out the violator's husband and punish him. I had seen a woman sitting on a bench in a mall. A religious policeman in plain clothes whipped the woman on her leg because she had revealed about an inch of her flesh just above her socks when she sat cross-legged. The crime rate was very low when I was there. The shops on the street often did not have to lock up their doors.

I heard from local friends that an absentminded German diplomat went to a store, grabbed a toothpaste in his hand, and walked out of the store without paying for it. He was caught and sent to the court. The trial and judgment came quickly; it was a guilty verdict. The punishment to theft was to chop the hand off. The German Embassy official went to the court and tried to exercise diplomatic immunity. The court rejected the request.

"How about letting us take him back to Germany and chopping his hand off?" asked the embassy official.

"No way." was the answer.

"Can we have the ambulance ready to take him and the hand to a hospital right after the hand is chopped off?" The official kept trying.

"We must hang the chopped-off hand in the square for three days before you can come and take it with you," the court told the embassy official.

This kind of harsh punishment never happened often in Saudi Arabia because potential thieves feared the severe consequences. Mugging and robbery were also very rare in Saudi Arabia. I felt very safe walking alone around the city at night in Riyadh.

Mohammed was an official of the information center assigned to escort me in the country. In Saudi Arabia, Thursday was a nonworking day, very much like Sunday in the States. Sunday, on the other hand, was a working day in Saudi Arabia. On one of the Thursdays, Mohammed drove me to the countryside of Riyadh. I saw Rolls-Royces and Mercedes-Benzes parked in front of mud huts—or more accurately mud *caves* because they were partially underground.

"Why do the rich people here prefer those mud caves?" I was curious.

"Most of our people like the natural coolness in the mud caves. They don't like the cold air from the air-conditioning," Mohammed told me.

"How did these people get rich? I don't see any oil fields in this part of the county at all," I asked.

"Well, the oil belongs to the king and his family. Most of the common people got rich by selling land their father or grandfather owned before the boom. They don't work and most of them are uneducated. All they do is trade lands or speculate on the land and buildings," Mohamed explained.

He took me to a vast palm forest. It looked like an abandoned park with marble benches and stoves for barbecues. At that time, the dates on the trees were ready for picking but no one was interested to harvest them. Many fell on the ground. I picked up a few and tried them out. They were the most delicious dates I had tasted.

A little fat puppy followed us around. "This is an abandoned dog," Mohammed told me.

"What does the dog eat to sustain its life?" I asked.

"At least for a while he can live on the dates," Mohammed said, pointing to the dates littered on the ground in the forest.

Not a bad living for the puppy, I thought.

Dr. Sagr was a visionary. He saw Saudi Arabia was totally dependent on oil output and every high-tech product was imported. Furthermore, the Saudi young people were unwilling to get their hands dirty in working as technicians and engineers; they all wanted to be bosses and managers. In 1984, the National Information Center had over five hundred civil service employees. Dr. Sagr came to Virginia Beach to talk to me about establishing a training facility in Virginia for engineers in the Ministry of Interior. The purpose was to train the engineers how to design Arabic language computers and then set up a facility to produce computers from ground zero.

"Richard, please draft a plan to train our engineers to design and actually make a computer and some peripherals in Arabic language. I'd like to see a production facility plan set up in Virginia Beach to train them and then transport the entire facility to Riyadh. Do you think it can be done?"

"Definitely. I will make a draft for you to look at, and we can discuss any changes you would like to make," I said.

Dr. Sage agreed and went back to Riyadh.

I spent about two solid weeks working at night after school and the whole day on weekends to draft a proposal to train Saudi engineers and a computer hardware production facility. I sent the proposal to Dr. Sagr in Riyadh for him to take to the Ministry of Interior for approval. That was in November 1983. Within two months, Dr. Sagr called me on the phone. "Richard, I have good news for you. The ministry has approved the proposal in total. How about coming here and letting us work out the details?"

"When would you like me to come?" I asked.

"Please come as soon as you can."

"I am not teaching any courses this semester. I can come right away. Is there anything you want me to bring to Riyadh? Like reference books?"

"If you can find some equipment catalogs for our people to get some ideas of the facility, that would be good. But if it takes too long to get them, just come here first and have the catalogs sent later."

I booked a flight the same day and left the States a day later. The initial plan was to be in Riyadh for two weeks to meet with the ministers and key officials involved with the project. When I arrived in Riyadh early in the morning, several Ministry of Interior officials were waiting for me at the gate. They took me through the gate for diplomats, and not a question was asked by the airline security or the customs official. They drove me in an official vehicle straight to the hotel and told me to get ready to meet the vice minister in thirty minutes.

"This appointment was made a few days ago. If we are late, I don't know when we can get another appointment with him. You know Dr. Awaji is the busiest guy in the ministry. He is the one who makes all of the day-to-day decisions, not the minister, Prince Nief," Dr. Sagr told me.

"I will be down in the lobby in five minutes," I promised.

The ministry was just ten minutes away by car. At the reception area, there were over fifty people waiting. Some of them were standing, some were sitting on the couches, and many were just sitting on the floor where it was cool. We did not wait and went straight to the second-floor executive office suite. Outside of Dr. Awaji's office, there was this huge, luxurious, and beautifully decorated waiting room. We were about to sink ourselves into the sofa when the secretary came out and spoke in Arabic to my escorts. I alone was led into the inner office where Dr. Awaji was. He got up from his chair and walked toward me.

"Hi, Dr. Cheng. I have heard a lot of good things about you. It is nice to meet you in person." He spoke in fluent English.

"Dr. Awaji, it is my honor to meet you," I said while shaking hands with him.

"I understand you are from Virginia. I received my degree from UVA a few years ago," he said. "I like Virginia very much."

"I hope you will visit Virginia again soon," I said.

"I will. Dr. Sagr has briefed me on the project you have proposed. I believe it will be good for our people. I am going to see the minister to get his blessing on this project."

"Thank you very much for your endorsement. There are a lot of people waiting outside. Please excuse me," I said.

"You are most welcome here. If there is anything I can help with, please let me know," he said.

The next day I spent about six hours with a group of Ministry of Interior officials. Some were engineers and most of them were administrators. There were several constructive suggestions about what to do with workshops and hands-on experiments. We decided that if the plan was approved, a group of thirty engineers would be selected to stay in Virginia Beach for six months and then the next group would be sent.

On the fifth day in Riyadh, I received a call from Dr. Sagr. "Richard, can you get ready and come with me in ten minutes? The minister, Price Nief, would like to see you."

"I will be waiting for you at the hotel lobby," I told him.

I waited outside the lobby waiting for Dr. Sagr. His big, black limousine pulled up to the hotel driveway in just a few minutes.

"Why do you take the big limo today?" I asked while hopping into the back seat.

"Well, the prince is swamped by people who want to see him. Without the limo, we will not be able to find a parking spot near the building," Dr. Sage replied.

I recalled the last time I was burned by the sun when I walked with another official to see the vice minister. This time, we got off right in front of the main entrance of the building. As a high-ranking official in the ministry, Dr. Sagr led me straight into Prince Neif's office. The prince's reception area was huge with at least thirty sofas for people waiting to see the prince, and the room was almost full when we entered. The receptionist talked to Dr. Sagr in Arabic and pointed where we should sit. We sank into the sofa and expected a long wait.

Within five minutes, the executive secretary of the minister's office came out from the inner office and talked to Dr. Sagr. We followed him into the minister's office. The prince was a tall and well-built man in his early fifties. He got up from his chair and shook hands with me and showed me the chair to sit in. He spoke in Arabic to Dr. Sagr and the two were engaged in a lengthy conversation. I was lost in what they were talking about exactly, but I knew it was about the project.

"The prince is very happy with your proposal and has entrusted me to implement the plan. I think he likes you," Dr. Sagr said while turning his head to me with a big smile.

"Please tell the prince that I am honored to have this opportunity to meet him in person. I am also very pleased about his approval of the project," I told Dr. Sagr.

When we stood up to leave the office, the prince walked toward me, extended his hand, and said in perfect English, "Dr. Cheng, thank you for working with Dr. Sagr on this important project. I hope you enjoy your stay in our country."

"Your Honor, the pleasure is all mine. Thank you for taking your busy time to see us. I will do my best to assist Dr. Sagr on this project," I said.

We left this elegantly decorated office very happy that we had obtained the final approval of the project.

"Now I will have students selected and contract your company in Virginia to implement the project," Dr. Sagr told me.

"I will start to work on the details of the program and the logistics as soon as I am back in Virginia Beach," I promised.

In the summer of 1985, thirty Saudi engineers arrived Virginia Beach. In addition to lectures, about 50 percent of the time was devoted to selecting production equipment and designing the plant layout. At the later part of the lecture, students were asked to participate in the design of computer mainboards and peripheral boards. Since the trainees were engineering graduates, they could easily grasp the practical aspects of computer system design.

The initial design was deliberated among three groups. As a result of discussions, refinement of the design was made. Parts were ordered by Saudi engineers to make prototypes. Intensive testing of the prototypes took several weeks to complete. After evaluations by instructors and Eastern Computers, Inc. (ECI) professional staff, the production was put into gear. Other than parts and the bare circuit boards, everything was done at the Saudi facility in Virginia Beach. Two groups of trainees went through the program in one year. They produced hundreds of Arabic-language terminals for the National Information Center to use in Saudi Arabia. In 1987, the facility was taken down, packed, and shipped to Riyadh, where it was reassembled to produce computer products.

The outcome pleased Dr. Sagr and his colleagues in the ministry. I had several thoughts about this experience with the Saudi trainees. I found all of them were very intelligent. But many of them had some attitude problems. For example, when the instructor pushed them to do homework, they would get upset. "We paid you money to teach. Why do you want us to do the work? You should do it for us."

They might be kidding a bit, but it was hard for me to tell whether they were serious. Although it was strictly forbidden, several of them did drink regularly. They had not caused any problem for ECI. We were concerned for what might have happened if they drove under the influence. A few of them applied for graduate studies in the States while they were in Virginia Beach.

A few years later, at least five of them received doctoral degrees in electrical engineering. One went back Riyadh and was hired by a television company as a newscaster. I continued communicating with many of the engineers for many years after the program was completed. One particular trait I found in my Arabic friends was that they were loyal friends and would do anything to help a friend in need. However, one must be careful not to offend them. The greatest offense would be an unjustified accusation of wrongdoing. One would have an enemy for life, if a Saudi friend was offended in such manner.

CHAPTER 18

Starting a Small Company

I had always believed that computing must be in each country's native written language. My work on such a project started in the late sixties. Several of my proposals to the National Science Foundation and other funding sources were all being turned down due to reasons of being "too costly," "lacking urgent need by the country," or "lacking national interest." In the late seventies, I saw the need of such development become more obvious and the technology had become more mature to take upon such projects at relatively low cost. I thought it was good time to test out my ideas by putting them on trial in the marketplace. I talked to Nancy and my oldest son, Jim, about starting a business.

"I think sooner or later people in other countries would want to use their own language for computer displays and printouts. Since I can't get any support from the government, maybe we will do it on our own," I said.

"Where do we find the money to do it?" Nancy asked.

"Well, we can start a small company to work on the project. It might be very slow, but it would be a starting point for the project," I insisted.

"It's worth trying. We really don't have to risk a lot by going slowly," Jim said.

"It would take a lot of your time to get involved. Are you willing to be part of it?" I asked Nancy.

"Definitely," Nancy said.

"Me too. I will be graduating in a few months from ODU," Jim said. He was studying computer science at ODU.

"Okay! I will get started by registering a company first. In order to save the expenses of paying lawyers, I will do it myself."

I typed the articles of incorporation and submitted it to the State Corporation Commission. We registered the business under the name Eastern Computers, Incorporated, simply because we were located on the eastern part of the United States. The effective starting date of the business was in July 1980.

Now we owned the business. But where was the funding? As a college professor for the past twenty some years, we did not have any savings to speak of. After scraping all we could muster, including selling our stock holdings and bonds, we had $14,000 for the start-up fund of our business. Because we had no credit history or any collateral, the banks just would not provide us with any loans or lines of credit.

Well, we just had to do with what we could manage. We rented a small one-room office with 120 square feet in the Koger office complex in Norfolk. The whole business place had just a used desk, two old chairs, and a telephone. A workbench was later added in the property list. The first full-time employee was a graduate student of mine: De-Yen Yen. De-Yen graduated with a Master of Science degree in computer science from ODU. He was ranked number one in the master's graduating class in 1980. Since there was no sale whatsoever during the first year, the entire business operation and my family depended on the basic funding and the salary of a professor.

De-Yen and Jim worked very diligently on the software algorithms, design, and programming. I devoted my time to the hardware design, construction, and testing. Because of my full-time job, I had to work at nights and on weekends. Jim was a senior during the first year of the business and worked part time just like I did. He became the second full-time employee upon graduation from ODU's computer science program.

By the end of the first year, we had a laboratory prototype of our product. It was just a device to demonstrate the concepts. It was a typewriter and doubled as a telex machine that could be used as a typewriter or to transmit and receive English, Arabic, Chinese, Korean, and several other alphabets. Although the machine could print in twenty-six different languages, it was a compact unit using the same computer keyboard for all languages. In 1982, we hired two more fresh graduates from ODU computer science program to further refine the software programs and to make a presentable demonstration unit. The company now had four full-time employees plus Nancy and me working part-time free.

After one year, the space was not large enough for the operations. We moved to a four-room rental space in Virginia Beach. The new space consisted of a large electronics laboratory, two staff offices, and my own small office. To pay for the salary, rents, utilities, parts, expenses, and equipment, we quickly exhausted our original reserve fund. I had to borrow a small amount of money from my relatives just to get by for the months. I also made a private placement to raise about $50,000 from friends. That was how we could keep the company going before we had any sales.

The working prototype multilingual typewriter and telex machine was a neat showpiece. We thought we had a good marketable product to be sold in the worldwide market. But to bring it from the prototype to production line would need a substantial amount of cash. To market the product overseas would require even more funding. It was obvious to all of us in the company that we must first get financing from investors before we could continue as a real business.

One day in the fall of 1982, when I walked into my office, I was astonished to see a young man in his early thirties sitting in my chair, and his feet were on my desk. "Hi! My name is Richard Hirschfield. I am a lawyer and a friend of Mohammed Ali. You know, he was the world boxing champ," he said, before I could open my mouth.

"Okay, Mr. Hirschfield, what can I do for you?" I said. I was a bit perturbed.

"I have a deal of the century for you. My client, Mr. Ali, would like to buy your company for a very generous price," he said, moving his feet back on the floor.

"What do you mean by 'generous price'?" I was a bit dumbfounded by the offer.

He smiled, got up from my chair, and walked around to the front of the desk. He made a gesture of putting something heavy on the desk.

"We will put $2 million on the table for your company," said he.

I was really surprised by how much he was offering me, and I was very glad someone knew the potential of our product. I was also taken aback by such casual approach for such a serious business matter.

"Mr. Hirschfield, have you studied our company and our product? We have had no sales at this point, and we don't even have our final product built. Two million dollars is a lot of money. Are you sure you don't want to study a bit more about us? I will be glad to provide you more information or show you our business plan," I asked.

"No need for all that. You have a good reputation and we trust you. So, what do you say, my friend?" he said while shaking his head.

"Gee! This is a big offer. I just do not know what to say. My company is not worth that much money. I really would like to talk to my lawyer before I give you an answer," I said.

"Okay, I want to let you know that my client is a very busy man. He is interested in the company today, but he might not be so interested in it the next day." He tried to push me.

I began to feel uncomfortable about the whole thing.

"By the way, if we come to an agreement, how are you going to make the payment to me?" I asked.

"We actually will do a better deal than just a cash investment. We will give you ten million shares of the common stock of our company, which is traded over the counter; you can call your broker to find out about it. Because of some misinformation, the stock is at its low and I am using the current value of the stock to give you this offer. When the stock bounces back, you will be a few million dollars richer," he said with a smile and gesture.

"Do you mind telling the ticker symbol of the company?"

"Sure, it is CPX listed on over-the-counter," he told me.

Although we desperately needed funding, I just felt the deal was too good to be true. I told him I had another appointment to go to and sent him off in a very polite manner. I then called my lawyer.

"Bob, do you know a lawyer named Hirschfield?"

"Yes, what about him?" he asked.

"He is offering a big price to buy ECI."

"Richard, I know this guy. He is not good. I would stay away from him with a ten-foot pole, no matter what he tells you."

"Thanks, Bob. I know what to do next."

The next day, my stockbroker told me the stock that was offered to me was worth absolutely zero. Mr. Hirschfield called me a day after his visit, about my decisions regarding his offer.

"Hey! Dr. Cheng, have you made up your mind yet? The opportunity to make these millions of dollars will not wait!"

"I have already decided not to take your offer. Thank for your interest in my company" was my answered to him.

I had never heard from him again. In later years, several national newspaper articles reported on him for unethical dealings and scandals. He became a fugitive of the law and had to hide somewhere overseas. I was glad not having mixed up with him.

Ted Chao, an old friend of mine, traveled to Hong Kong with me in 1981, to raise funds for the company. I carried the demonstration unit with me to show people there. Ted knew the owner of the largest bank, an industrialist named Mr. Gin-He Fung, and made an appointment for me to see him. The appointment was made for the next morning. We went to the SHK building at Central and to Mr. Fung's office on the twentieth floor.

A secretary came to the reception area. "Mr. Fung is expecting you. Please come with me."

We walked into this large and gorgeously decorated office. Mr. Fung got up from his chair and greeted us.

"Good morning, gentlemen. How are you, Ted?" he said gently.

"This is the Professor Cheng from Virginia Beach I have told you about." Ted introduced me.

"I have heard a lot of good things about you, and I am pleased to see you," Mr. Fung said. He walked over to shake my hand.

"Thank you for taking time to see us. I am honored to see you in person," I said.

"Professor Cheng has brought his Chinese computer and telex machine to show you, if you'd like to see them," Ted said.

"I would like to invite a group of business leaders in Hong Kong to join me in seeing a demo of your invention," Mr. Fung said.

"We will be ready to demonstrate the unit at any time that is convenient for you," I offered.

"I will invite a group of my friends to a banquet for you tomorrow—those are the who's who in Hong Kong. They would have the money to invest if they want to. Tomorrow six o'clock in the evening at the Hong Kong Club," he said. "You may want to come by five and set up the demonstration."

"We will be there at five. Thank you for the help," I said.

The next afternoon, we went to the very exclusive club. Ted helped me to set up the demo systems that included a multilingual telex machine and a Chinese-English microcomputer. Before five o'clock, many people came to preview the demonstration units. Mr. Fung introduced me to each of them. I met the famous bankers, publishers, factory owners, and other business tycoons. That must have been the most powerful group of people gathered in one room in Hong Kong that day. By the time I started the demonstration, there were more than thirty-five VIP guests there. That spoke for Mr. Fung's prominence and influence in Hong Kong business circles. I gave a brief introduction to the concept of the systems and proceeded with a live demonstration. A telex message drafted by a guest in Chinese was sent to Virginia Beach. The answers came back in Chinese printed out on the paper right in front of their eyes.

After the demonstration, all the VIPs came up, shook my hand, and congratulated me. I thought everybody was so impressed and my company would have more investors than we could handle. Ted and I went back to the hotel elated.

"You know that was the group that practically owns the entire Hong Kong. A few million dollars to them means nothing. The way I see it, they will give you a positive answer," Ted said.

"I feel pretty good about the responses. I hope they will invest," I said.

Mr. Fung's secretary called me and said Mr. Fung would like to see me. "Give me fifteen minutes. Ted and I will be there," I told her.

I called Ted to meet me at SHK lobby. "Ted, Mr. Fung wants to see both of us. I think it is good news," I said.

"It is fast! I will meet you at SHK in a few minutes," he said.

We walked in to Mr. Fung's office with great expectations. Mr. Fung greeted us and showed us to sit down in the large sofa.

"Professor Cheng, that was a brilliant invention and my colleagues were quite impressed," he said. My heart started pounding rapidly. He continued. "After we discussed the product among a few of us yesterday, the consensus was that your products are too far ahead of their time. In addition, we have been using computers for more than ten years. English has been the language we use here. It would be very difficult to change over to Chinese."

I realized there was no use to argue about their decision.

I said, "I am sorry that you feel the product is not practical at this time. And what you just said about the product being ahead of its time is not quite true. I believe in the not too distant future native language computing will be mandatory in non-English countries." Then we just exchanged some nice words to each other and departed with great disappointment.

About a month later, in November, Jerry and Dai invited Jim Wang from Hong Kong to visit the company in Virginia Beach. Jim Wang was a very successful businessman with business in the States as well. When Jim arrived Virginia Beach, Dai and Jerry were also there to greet him. I gave Jim a demonstration of our systems and explained the company business plan. He asked a few key questions and was quite impressed with the business prospects.

The next morning, Jim Wang and Dai came to my office. "I know this company is a start-up without any track record, but I am willing to invest $1.5 million for 40 percent of the company," Jim Wang told me.

It would make him the largest shareholder of the company. With the other investors like Jerry, Dai, and Stanley holding 15 percent, and the Taiwan group 10 percent, my family still had 35 percent of the company. I thought if we got the company to grow and become prosperous, 30 percent of the company would still be very good. I agreed for his 40 percent shares and, also offered Dai some bonus options for introducing Jim Wang. That was very good news for my family, although our family holding of the stock would drop to 35 percent from 75 percent.

Now came the time to discuss the company organization.

"We suggest asking Jerry to serve as the CEO and you work as the COO," Dai told me on the phone.

From the surface, it sounded very logical. I had been a professor all my life and had not been in any management position in a real business, nor had I any marketing or finance experience. On the other hand, Jerry was a brilliant corporate executive who led the company he founded ten years ago to a large corporation. While Dai was totally convinced that Jerry was a much better choice to run the company, I had my misgivings about the arrangement. The difficulty was that I had real problem of taking orders from people who might treat me less courteously.

"I don't think it will work," I said.

"You don't have the experience to run a business. Jerry has many years of corporate executive experience. We strongly support Jerry as the CEO," Dai insisted.

"If Jerry becomes the CEO, I would like to stay full time with the university and just function as a consultant to the company," I offered.

"In that case, your family stock shares must be reduced to below 5 percent," Dai told me.

"If I remain active in the company, I don't want to report to Jerry. I believe it will destroy our friendship," I told her.

I knew that I'd rather be out of this deal instead of having the unhappy situation my family and I might be subjected to. The $1.5 million was an astronomical figure to me and to the company, but the trade-off was much worse. Dai and Jerry knew that it was a tremendous opportunity for me and it would be very foolish for me to turn the money down. It was to their biggest surprise that I called Dai the next day.

"Ay! Dai, old buddy, I want to thank you for bringing Jim Wang to me. I think I will just try to make it entirely on my own."

"Oh! Richard, of course it is up to you. We were just trying to suggest the best for the business," he said. He was my oldest buddy in the world. I trusted everything he told me.

In March 1982, ECI started to export the ACG (Arabic Character Generator) into Saudi Arabia and other Gulf states and the CCG (Chinese Character Generator) to Taiwan, Hong Kong, and China through Hong Kong. The annual sales revenue of all circuit boards was less than $500,000. By the end of 1982, we had six full-time employees and had moved to a larger space. We had five software engineers and one electrical engineer. There was not a full-time administrative staff. Nancy worked for no pay to handle all the administrative and support matters. I was moonlighting as an electrical engineer, marketer, and custodian at night. The circuit cards we sold to Hong Kong and the Gulf states were specially protected with software codes and hardware circuits. We were very concerned that people in other countries might copy our products and the CCG technology. We had copyright statements etched on the boards and put warnings on the packages and instructions. We knew the products would be copied, but we did not know when it was going to happen.

In May 1984, I was in China as a UNDP advisor to give talks to groups of scientists in different cities. To my great surprise, I saw large number of computers using our products in their computers.

I asked the host to open the cage and pull the language card out for me to inspect. The card looked quite like our card. It even had the same logo and the copyright statement on the card. But a close look revealed the chips were not the same brand; the components were all slightly different from ours. I knew the card had been copied and sold in large quantity to China by our distributor in Hong Kong. There was a picture of the card in a color advertisement on a trade magazine by the distributor.

When I went to Hong Kong after the lecture tour, the distributor simply changed his address and was nowhere to be found. In Saudi Arabia, the distributor sent our card to Japan and had it copied. The orders on ECI cards suddenly dried up from Asia and the Gulf states and we all knew why. ECI did not have the time or the means to take the distributors to court, so we just changed the company focus to do business on other products.

In January 1982, a friend of ours, Frank Lee of Washington, DC, called me one day. "Hey! Richard, have you read the latest CBD? It has a request of information that looked like what you are doing with your language thing. Go look," he told me.

The *Commercial Business Daily* (CBD) was a government publication that announced government contract opportunities. It also listed the government requests for information (RFI) and requests for quotations (RFQ) from interested parties. Most businesses in the nation subscribed to the CBD for contract opportunity announcements by federal agencies. It was like the Bible for government contractors. In the stacks of CBD issue, we received in the past week, I did find an announcement of RFI by the US Information Agency (USIA).

In the announcement, the agency was seeking a contractor to provide computer networks to be installed in all USIA overseas posts throughout the world. It was mandatory that native language be used for input and output. I thought that was the kind of product we had been trying to sell all along. I called a meeting of the company staff and showed them the CBD.

"This looks interesting. We should respond to it. I am quite sure we have a shot at this," I said.

"I think we should check into it," Jim said.

I immediately wrote a letter to USIA indicating the interest and capabilities of ECI. Two days later, I received a phone call from a Mr. Gerald Huss at USIA.

"Would you be interested in giving us a demonstration of ECI foreign-language capabilities? Of course, there is no assurance the government will buy any of it," he told me.

"I understand what you just said. I am willing to show it to you. Are you coming down here, or do you want us to go up there in DC?" I asked.

"There will be several people that would like to see the demo. Can you bring the computer up here?" he asked.

"We will be glad to do it. Just tell me when we should we do it," I said.

Jerry called back an hour later. "I have talked to my boss and other interested parties. They would like to it as soon as possible."

"Today is Friday. How about Monday next week in the morning?" I asked.

"Which hotel do you plan to stay?"

"We normally stay in the Ramada Inn off I-495 near Tyson's Corner," I answered.

"Is eight o'clock okay? That will be in your hotel room," he told me.

"I will be ready. See you on Monday and have a good weekend."

"You too," Mr. Huss said.

My son Jim led Tommy Ho and Brian Dailey and I worked through the remaining days of the weekend to get the demonstration software tailored for the situations that USIA might want to see. That Sunday night, we checked into the Ramada Inn just before midnight. We set the computer up in my room and ran some test programs to make sure the demo would go smoothly. It was almost two in the morning before we said good-night and turned in, trying to get some rest before the big day. I was very tired from driving and the lack of sleep in the past week. Now that we were ready for the demo, I was relaxed. I fell into deep sleep as soon I hit the pillow, until the alarm clock woke me up at six fifteen.

I woke Jim up next door at six thirty. We went downstairs to the hotel café to have some breakfast at seven. When we returned the room at seven thirty, the phone in my room was ringing. It was Jerry on the other end of the line.

"Dr. Cheng, good morning. I just want to make sure you are ready. My boss and some other people have decided to come with me this morning," he said.

"No problem at all. I may not have enough chairs in the room. If they don't mind to sitting on the bed or stand around, the demo will take just ten to fifteen minutes. How many people do you know will be here for sure?"

"Counting myself, it will be seven people. We will be there shortly."

"See you soon," I said.

At ten minutes after eight, I heard the knocks on the door; they were here before the agreed time. We were ready, and I thought, *If, they are here early, it could be good news for us, because government officials are like the doctors: they like to make people wait for them.* This indicated their interest on my products was very high. Jim and I were both a little anxious about meeting these folks from the USIA. That was the first time we were dealing with federal officials. When I opened the door, a tall, red-haired man extended his big hand to me.

"I am Jerry Huss. This is my boss, Felecia Carpenter. This is George, our expert in languages, and other officials in the overseas programs," he introduced.

In all, there were seven people, just like Jerry had told me.

"I am Richard Cheng. This is my son, Jim. Tommy Ho and Brian Dailey are our engineers. Please squeeze in."

The small room was not designed to have so many people in it at one time. No one sat down because there was just one chair in the room. I wished I had rented a bigger room.

"I apologize for the tiny space. Maybe Tommy and Brian can just stand by outside the room. I will call you when we have trouble." I had to make some space just for the visitors.

I made a short introduction to our company and the system and then turned on the system. Jim was on the terminal. He showed them all the languages and how to use the system for foreign-language word processing and data transmission.

After the demonstration of the operations, many people asked questions. Between Jim and me, we provided all the technical answers. By the time they were leaving, it was half past ten o'clock.

"The system is very impressive. I believe your company has a lot of potential in the computer business," Felicia said to Jimmy. She then turned toward me and said, "If we do decide to acquire the foreign-language capability on the open market, I hope you will participate to bid on our RFP."

"I definitely will throw my hat in the ring for that opportunity," I replied.

"Thank you all for visiting us. If you need me to answer any questions, please feel free to give me a call," I told them.

"We will do. See you around," Jerry said.

Jim and I felt quite confident that USIA folks liked what they had seen.

"Jimmy, what do you think?" I asked.

"I think they really liked what they had seen," Jim told me.

"Let's watch the CBD closely for the RFP to be announced," I said.

"If this goes through, it would be a gigantic contract worth million," Tommy said.

"If we should get the award of a contract, it would be the biggest break for ECI," I said.

"Let's keep our fingers crossed," Brian said with his fingers crossed.

We checked out of the Ramada Inn and headed back to Virginia Beach before lunch. We knew this could be a big project, but we did not know how big the scope was. We were very confident that we would have a shot at the competition against bigger companies.

Nothing was heard from the USIA for the next three months. We kept close watch on the CBD for the USIA announcement. Finally, in January 1983, an announcement of an RFP by the USIA of the Overseas Post Network appeared in the CBD. We requested a copy of the RFP from the USIA. We received the RFP stack about one and a half inches thick in three days. I studied the RFP and found we had all the answers to the project. The project was to put a small computer network in each of the overseas USIA posts, normally housed in the embassy. The local area network at each overseas post must use the native language to process information. All the foreign posts were to be networked with the central computer in Washington, DC. In all, there were 156 overseas posts at the time of the RFP. The requirement was immediate and the time to turn in the proposal was less than two months.

At ECI, we had only technical staff and no secretary or typist. There was no technical or proposal writer in the company. The proposal was not just a technical solution but the complete package of technology, management, finance, and logistics. We were quite hopeful to win the contract, but there was no assurance. I did not want to risk the company by hiring high-priced proposal writers. The only answer to this was to have it done by myself.

I spent the next two weeks working after school and on weekends at home. I had to survey the market for costs of the equipment and to select a suitable computer system for the project. We had experience with the new Victor Technology computer that had the highest screen resolution. The screen resolution was the most crucial factor in displaying foreign characters on the monitor screen. Other computer systems with the same resolutions were many times costlier. Once the basic system was determined, I could then design the solution of the project around the computer system. After a hand-sketched concept of the approach was done, I started the proposal writing by typing on an old IBM electric typewriter. Word processing was not heard of at that time. Not well versed with typing plus, thinking while typing, it was a slow and trying process. I could hire a typist to do it, but still I had to put my ideas on the paper before the formal typing. There was not time to do all that.

The technical section of the proposal was easy for me, but the management and logistic support portion of the proposal took me much more time to understand and come up with an answer. I had to consult my friends who had done business with the government before. My greatest problem was that typos had to be whited out with a white paste. If I needed to change a sentence, I had to retype the whole page. I struggled with the typewriter until early in the morning, every day for ten days straight, to complete the technical section that included the management and logistics of the project.

With ECI Senior Members

The next section was the price section. Since ECI produced only the language boards and corresponding software for the proposed system, we had to purchase all other hardware and software from the microcomputer to operating system on the market in case we were awarded this contract. I searched and tested out the Victor Technology Company's Victor 2000 model computers to be most suitable for the USIA requirements. Not only did it have the highest screen resolution to accommodate the foreign language, it also had the highest hard disk drive capacity available and extra space to put a removable hard disk drive. The project also called for several other subsystems and many software applications that were specified in the RFP. We had to purchase all that hardware and software from other companies in order to comply with the requirement of the USIA RFP.

It took a whole two-week effort to search, test out, and select the right components. We negotiated prices with all selected vendors to reach an acceptable price level in order to gain price competitiveness. After that, I began to put the price proposal together. Spreadsheets were not heard of at that time. The extensive pricing matrix was just very difficult for me to do on an old typewriter. It was truly a nightmare for me!

I finally finished the price section in eight nights of typing; it was just three days before the deadline of proposal submission. I knew there were a lot of typos in the text, but to correct them would be impossible. There simply was not enough time to retype the whole proposal. In all, there were seven sets of proposals. Each proposal was for a region in the world and each region represented several countries. Bidders had the choice of proposing one region and up to seven regions. We proposed all seven regions around the world.

On the day of the proposal submission, Jim and I drove from Virginia Beach to Washington in the morning. Although the deadline was set at four o'clock, that afternoon, we left Virginia Beach at nine o'clock, so we could get into DC ahead of time just in case of traffic problems.

"Jimmy, did you have a chance to look at the proposal?"

"Yes, I did," he said.

"What do you think?"

"I believe you answered all of the questions," he said.

"I am afraid there are too many typos and bad English in it." I was truly worried.

"Well, if they really want our technology, I think they will overlook the typos."

"I sure hope so." I hoped Jim was right.

We arrived at the USIA building on C Street at twelve thirty. We had heard that the best time to submit a bidding proposal was just a few minutes before closing. We decided to take the advice and sit in a nearby cafeteria for a long lunch and many refills of coffees. At three twenty in the afternoon, we went to our parked car, retrieved the seven copies of our proposals, and proceeded to the USIA office on the second floor.

As we walked in the hall of the USIA office complex, we saw Wang Lab, IBM, and another company each had two persons and a hand truck. On the hand truck, there were seven volumes of two-inch binders and seven one-inch binders. All we had in hand were seven "technical section" volumes in soft cover and the total thickness was less than two inches. Our "price section" was even thinner.

"We must have missed something. How come they all had so much to submit and we had so little?" I asked Jim.

"Maybe we missed some of the attachment or supporting documents." Jimmy was puzzled as well.

"Maybe we just go home and forget about the whole thing!" I was serious.

"Since we are here, why don't we just submit the proposals and see what they say?" Jim said.

"Okay! The worst they could do is to laugh at our face. What the heck! We may never see them again anyway," I said.

We made it to the counter, handed the proposal to the clerk, and felt somewhat embarrassed by our small stack of paper and less than formally packaged proposal. Jimmy and I rushed out of the USIA office as if we had done something to make us feel guilty. We drove straight to Virginia Beach and felt we must have lost the opportunity.

"Well, let us just treat this as a lesson learned. We need to hire someone who had experience in government business to do the proposals," I said to Jim.

"It is a good idea, but it cost us an arm and leg to find a good proposal writer," said Jim.

After the proposal submission, Jim and I both felt that we were up against some most formidable giants in the computer business. We heard there were over one hundred companies that requested the RFP. Thirty-eight companies submitted the proposals. These companies were industrial giants like IBM, Xerox, Wang, and Mohawk Data Sciences, just to name a few. We were too small to compete with any of them. Our hope for a business breakthrough seemed very dim indeed.

We knew that ECI had the most advanced language capability at that time. We just did not know what else the other companies had done in order to put their proposals into such big volumes. Did we miss read something in the RFP? At that juncture, we could only wait for the review of our proposal. We had no idea what was the next step that the USIA would take. We were discouraged and had very little hope to win the contest.

A month after the proposal was submitted, we were surprised to receive a letter from the USIA stating that ECI was one of the several companies selected to give a live-test demonstration (LTD). A list of procedures and items to be tested was specified. ECI was scheduled on a Wednesday, about three weeks from when the notification was received. Everybody at ECI was elated and overjoyed by such a request. It meant that we had passed the first round of scrutiny. Jim and I just could not believe it was true.

"I don't believe this is true! We really got through. That means our proposal was accepted," Jim said in elation.

"Now we need to pass the next phase, and I can tell you it wouldn't be a piece of cake to anybody. We need to be sure we are well prepared for the LTD," I said to the group of staff standing around in the office.

Based on the instructions, there were many special and difficult requirements in the test that we had to write software to achieve such requirements. The six full-time employees including Jim were working day and night for the next twenty days on the software. I was working at nights and weekends with our staff as well on the hardware. The system was totally tuned to the requirements of the USIA and working flawlessly just a day before we needed to pack up and go to Washington, DC.

We had to take four identical PC systems to show the local area network and linking the local area network to the USIA main computer. This time, I had Tommy Ho, Brian Daily, and Jim to go with me to Washington for the LTD. We loaded two cars full of computers and accessories and drove to DC on Tuesday afternoon, a day before the LTD. We arrived in DC at about seven o'clock at night. We inspected the equipment to make sure no damage had been done on any equipment during the trip before we went to the hotel restaurant for supper. There were the three big days ahead. I urged everybody to rest early and be ready for the biggest challenges in our life.

The morning of the LTD, we moved our systems to the designated room on the third floor of the USIA building at eight o'clock sharp. Carl Vesper and Jerry Huss were overseeing the LTD. There were another half dozen USIA officials acting as judges. We were never introduced to them throughout the three-day LTD. The first day of the LTD involved the basic system functional characteristics and its operations. The actual LTD started at ten thirty in the morning. We showed them the procedures of setting up the system and the network. At eleven, we demonstrated the system basic functions and system software as outlined in the USIA statement of work specifications.

After lunch, we also demonstrated the networking characteristics and operations as required. There had been no breakdowns or any problems with our equipment during the first day of LTD. The judges were closed mouthed and not a single question was asked. At four o'clock, the first LTD day was over. We were asked to leave our equipment there and go back to the hotel for the day. We thought we did everything as required without any problems, but we did not know what the judges were thinking. Anyway, we just had to do our best and hope for good evaluations by these judges.

The second day of LTD started at eight thirty in the morning at the same room. This was the day of foreign-language demonstration. A new set of four judges was there to see the LTD. We demonstrated each of the seventeen languages as required. Among the languages, the Chinese and Arabic were the most interesting ones to the judges. Unlike the first day, questions were abundant about how and why did the foreign-language system work, the input method, the printout, and the data transmission conventions. We could see how much they were impressed by our demonstration. The questions and answers did not end until six o'clock; our confidence of winning was creeping up inside our minds.

"The judges are quite happy with the demo. What do you think, Tommy?" Jim asked.

"I believe they liked our solutions to some of the toughest problems such as the input methods of different languages," Tommy said.

"From the looks of their eyes, I feel they really liked our system. I have good feeling about winning the contract," Brian said. He was a normally quiet person.

"You guys did a real first-rate job today. I am very proud of all of you, but we still have another day to go. Let's keep doing the best we can and not to count our chickens before they are hatched," I told them.

The third and the final day of the LTD was in the same room at the USIA headquarters and it did not get started until ten in the morning because the communications connection from the tested units to the mainframe computer had some problems. The main test on the third day was communication links between the local area network to the USIA mainframe computer. One of the requirements was to have a very large block of data being transmitted to the mainframe without interruption and vice versa. We set up our system easily to achieve such a task, and within one hour, the life test demonstration was over. The six judges from the first day were there to judge the LTD. They asked very few questions. We thought that was because the test was too easy for everyone asked to perform the LTD. However, we learned later that most of the companies taking the LTD had failed to perform this very same test. But at this point, we did not know who the semifinalists were and how many participated in the LTD.

We packed up our gear and headed home the same afternoon. We knew we had done everything in the test well, but the competitors might have done just as well. "You have done a tremendous job in preparing and demonstrate the system. I think they like our products, but it is difficult to predict what's going to happen. There are so many big guys in the contest. We just don't know how good they are," I told the three colleagues who went to DC with me.

"Winning the contract or not, we have tried our best. I am happy what has happened during the LTD process in the last three days," Jim said.

"Right you are. Let's now find a good restaurant to have a good dinner and then get on the expressway," I said.

"That's what I was hoping for in the last thirty minutes. I am hungry," Tommy said.

We pulled the car to an all-you-can-eat seafood restaurant. I had never seen these three young men eating so much food in a single meal. Winning the contract or not, they were all very happy. I could sense that they were also very confident that after the LTD we had a better shot at this big contract.

It was a rainy November day at noon when the mailman came and dropped off our mail stack. I looked through the stack and found an envelope from the USIA. My heart was pounding rapidly. Was this the good news or another disappointing news? I opened the envelope and saw the form letter that was something new to me. It was clearly titled "CONTRACT AWARD." I could not believe my eyes.

"Nancy, Jim, come quickly!" I yelled.

They were in the office next door. Jim came in first and Nancy followed.

"Read this and tell me what you see," I said.

"Wow! We've got it!" Jim yelled out loud.

"Do you mean we have won the contract?" Nancy asked.

"Of course, we won. Look at this award letter, Mom. I just can't believe this yet," Jim said.

"I am going to give Jerry a call and see what he says," I said.

"It is on the government letterhead. I think this is it. Let me read the details," Jim said.

"Look! The award is for a multimillion-dollar five-year contract. We are going to be busy," I said. "Why don't you go tell the rest of the people?"

"Everybody is out for lunch. Why don't we do something more exciting like a party?" Jim said.

"Let's do it before they come back from lunch," I said.

Nancy and Jimmy went to the nearby store, bought some refreshment, and set it up in the crowded laboratory. A big sign was made that read, "ECI has WON the USIA contract." When people came back from lunch and saw the announcement, they were just overwhelmed by the good news. Tommy Ho and Brian Daily just jumped up and down with their fists in the air. De Yen, usually a very quiet fellow, was joining Tommy and Bryan. All of them were overtaken by emotion because they had worked so hard for so long and this was the biggest break anyone dared to dream about.

That evening, I hosted a seafood dinner for the entire company of six people plus Nancy and me. No one had any alcohol beverage that night, but we felt like we were floating above the clouds.

The next morning, Jerry called me on the phone. "Congratulations! Dr. Cheng, you guys have done it," he said.

"Thank you very much, Jerry. We will do a good job for the USIA. You can count on it," I said.

"You know your prices were not the lowest. I would like to negotiate it down a little. If you don't mind, I will bring Rich Hyneck, my assistant, down to your office to go through the price item by item."

"I understand we need to do this before you will put any order through. Right?

"I am afraid so," he said.

"So, it is to both ECI and the government to get the price negotiated. I am at your disposal. Any time would be good for me."

"How about next Monday? We will drive to the Beach and stay there overnight. I'd really like to try to complete the work before we return DC on Wednesday," he said.

"That will be fine. We will be expecting you late morning on Monday."

Jerry came into our office at eight o'clock sharp on Monday morning with his assistant, Mr. Rick Hyneck. We sat down in a small room with just a small round table and four chairs.

"You will afford better furniture after you get the contract started." Jerry made a joke.

"Mr. Huss, it all depends on how deep you want to cut into our prices. Our margin is not really that high," I said.

"We have general ideas of how much each hardware and software item costs on the open market. We will go from there," he said, Indeed, both Jerry and Rick were very sharp and kept up with market prices. However, there were many items that were produced by ECI. We set the prices based on our research and development cost plus a healthy markup. When they questioned the cost, I had prepared a cost analysis for each item.

"How about just give us a flat 7 percent discount on your own products?" Jerry said.

"You are driving a real hard bargain. I will do that for the sake of the country!" I said.

We shook hands as the deal was finalized. They told me a purchase order would be prepared by USIA purchasing department and sent to ECI.

"Jerry, how soon do you think we will get the purchase order?" I heard how slow the government purchasing agents were.

"We are in a hurry to implement the project. I think it should be here in two weeks," he said.

The big envelope from USIA arrived at ECI about ten days later. It was about two inches thick and contained orders for each USIA overseas post in the fifteen countries. It was separately outlined for each hardware item and software item. The training requirements and maintenance procedures for each location were also separately itemized. This indeed was a very complex operation. The first-year contract totaled over $3,500,000 of equipment. Additional amount was cost plus fixed-fee type for overseas training of USIA field staff and maintenance of equipment. We immediately proceeded to hire six more new software and hardware staffers to meet the workload. As the current space was too small, we contemplated leasing a larger space and a warehouse just to meet the minimal requirement of the contract.

On the third day after we had received the formal order, very bad news came from the Victor Technology Company, maker of the computer we proposed to adapt in the USIA contract. The company suddenly announced that it was forced into chapter 13 bankruptcy protection because it had overspent the huge amount of money it had raised but the sales volume was far below expectations. The financial institutions that supported Victor Technology Company decided to pull out their support.

At that time, the Victor computer was the best on the market. The CEO of the company knew that his product was going to sell well so he started to build his distribution system by putting at least one sales office in each city. Each office was equipped with the most expensive furniture and paid handsomely to all the salespeople a high salary plus health club membership. I had visited the local Victor office and the headquarters in Atlanta. All the offices were furnished with top-grade teak wood furniture, expensive paintings, and luxurious carpeting. I also saw other kinds of extravagance everywhere in the company. I first thought it must have done well in business and made a lot of profit.

In fact, the CEO was not using any common sense or any expert planning. It was all based on his own ideas on how to spend the huge amount of money he raised from his supporters and not from the money he earned from the business. I realized this was bad news for ECI, but I did not know how bad it could be. I thought the worst thing that could happen to the contract was to find a new computer with comparable capabilities to be used on the contract.

The next morning after the news about Victor Technology, I received a call from Jerry Huss from USIA early in the morning.

"Dr. Cheng, I think the contract is in trouble. You'd better come to our office and meet my top boss to discuss this before we terminate you," he said.

Termination of the contract? That was like big thunder from a blue sky! That meant all our efforts and plans were going down the tubes.

"Jerry, it is only the computer supply company going out of business. We can just get a comparable computer to replace the Victor computer," I said to Jerry, after the initial shock.

"Well, it is not that simple. We are talking about the government contract. It has to follow the contractual statement to the dot," Jerry said.

I still could not comprehend the reasoning for termination of the contract.

"Okay. Jerry, I will be in your office at eight in the morning tomorrow and then we will meet your boss," I said.

"Okay. Just be prepared. I don't know what he is going to say about it," he said.

I figured out the concerns of the government by talking to some experienced friends. They told me that if the contract was awarded for a certain brand of computer, then it could not be changed to another brand even if the specifications met the contract statement. If I had used the same computer but called it an ECI model name when proposed to the government, there would be no problem at all, even if the computers were replaced with another equal product made by some other computer makers. Now that Victor Technology was going out of business and the supply of such computer was in question, the government had to be assured that there would be enough Victor Technology computers to supply for the complete three-year contract.

Knowing the specific problems, I called the president of Victor Technology, Mr. John Ranch, after I was off the phone with Jerry.

"John, we are in big trouble. The USIA is going to terminate our big contract if I cannot supply Victor computers to them," I told him.

"Let me think. Ah! I know how to do it. Our European subsidiary is still going strong. I can drop-ship all of the Victor 2000 computers you need for the USIA contract," John told me.

"Where do you produce the Victor 2000?"

"We produce them here in the States and ship them to the Europe market," he told me.

"This is good news to me. Would you write a letter to me and assure me the supply of Victor 2000 computers for all USIA needs?" I said.

"I am glad to do it for you," he said.

"Do you mind if I ask the USIA official to call you to confirm this?" I asked him.

"By all means," he said.

"Thank you so much for your help," I said.

After I got off the phone with John Ranch, I felt much better. I was quite sure this was a good solution. I called Nancy and Jim to meet with me on this unexpected bad situation.

"The USIA wants to terminate our contract because the Victor Computer Company is in chapter 13 bankrupt proceedings," I said,

"Jerry Huss just called me. I found a solution, but I don't know if they would accept it or not."

"What is your solution?" Jim asked. Both Nancy and Jim looked pale.

"I just talked to John Ranch, the new president of Victor. He promised to supply all Victor 2000 computers the government needs from the Victor European operations in the coming three years," I said.

"In that case, I believe we are not that hopeless, because the government really needed the systems in a hurry," Nancy said.

"There is no one on the market who can provide a better system than the Victor 2000. I think we are in pretty good shape," Jim said.

"I am going to DC to see Jerry's big boss. I don't know what he would say. Don't tell the bad news to our people yet. They would be very disappointed. Wait until it was final. Okay?"

"I will not tell anybody. Do you want me to go with you?" Jim asked.

"I will go alone. Just proceed with the contract work. I will call back here as soon I know the answer, one way or the other," I said.

I drove to DC alone that evening and stayed in a hotel at Crystal City, which was very close to the USIA office complex.

In the hotel, I drafted a two-page brief proposal in a talking paper discussing how to assure the delivery of the Victor 2000 computers to the USIA. I made ten copies of the handwritten talking paper in the hotel business center.

The next morning, I want to the USIA building at eight o'clock sharp. Jerry was waiting in his office. He immediately took me to the third-floor conference room where his boss, Mrs. Carpenter, her boss, James Mahman, the division head, and two staff members were already waiting.

"Thank you for allowing me to present a solution to the delivery of the Victor 2000 computers for the contract," I said, after I had greeted each of them.

"You know we could have simply canceled the contract. Mr. Huss insisted that we give you a chance to tell us how you can assure us the delivery of computers made by a bankrupted company," Mr. Mahman said.

I handed each of the attendees in the room my simple proposed solution of the problem. After reading my two-page proposal, they seemed relaxed a little.

"Let us call Victor Technology now and see what Mr. Ranch has to say about this," Mr. Jerry Huss suggested.

A phone call was made to Denver, where John Ranch was residing at nine o'clock EST. Mr. Ranch was in his office already at seven o'clock Denver time. We put him on the speakerphone.

I told him, "Good morning! John, I have Mr. Mahman, the administrator of the information systems department of USIA, Mrs. Carpenter, division chief of the overseas operations, Mr. Huss, the head of overseas operations, and his deputy, Mr. Rich Hyneck. They would like you to confirm that your European division will provide Victor 2000 computers to ECI."

"I will be glad to answer any questions you have," John said.

"Mr. Ranch, please tell us how you can supply the government your Victor 2000 computers when your company is in chapter 13," Mr. said.

"This is not a problem at all. Our European operation is a profitable one. We are still shipping thousands of units of Victor 2000 to our European subsidiary each month. A different owner owns the European subsidiary and is not affected by the home company. I can assure you the delivery of all of the Victor 2000 computers you need for the overseas posts," Mr. Ranch said.

"Would you put this in writing to us or to Dr. Cheng?" Mr. Mahman asked.

"I will send the letter out to Dr. Cheng today," Mr. Ranch said.

"Mr. Ranch, I thank you for saving my day," Mr. Mahman said.

"John, thank you very much for taking time to talk to us. I am looking forward to receiving your letter," I said.

"Richard, I am happy that we don't have to redo the solicitation again. It would cost the government a lot of money and time," Mr. Mahman told me.

I was so happy that the USIA officials were satisfied with the solution. A devastating disaster for ECI was averted. What a cliff-hanging twenty-four hours we had! I called the office back home and talked about the meeting.

"Nancy put the phone on the speaker. I want Jimmy to hear this too. Is he there?"

"Dad, I am here," he said.

"Okay! Good news. The USIA has decided to keep the contract. I will tell you the rest when I arrive at home," I said. And then I started my journey home.

Implementation of the contract was the next hurdle. The immediate question was where to find money to pay the additional staff and to buy computers and parts for the contract. Victor Technology was in financial trouble. We had to pay them the money in advance before they would build the Victor 2000 for us. The company certainly could not do business as usual by building the equipment first and giving ECI certain payment terms. The government does not have the mechanism to advance any payment to ECI for this contract. It was the way the government always has done business.

My challenge was to find $150,000 before we could start to implement the contract. The only way at that time was to borrow money from a bank. When I went to my bank where I had my account, the Virginia National Bank, the vice president told me that ECI did not have enough credit to borrow the $150,000 ECI needed to buy the first batch of Victor 2000 computers. A line of credit would take too long to get approval. When I showed him the contract, he said he was not sure that ECI could deliver and satisfy the contract and the bank could be risking too much by doing any business with ECI. The Virginia National Bank suggested to me to seek another lending institution.

A friend introduced me to the chairman of the board of the United Virginia Bank, Mr. Lee Payne. Lee called a meeting for me to talk to the president and some staff. I gave them a presentation of what ECI was doing and the big contract ECI just received. After the meeting, someone suggested that the bank could invest some money in ECI and set up a line of credit to support ECI contract activities.

I thought that was a great idea and agreed that the investment would be helpful. Mr. Payne told me that they would contact me in a day or so to visit ECI before the final decision was made by the bank.

The bankers came to ECI to look at the operations and some software demonstrations. They also checked out our small production facility. The bank offering letter came within a week that the bank would invest $150,000 cash for 7 percent of the company equity. ECI needed to hire a person designated by the bank as the vice president and COO to run the operations and finance. ECI needed to pay the new person $60,000 a year plus all benefits. The bank would provide a line of credit for up to $300,000. I thought it was a good deal, since ECI did need a professional businessman to run the business. We signed the agreement in a matter of days. I was eager to get started with the implementation of the USIA contract.

CHAPTER 19

Running a Million-Dollar Company

Mr. Willard Andrews, a former banker, was named executive vice president at ECI. He was a friend and confidant of Mr. Payne and Mr. Larry Smith, the United Virginia Bank president. Willard was a very nice and polished man in his late forties. He was the highest-paid employee at ECI at that time. Although Willard was the executive vice president, he knew nothing about computers, corporate finance, or government contracts; therefore, his responsibilities were limited to furnishing of offices and laboratories, purchasing supplies, and serving as an interface person to the bank.

He had a habit of being extravagant, like when he bought those $3,000 murals for the company hallways and $200 ashtrays for the conference room.

"Willard, these items are too expensive for the little company. Do you think we need them?" I asked him.

"I have got the okay from the bank to spend the money," he told me.

"Willard, the bank agreed to loan us the money, but we have to pay them back plus the interest. The money is not free to us," I said in amazement.

In addition to his expensive taste of furnishings, his preoccupation was duck hunting. He often spent hours on the phone to arrange duck hunting events with his friends. We all thought, *Well, if he can make the company profitable, we can tolerate all his shortcomings.* At the year-end, our accounting record showed a loss of over a quarter of a million dollars that year.

I went to the United Virginia Bank and asked for a meeting with Lee Payne and Larry Smith. My complaints about Willard were not acceptable to them by phone. From their point of view, I did not know what I was talking about.

"We have sent you the best person in your business you can find," Lee told me.

"Look! Lee, we are losing money because we have spent too much on unnecessary purchases. I really need to borrow more money to sustain the operations," I told them.

I was trying to be polite and pleasant to them. Not only had they refused to loan ECI any more money, they were also trying to insult me.

"We are not about to loan you any more money. Why don't you wipe the smile off your face?" Lee Payne said.

I felt the insult was highly unprofessional. I got up from my chair and said, "You really have no right to insult me. I will pay back your loan, buy back your shares of ECI stock, and I am firing your man Willard as of this moment."

I just walked out of their boardroom without saying another word. I went to Sovran Bank upstairs right after this meeting. The new vice president, Eddy Witcher, was happy to take ECI's account back and agreed to loan the money to pay off United Virginia Bank immediately.

At this point, I did not have any other options but to run the company myself. I requested a leave of absence from Old Dominion University for one year and stepped in as the president of the company. That was in January 1985. I had no experience to speak of as a serious businessman. The only financial background was preparing requests and spending the departmental budgets in universities. That was not quite the same as running a multimillion-dollar business. I was very concerned about my ability to run the company, but I had to do it regardless. I was also excited about the challenges that I might be able to conquer the difficulties in the company.

The first thing I did was to control expenditures. I had to review all purchases regardless of the amount. Often, I rejected the purchase request if I felt it was not critical for the business. Travel and long-distance phone calls were drastically reduced. The next thing I tried was to close the gap on cash flow. The government payments were always delayed from thirty days to sixty days or beyond. But we had to spend money to buy and work on the goods to be delivered to the government. It caused the negative cash flow to be a constant problem. It was caught in a vicious cycle, and the problems became more severe as time went.

I negotiated with our suppliers to give us some more slack in payment terms, and I talked to the government contract office to move a bit faster in our invoice processing. I was also very strict in approving all indirect contract expenses. ECI now had twenty-six employees, including me. The contract deliveries were smooth and uneventful. We had sent instructors throughout the world to train USIA staff on how to use the network system and how to get help from ECI's twenty-four-hour help desk.

During the first twelve months, ECI had delivered network systems to USIA overseas posts in sixteen countries. Overseas posts were sending broken units through diplomatic pouches back to ECI for repair and for preventive maintenance. Officials at USIA were quite pleased with ECI's contractual performance.

In the year 1985, ECI did about the same amount of business as in 1984 by the year-end. But instead of losing money, ECI had a net gain of over $280,000. That result had boosted my confidence in running a business. I was not as scared as when I first took over the helm a year before. The company now needed my service to sustain the stability. I requested a second annual leave from the university and was again approved by the provost. The year 1986 was at about the same revenue level as in 1985, somewhere around $3,750,000. Again, we made it in black, earning about $350,000 after tax. Not only I gained the confidence in running a business, I had a lot of fun and satisfaction in doing my job. I requested the third-year leave of absence and was again approved by the university.

CHAPTER 20

Trips to China and My Career Cross Road

In early 1984, I was appointed by UNDP as a technical consultant to give lectures in China. I had my concerns for going into China in the past because of my dad's previous position in the military. But with the United Nations' appointment, I felt much more comfortable about going there on my own. Because there was no direct flight from the States to China at that time, I flew to Hong Kong and from Hong Kong to Beijing.

I had planned to take a two-day tour in Beijing since I had never been in Beijing before. A visiting scholar of ECI, Wei-Lin Zhu, was in Beijing working in a semiofficial business. He picked me up from the airport and checked me into the Beijing Hotel.

"Dr. Cheng, please be careful what you say to people here. This is not America," Wei-Ling told me when we were alone.

He also accompanied me to see the Forbidden City and the Summer Palace. I was awed by the magnificence of the ancient constructions and architecture. How could they accomplish all that without machinery to construct such enormous fine buildings? One of the sculpted marble slabs—fourteen feet by over one hundred feet—was moved to the palace site from a thousand miles away. I heard it was transported in the wintertime by pouring water in its path to make a road of ice to slide its way to Beijing.

In the Forbidden City, I saw the huge golden pot that was the size of the Liberty Bell in Philadelphia. The gold layer had been scraped away with knives by foreign soldiers during the eight-country invasion of China. I also saw the damages done by the Cultural Revolution to ancient Chinese artifacts. That really broke my heart.

In Forbidden City in 1985

At lunchtime, we went into a large and clean-looking restaurant, where we found a table to sit down and saw a few guests. A group of young waiters and waitresses was having fun talking and laughing. I raised my arms several times but could not draw anyone's attention. Wei-Ling was upset and yelled aloud. A waitress reluctantly walked over and asked, "What do you want?" She was very impatient.

"We'd like to have lunch here," Wei-Ling said.

The waitress did not say anything. She just went to the back and returned with two sets of tableware that she threw on the table. Wei-Ling was so upset he got up and dragged me to leave.

"This is a typical restaurant run by the government, and those young waiters and waitresses are children of high-ranking officials. They don't care if the business is making money or not. They just want to get paid and have good time. We ate in a smaller restaurant after that lesson.

Wei-Ling also showed me the city. Baba had lived in Beijing for several years when he was young, so I had heard so much from him about Beijing in the past years. The late spring in Beijing was a beautiful season. I was impressed by the grandiose tall ceilings, the wide and straight streets, and Tiananmen Square. People in Beijing were very polite comparing with what I could remember of those places I had lived in before. Baba had told me that since this was the ancient capital, people here were proud to be civilized as residents of the city.

In 1984, there were very few cars in Beijing. Taxicabs had to be arranged by hotel personnel ahead of any service. You could not get a cab by waving at one on the street. Some old limos designed for dignitaries now were used as taxicabs. I rode in one of those gigantic black limos just for my curiosity. It was not comfortable and certainly very inefficient in terms of gas consumption. I was trying to carry a conversation with the driver, but he was very careful and closed mouthed. As someone who had been absent from his homeland for thirty-six years, I was most curious and felt a sense of closeness to people I had seen on the street. But after several attempts to get closer to them, I felt a strong resistance to open and talk to me, which disappointed me deeply. Of course, I understood where they came from. I was a foreigner in their eyes and they were afraid of the watchful eyes of security folks and being branded as counterrevolutionary.

Food service in Beijing Hotel was quite unique indeed. It was supposed to be the best hotel in Beijing at that time, so I invited Wei-Lin to have dinner with me at its main dining hall. I looked the menu over and found many nice dishes, and the prices were right. I ordered four dishes for the two of us. I thought there would be leftovers. But when the dishes were served, I was astonished. They were very, very small. I couldn't believe it.

"Wei-Lin, look at those damn dishes! They are so small like coffee cup saucers! I don't think that's enough for the two of us. Let me order some more," I said.

"I have never been here before. The dishes are indeed too small, and I am hungry," he said.

"This is really a stingy place. I thought this hotel is for foreign dignitaries as well."

"They would not eat here. Did you see the many special banquet rooms on the second floor? There you can have the big dishes and really good food," Wei-ling told me.

I ordered four more dishes. The two of us finished every bit of the food served. They all tasted right. Just the portion was so small. That meal caused me to wonder what the other restaurants were like.

Although food was inexpensive, we had to use the "foreign exchange bill" instead of the currency used by residents. My first impression of Beijing was overall favorable.

Flying commercial inside China was very difficult in 1984. Wei-Lin and I traveled by train to Shanghai instead of flying.

"You don't want to ride in those Russian AN-24s. They have the reputation of most crashed planes in China. I would take the train instead, since you are not in a hurry," Wei-Lin told me.

"Sure, we'll take the train. Besides, I want to see the country along the railroads," I said. "I don't have to be in Wuxi until three days later. Why don't we tour Shanghai before we go to Wuxi?"

"We sure can do that. I will get the hotel booked in Shanghai."

"Do you know Shanghai well?"

"I am a native of Shanghai. I grew up there," Wei-Lin said.

"That's great! I was in Shanghai when I was only fourteen years old. I would need you to show me around the city," I said.

"I will be glad to show you around."

We took a night train in the sleeping car. It was comfortable. Next morning, we arrived at the Shanghai railway station. We took a taxi just to drive around the city. Shanghai looked pretty much the same as I'd left it in 1948. Very few new buildings were added to the commercial or residential districts. My recollection of old shanghai was more glamorous than it was thirty-six years later. I thought the city in 1984 would look thirty-six years older, but it also seemed to be covered with a layer of dust. The city had lost the shine I had had in my mind since I last had seen it.

In the downtown business district, most of the storefronts were closed or boarded up. The most popular shopping district, East Nanjing Road, now had just a few government-owned stores. The stores were teeming with shoppers but had very limited varieties of merchandise for sale. East Nanjing Street was as crowded as I remembered thirty-six years ago, but now it had very few choices of what to buy.

People dressed in unisex clothing, either in gray or blue; the colorful displays had disappeared from the crowd. Of the people on the streets, many wore old clothing with patches. The glamorous Shanghai in my memory was no longer in existence.

We went to where my granduncle's huge building and his apartment were located. The building looked rundown and in disrepair. The downstairs offices had turned into dwellings for many people. I knocked on the door, and an elderly lady opened the door.

"Excuse me! Is this the Cheng residence?" I asked.

"No. This is not Cheng's residence. They were kicked out of here when Shanghai was liberated. My family and five other families were assigned to live here thirty years ago," she said.

I heard this sort of thing had happened in China after the revolution, but this was the first real one I saw with my own eyes. I also found some leads to my long-lost relatives, but I did not have time to look them up on this trip.

We took the train to Wuxi the next morning at eleven thirty, arriving at one thirty in the afternoon. Two officials were waiting there with a name sign to locate me.

"I am Richard Cheng from UNDP. This my friend Wei-Lin Zhu from Beijing."

"Welcome to Wuxi. We are from the Technical Conference. We will take you to the hotel," one of the officials said.

"We have not eaten lunch. Can we stop by some restaurant to eat something before we go?"

"I am sorry. All of the restaurants stop serving food at one o'clock here," he said.

"Why don't you help us to find some biscuits or something for us? We are very hungry," Wei-Lin said to them.

"Okay! Why don't you sit here and have a cup of tea? I will go with the driver to find something."

About fifteen minutes later, he brought a birthday cake to us. That was the only food he could find for us that day.

"We are very sorry. Next time, please eat before one o'clock any place you go," the official said.

On the way to the hotel, I asked Wei-Lin about it. "Hey! Wei-Lin, how come you didn't know about this one o'clock in the afternoon business?"

"Well, we didn't have time to eat before we left Shanghai. Then I thought we would get in town before one o'clock and in Beijing I could go home to eat. I did know the rules. Sorry about it," he said.

Wuxi was a quiet small city, a famous tourist lakeside resort on the beautiful Tai-Fu (Grand Lake) where the ageless beauty Si-Tze lived over two thousand years ago. The officials took us to the lakeside guesthouse reserved for VIPs. Wei-Lin had to stay in a different hotel. The guesthouse was built right on the water with a wooden walkway connecting to the dinner room and to buildings on the land. I thought it was really nice place for vacations.

The UNDP appointment was designed for six lecture sessions. I prepared six sets of material for four-hour sessions each. I planned to give four hours of lecture each day. That evening, Mr. Gi-Chien Wang, the organizer, came to my room to see me.

"Welcome to Wuxi. We are very honored that you can come to our small city. Is there anything I can help you with?" he said.

"I have only the letter from UNDP telling me to give six lectures. I plan to lecture four hours a day," I said.

"Oh! That, that…" He hesitated.

"Is there any problem?" I asked.

"I am sorry. We have announced that you will give six hours of lectures per day and six days for the program," he said.

"I have prepared a total of twenty-four hours of lectures. Now you want me to give thirty-six hours of lecture. I just can't do it." I was a bit upset.

"You see, these participants have come from all over the country on their own expenses. They will be very disappointed if we don't give them what we have promised in the brochure."

"I wish I had been informed of that. Okay, I guess I have to figure out a way to do that," I said.

"Oh! Thank you! Thank you! I will meet at the lobby at eight forty-five and walk you to the auditorium. Good night!"

The morning scene on the lake was just breathtaking, I got up early and ate the breakfast alone in the separated dining room because I was the only foreign guest in that big guesthouse. The food was great with the famous Suchow dumpling soup and many other dishes—far better than in Beijing Hotel.

My lecture started the next morning at nine o'clock sharp. The auditorium was crowded with over two hundred representatives from all over the country plus countless local people. I used my folding overhead projector and slides to assist my lecture. My topics were networking and communication standards and the latest technology-related subjects. The morning session and afternoon session used up two sets of my lectures. Each session went over time in order to complete the presentations.

As it went, I would finish the material I prepared in three days. I needed to make six more lecture materials from my head. And I did not have any references with me. I planned to write the lecture material after dinner. After all day lecturing and answering questions, I quickly finished the dinner and hoped to relax a few minutes before I started writing notes. Knock! Knock! Someone was at the door. I opened the door and saw a group of about eight people.

"Good evening, Dr. Cheng. May we come in?"

"Please come in. I may not have enough chairs for you to sit down," I said.

"We just want to ask some questions. You were swamped during the day, so we thought we would come to ask you now," one of the participants said.

They were eager to learn more and were very sincere. I had no heart to kick them out. The question-and-answer session lasted beyond ten o'clock before they left. I was totally exhausted, but I still had to write the new lecture notes until after one o'clock in the morning. This went on every day until the fifth day. It was a very hot day and there was no air-conditioning. I was tired from the morning, but in the afternoon session, I felt light-headed at about four o'clock in the afternoon. When I showed some sign of losing balance, the organizer talked to me about taking a break. He took me to the clinic for a checkup. The doctor there found me feverish and with very high blood pressure.

"You must rest and stop your ongoing activities," the doctor told me.

"I have one more day to go to finish the job I was hired to do. Can I make it, Doctor?"

"No. You will kill yourself if you do. I will tell Mr. Wang to cancel the lectures tomorrow."

The lecture for the Saturday was canceled.

"I am sorry that we have worn you down like this. Let me take you to tour the lake on the boat tomorrow. It is very beautiful. I am sure you will enjoy it," Mr. Wang told me.

He hired a large boat on the lake and took three of his staff members with us. It was a sunny and mild day. The wind was soft, and the lake was smooth like a mirror. With the green mountains surrounding the light-blue water, I was totally absorbed by the natural beauty of the surroundings. The boat sailed through the vast water to an island. We stopped at a small food vendor for lunch and returned just before dark. It was a most enjoyable and memorable tour for me. I believe my blood pressure returned normal that day.

Weil-Lin and I returned Shanghai the day after.

"Wei-Lin, I appreciate all of the help you have provided me since I arrived in China. I am going to Hong Kong, Taiwan, and back to Virginia from there. I'll see you later in the States."

"It's my pleasure to be with you these days. Take care of yourself and say hello to Mrs. Cheng and my friends at ECI," he said.

I flew to Hong Kong and stayed for two days and then took a flight to Taiwan to see Mama and Baba. They were doing quite well. Baba was teaching a class to a group of devoted students at the Confucius Research Institute. He had a houseful of students two or three times a week. That kept both Mama and Baba very busy and happy. I did the usual by treating them in restaurants. It was always very difficult to say good-bye to them, especially Mama.

Back in Virginia Beach, I began to write to my friends in China to look for my relatives in Shanghai and Beijing. The first relative I found was Uncle Xie-Fu, the one who fed my dog with sticky candies in Chunking. I wrote to him first, and he responded immediately. He also gave me Grandma Liu's address in Shanghai. She lived with my Mama's brother and his family. I wrote to Grandma Liu, and the uncle responded. I called Mama and Baba in Taiwan. They were just happy beyond words.

"Ren, can you go to Shanghai and visit Grandma for me?" she said. "Tell her, I miss her, but I can't even write to her now," she said. I knew she must be crying.

"Mama, I will go. Maybe in October or November. I will go to Shanghai to see Grandma."

"When you see Grandma, be sure to give her some money and tell her about us."

"I will, Mama. I will tell you all about it when I come home to see you after I come back from China," I said.

In November 1984, I went to China again on my own. I flew to Hong Kong first. Took the electric train to Lo-Fu, the border town between China and Hong Kong. I had to stand in line for two hours to get through the border checkpoints. My passport was not stamped because I was going to Taiwan. The official would make the "red star" chop on a separate paper instead on the passport. I flew the AN-24 to Xiamen via Fu-Chow to Shanghai because I needed to have some business meetings in those two cities for ECI. Wei-Lin was right. The AN-24 was a very flimsily built aircraft. After the engine was started, I could see the rivets on the sheet metal seemingly vibrating out of place. It also scared me that the pilot would put the landing gear down hundreds of miles before landing. I thought I was foolish to take such chances. But I wanted so badly to see Grandma that I took the risk because it saved me time.

I arrived at Shanghai's airport and found the luggage bags were randomly put on the ground for passengers to locate. Fortunately, Uncle Xie-Fu and his son-in law, Mike Su, came to help me at the airport. They helped me to check into the Shanghai Hotel. After I cleaned up and changed my clothing, I hired a taxi to take me to Grandma. With thought and emotions running fast in my mind, I wondered what had changed in the thirty-six years since we sneaked out of the house on that August evening. What did happen after that? Uncle I-Quon was her eldest son, just a few years younger than Mom. He was married with two sons. The older son was married and lived with them. The other uncle, I-Quay, was elsewhere at that time.

I walked into this very long and narrow alley to find the number. It was a large, multistory brick building. When I arrived at the house, I saw this very old lady standing at the door with one hand holding the doorframe. I recognized her. She was Grandma Liu. I rushed forward to hug her and told her who I was.

"I knew you are coming. I have been waiting for you. Come on in the house," she said.

"How are you, Grandma? I have not seen you in thirty-six years." I followed her in the house.

The uncle, the aunt, and their son, Yu-Ming, were at work. Only the cousin's wife, Jan, was at home. She served me a cup of hot tea.

"Ren, how are your Mama and Baba?"

"They are just fine. They want me to greet you and give you this," I said as I gave her an envelope with $200 in it. It was big money in China at that time.

"Do you know how old I am?" Grandma Liu asked me. She could speak Mandarin now.

"Let me see. You must be over ninety years old now."

"I will be ninety-four after the New Year," she said with a big smile.

"Grandma, do you still drink?"

"Not much nowadays. I only drink when we have celebrations of something."

"Grandma's memory is so good. We always ask for her help when we are not able to find something. She has a memory like an elephant," Jan said.

"Grandma, do you remember the day we left Fu-Chow?" I had had this question for thirty years.

"Of course, I remember. When you and your Mama didn't come home after midnight, someone came to the house to question me and I-Quay about your whereabouts. I told them we did not know. They were very unhappy and took us to their place for questioning. Two days later, they found out all of you had gone to Taiwan. They just let us go. We were branded as relatives of the enemy. The new officials took your property after the liberation. I moved here to live with your uncle about thirty years ago."

"Grandma, I hope we did not cause you too much trouble."

"You did, but that was fine with me because I knew you were safe," she said. "Jan, come with me. I want to shop for my grandson's favorite food."

She went out with Jan to the market. I stayed home for more tea. I looked around the place for the family of five adults and a year-old baby. It has just one single room of about twenty by fourteen feet. A blanket was used to divide the room into two parts for the generations. Grandma had her own corner near the door. Kitchen and other facilities were shared with families to live on the first floor.

Grandma and Jan came back with two baskets of groceries. My uncle, my aunt, and Yu-Ming came home individually after five o'clock. Grandma Liu introduced me to each of them. I had never met them before. We had the dinner in the public quadrangle shared by the eight families. My uncle's family used it that day. I recognized how severe was the shortage of housing units for Shanghai residents. Uncle I-Quon was a finance expert, my aunt was a nurse, and

Yu-Ming was an electrical engineer. The combined income of the household was about one hundred RMB a month. That was less than a day's income for a young engineer in the United States.

From this visit, I found several relatives whom I visited during later trips to China. Of the uncles—the granduncle's children—I met in Shanghai in 1948, Jan died at the age of fifty, and the younger one Ming was an engineer in Beijing.

Mama and Baba could not communicate with any of them in 1987, through the effort of Uncle Xie-Fu, we were related to the aunt that was put in an orphanage during the war. All their correspondences had to go through me or friends in Hong Kong. I had made business trips to China for the company two to three times per year for several years. Eventually, I had seen most of my relatives in China, except Uncle I-Quay, who taught me to make the crystal radio, which led me into the electronics profession. He was a chemical engineer in northern China.

Grandma Liu passed away at the age of ninety-nine, after a fall from a stepladder. Uncle Xie-Fu emigrated to the States to live with his son. I visited him often at his home in Washington, DC. He was retired but kept busy with his duty as the chairman of the overseas branch of the Jao-Tung University alumni association. He was suffering severe back pain.

"Ren, I had been through hell during Cultural Revolution. I was near death more than once."

"Why did they do that to you?" I asked.

"Well, during WWII, I worked as an interpreter for the US Army. That was one of the crimes," he said. "I also did not go along with some of the things the leaders in the railroad organization were doing. They first put me in a jail and then sent thugs to beat me up."

"Did they beat you, so you will cooperate with the leaders?"

"It was too late for that. They wanted to kill me, and they thought I was dying. I had god help me to have this good-hearted jail guard who told the thugs that I was dying, and he would take me out and bury me. Instead, he took me to a place and hid me in a closet. After a few days, I regained my strength, and I escaped to a different city. Later I reunited with my family after the crazy period was over. Since then, my stomach and my back have bothered me all the time. I have been taking painkillers and sleeping pills ever since."

I visited another uncle, Mama's youngest sister's husband, Jiou-Yu Lin, in Xiamen in 1986. When I was in Nanking back in 1947, he came with his girlfriend, my aunt, to visit us. I remembered him as an unusually handsome young man in his twenties. He married my aunt a few years later. They had a daughter, Tsan-Tien, who had just graduated from college. Both the uncle and the aunt were retired. He was the principal from Xiamen High School and she was a teacher in a different school. When I went to his home to visit him and my aunt, I saw a deep scar on his neck that I didn't see when I last saw him in Nanking thirty-eight years ago. After the revolution, he was a newspaper reporter in Hong Kong and was talked by a relative into returning to China to serve his country.

"Uncle, what happened to your neck?" I asked.

"Well, it's a long story and a bad memory. Since you asked me, I will just briefly tell you about where the scar came from." He took a sip of his green tea. "I was branded as the bad element of the society because I was 'highly educated.' They put me on an insulting public trial; I was beaten severely during the trial. Afterward, they put me in a cage just like an animal." He became excited and tears were welling in his eyes.

"Wow! It is unconceivable people would do such a thing to you. Just who are those people anyway?" I was puzzled.

"Those were the unhappy people at school while I was the principal. Because we had some small disagreement when I was the principal, they wanted to take their anger out on me. Those people incited the students in the high school about how bad I was and encouraged the students to punish me." His voice was trembling as his past flashed though his mind.

"Uncle, why don't you have some tea and rest a few minutes?" I asked him.

"I am just a little upset when I think of those days. Anyway, inside the cage, I had no bed and no blanket. I had to sleep on the dirt floor. They put the food in a dish and pushed it into the cage under the iron grid. I was forced to lick my food from the floor like a dog, or I would starve to death. When it was very hot in the summer, they would make me hold a heavy stone and stand under the burning sun. If I fell asleep, the stone would drop on my feet and crush my toes. You see, I still have the scars." He showed me his deformed feet. After sipping his green tea, he continued. "I wanted to make sure your aunt and Tsan-Tien were safe, so I endured all of the insults and harsh treatment. But after a few months, I could not take it anymore. I hanged myself with the rope they used to tie me up. Someone cut the rope and put me down after I had lost my conscious. The rope cut deep into my flesh, and the wound was infested. After the wound healed, the scar remained. But I can tell you the scars in my heart are much deeper than what you can see," he said with tears rolling down his face. I felt very sorry for him. He was no longer the handsome young man I had kept in my mind for so many years.

I visited Fu-Chow in 1985. Because local people viewed me as a more successful native son now living overseas, the governor of Fujian and the major of Fu-chow hosted a banquet for me. They also provided me with a car and interpreter the next day to accompany me wherever I wanted to go in Fu-chow. The first stop was to my old residence where Grandma Liu used to live. I wanted so badly to see the library and bring some of the books with me back home to the States. The road to our house was unchanged but the house was the same as I remembered, although it looked very, very old. It needed a lot of repairs. When entering the second-floor apartment, where one of my aunts lived, I saw the library was made into a bedroom. All the wood bookcases were gone, and none of the treasured books were in sight. I found an old tenant, Mr. Huang, downstairs.

"Mr. Huang, do you recognize me? I was here in 1949," I said to this frail old man.

"I can't see too well, but I know who you are," he said.

"Do you know what happened to our library upstairs?"

"I sure do. I tried to stop them, but they just beat me up."

"Who were those people? What did they do?"

"Those were the punks from the neighborhood. They reported to the security people that in the upstairs apartment was property of enemies of the state. You know that's a big crime. The security people came, took all the books, and burned them right on the street. Some other people came and took all the bookcases. I do not know what they did to the bookcases. Anyway, I just minded my own business in those days."

My heart sunk as I heard the old man's story. I was hoping to see some of the books that had caused Baba so much trouble when he was young. The library was my favorite place when I lived there. What a pity! I didn't understand why people could become so stupid and crazy as to destroy anything of historical and cultural value. But it really happened during the Cultural Revolution, between 1961 and 1969. The country was driven backward for more than twenty years and an entire generation of youth was lost. The economy of the country was put into a tailspin.

Our old building was divided into small apartments and housed many families. As a gesture to overseas Chinese, the authority would return the house to me. I was reluctant to accept the offer, because if I took it back, I had to repair it and then rent it to people at a government-determined price. I thought it would be foolish for me to spend money to repair the house and then get into a lot of headaches of maintaining the house. I talked to Baba first and asked Nancy. We decided that we would not respond to the offer for the returning of our properties.

My next stop was to see Trinity College, where I had spent one semester. I was astonished by what I saw of the once beautiful, red-brick, English campus. Several grayish concrete buildings were added to those red-brick buildings in disrepair. The church was converted into a foundry to produce plumbing fixtures. The sounds of blowers and the roaring flames replaced the voices of prayers. The once glorious stained-glass windows were coated with black soot from the coal-burning furnace inside the church. I did not have the courage to venture inside the church, but I could imagine what was inside the sacred gathering place. It certainly pained me to see the deterioration of this old school of mine.

All the British teachers had left for England right after the "liberation" of the city in 1949. I did not find any teacher or classmate from the time I was there. The principal, Mr. Chun-Hsin Chen, was over seventy years old and lived near the school. The driver drove me to his house. It was a ten-minute drive through the Drum Hill district. I saw a large villa-type of house with high fences. I knocked on the double wooden door. A young woman about twenty years old opened the door.

"May I see Mr. Chen?" I asked.

"Which Mr. Chen?" she asked me.

"Oh! Mr. Chun-Hsin Chen, the former principal of Trinity College," I said.

"He is my grandfather. May I have your name and who you are?"

"I am his student in 1949. My name is Tien-Ren Cheng."

She left the door open but went back to the house. I assumed she had to talk to her grandfather for permission to allow me inside the house. After about two minutes, she came out with a light smile on her face.

"I am Mei-Chi. My grandfather would like to see you. Please come in."

"Thank you!"

I followed her into this very old but very clean large house through a tearoom to the living room in the rear part of the house. Mr. Chen was sitting on a couch. He had all-white hair, was skinny, and looked much older than his age.

"Grandfather is not able to walk easily. His knees are weak from arthritis," she said while Mr. Chen struggled to get up.

"Good afternoon, Mr. Chen. Please don't get up," I said as I walked over to shake his hand.

"My granddaughter has told me who you are. I remember you. Your father and I were schoolmates at Yin-Hwa High School many years ago," he said.

"I still think about the help you gave me to allow me to stay in my class after I failed the first monthly examination," I said.

"Well, I recall you did well in the following exams. I am glad you worked hard for it. How is your father? I heard he went to Taiwan."

"My dad lives in Taiwan. He is retired now."

"Now tell me what you are doing."

"I live in America with my family. I am teaching computer science in a college."

"Very good! I knew you would do well. Have you seen the school?"

"Yes. I just came from the school."

"You don't recognize it now. It is ruined."

"I feel so bad about it. It was such a beautiful campus."

"I was jailed and beaten during the Cultural Revolution. Fortunately, some good-hearted people saved me from sure death. It was a terrible period in our history."

"I am glad the country is going in the right direction now. It is more prosperous each time I come back."

"It is about time we recover from the ruins." He sighed.

"Thank you for seeing me. Good-bye! Please take good care of yourself," I said. He looked very tired.

I felt depressed to have come back to my ancestors' hometown. What I had seen on this trip had wipe out my beautiful memories of the school, our library, and the entire city. Suddenly, I lost my feelings of keenness and closeness to the place I had longed to visit. I wished I had never come back.

During 1987, ECI won several government contracts, including the Pentagon broadband computer network, Defense Nuclear Agency, Department of Labor, the Department of Education, and the US Navy. The annual company revenue had grown to over $13 million. Employee numbers had also grown proportionally to over one hundred. We moved again to a new location to accommodate the number of people. I was constantly on the go, meeting with government officials, business counterparts, and foreign suppliers. I was traveling around the world four or five times a year. Should I go back to school where I had been almost all my life? I had one of the highest-paid and most prestigious positions in the university. I could go back and live a quiet life and wait for my retirement. On the other hand, I would be facing the day-to-day challenges of running a large and complex business that might age me faster.

"Nancy, I have been on leave for almost three years now. I am not sure I should return to the university. The company is just getting stabilized. I really like the business world," I told her.

"Well, you have been in universities for over twenty-five years now. I am sure it is hard for you to break away from academics, but I know you enjoy the challenges in business as well. Whatever you decide to do, I will support you." She knew me well.

"I'd like to go back to ODU. That eminent professorship is something I always treasured, but I think I am having fun with running the business now," I said.

"You have too much going on in the business and it seems to me you really enjoy it. I believe deep in your heart you still want to do more in the business." She read my mind correctly.

"Since you can tell what's in my heart, and in my mind, I'd say you are quite right. I've decided to stay in business for good and resign my position at ODU. What do you think?" I asked her.

"I think it is good for you and the business. You can always return to teaching, if you want to teach again later," she said.

"Okay! That's the way it will be. I am going to call the dean and tell him about my intention, so he can get ready to find a replacement. But once I am out, I don't think I want to go back to school again."

"I am not going to worry about that," Nancy said.

Although I did miss teaching and academic work, the business world was much more challenging and interesting. I also had built up my confidence in running a company and I had a bunch of ideas and plans that I wanted to carry out. To me, meeting the challenge was fun instead of being a burden. Just before the end of the 1987, I officially resigned from my position of tenured eminent professor in computer science. That was the end of my academic career that had spanned thirty years from 1957 to 1987. Although I was still formally contracted as the adjunct professor of computer science, I would never have time to teach any courses.

Lightning Source UK Ltd.
Milton Keynes UK
UKHW011411030720
365982UK00001B/151

9 781952 835254